# Environmental Political Theory

# ENVIRONMENTAL POLITICAL THEORY

Steve Vanderheiden

polity

First published in 2020 by Polity Press

Polity Press
65 Bridge Street
Cambridge CB2 1UR, UK

Polity Press
101 Station Landing
Suite 300
Medford, MA 02155, USA

ISBN-13: 978-1-5095-2961-2
ISBN-13: 978-1-5095-2962-9 (pb)

A catalogue record for this book is available from the British Library.

Names: Vanderheiden, Steve, author.
Title: Environmental political theory / Steve Vanderheiden.
Description: Cambridge, UK ; Medford, MA : Polity, 2020. | Includes bibliographical references and index. | Summary: "A systematic outline of how the environmental crisis is transforming political theory's fundamental concepts" -- Provided by publisher.
Identifiers: LCCN 2020008758 (print) | LCCN 2020008759 (ebook) | ISBN 9781509529612 (hardback) | ISBN 9781509529629 (paperback) | ISBN 9781509529643 (epub)
Subjects: LCSH: Environmentalism--Political aspects. | Environmental policy. | Environmental ethics.
Classification: LCC JA75.8 .V36 2020 (print) | LCC JA75.8 (ebook) | DDC 320.01--dc23
LC record available at https://lccn.loc.gov/2020008758
LC ebook record available at https://lccn.loc.gov/2020008759

Typeset in 10.5 on 12pt Palatino
by Fakenham Prepress Solutions, Fakenham, Norfolk NR21 8NL
Printed and bound in Great Britain by TJ International Limited

For further information on Polity, visit our website: politybooks.com

# Contents

# Glossary

All words defined in this glossary are **in bold** at first occurrence in the text.

**all-affected principle**: under this principle, accountability binds decision makers to those affected by them by allowing the latter to hold the former to account in their decisions

**Anthropocene**: the proposed current geological age, characterized by human activity having a dominant influence on climate and the environment

**biotic community**: group of organisms that interact with each other in an ecosystem

**carbon offsets**: reduction in carbon dioxide emissions to counterbalance emissions made elsewhere (for example, offsetting one's emissions from airline travel by planting trees to sequester a comparable amount of carbon)

**carrying capacity**: capacity of a system (usually measured in population size) to support life without ecological degradation

**choice architecture**: design of different ways of presenting choices in terms of the behaviors that they tend to yield

**considerability**: the status of being worthy of moral consideration

**consumerism**: a social and economic order that encourages the private acquisition and consumption of goods and services in continually increasing amounts

**distributive justice**: an account of justice that focuses on how laws, policies, and institutions result in unequal distributions of benefits and burdens in society, often including principles defining a just distribution

**ecological modernization**: a school of thought within the social sciences which maintains that economic growth can be reconciled with sustainability imperatives, typically through the use of efficient technologies and design

**ecological steady-state**: an economy with a constant stock of natural capital and stable population size that does not exceed the capacity of its ecosystem to sustainably yield resources and absorb wastes over time

**epistemic authority**: a type of authority or persuasive power vested in certain persons by virtue of their expertise (in contrast with democratic authority, which depends on claims to represent or be responsive to the people at large); lay persons may defer to the judgment of experts or otherwise attach undue weight to their opinions on prescriptive matters due to their knowledge claims on related facts

**ethical holism**: claim that wholes such as ecosystems have moral standing, apart from that of their individual members

**externality**: unremunerated cost of economic exchange that is borne by neither buyer nor seller, but imposed on society at large

**food security**: according to the FAO, "food security exists when all people, at all times, have physical and economic access to sufficient, safe and nutritious food that meets their dietary needs and food preferences for an active and healthy life"

**global justice integrationists**: following Caney, a global justice "isolationist" applies distributive justice principles to particular goods, like greenhouse emissions, while an "integrationist" refuses to do so, insisting that such principles can apply only to whole bundles of goods (social, political, economic, environmental), such that shortages of one kind of good can be compensated with more of another

**green consumerism**: movement or practice of buying "green" products or services in an effort to reform production processes through consumer demand, and thus to mitigate environmental degradation

**human exceptionalism**: the belief that humans are categorically different from other animals in fact, typically used to justify differential status or treatment of nonhumans

**human security**: protection of persons and peoples against serious threats, including violence and deprivation

**humanitarian intervention**: use of force by a state or coalition of states against another state for the purpose of protecting human rights

**instrumental value**: value that we attribute to things in the world because of their potential to contribute to human welfare (in contrast with intrinsic value, which is when such things are viewed as valuable in themselves)

**international Paretianism**: condition (cast by Posner & Weisbach as a constraint on international politics) in which an international agreement advances the interests of all state parties to it and no state is made worse off by it

**jurisdiction**: practical authority to make legal decisions and administer justice

*laissez faire*: policy of governments to refrain from interfering in markets, e.g. through regulations to protect workers or the environment

**land ethic**: from Leopold's *A Sand County Almanac*, the ethical principle that "a thing is right when it tends to preserve the integrity, stability, and beauty of the biotic community"

**nation**: a community of people, when conscious of its unity, desire for autonomy, and shared interests

**necessitous migrants**: forcibly displaced migrants, whether stateless due to fleeing violence or through loss of territory, who lack a practical ability to return to their territories of origin or recent residence

**negative liberty**: a conception in which persons are free from impediments posed by others

**overshoot**: temporary condition of a population exceeding its carry capacity, resulting in ecological degradation and consequent reductions to or collapse of that system's carrying capacity

**peoples**: particular groups of persons that share features such as a common language or culture, historical residence of a place, or other distinguishing contributors to group identity

**popular sovereignty**: principle that state authority originates in, and continues to require, popular consent

**positive liberty:** requires that an individual have the power and resources to fulfill their potential

**postmaterial values**: values not associated with physical or economic wellbeing; thought to manifest more strongly in persons or societies where material (i.e. related to physical or economic security) values have largely been met

**prior appropriation**: principle that the earliest users of water for beneficial purposes have rights to continue using that water (key legal principle of water law in the American west)

**private sphere**: domain of activity in which individual actions are considered private, to be protected from the interference of others (in contrast to the public sphere, which is properly subjected to political scrutiny)

**procedural legitimacy**: quality of a political decision that issues from the processes by which it was made, yielding the belief by those bound by it that the decision is valid

**Promethean**: view (named for Prometheus from Greek mythology) that technological innovation would allow humans to overcome ecological limits, making resources practically abundant

**remedial liability**: requirement entailed by an agent's responsibility for an outcome whereby the agent must provide some kind of remedy (e.g. compensation) for that outcome

**scientific racism:** pseudoscientific belief that empirical evidence can justify beliefs about racial superiority or inferiority

**self-determination**: a collective prerogative of peoples to govern themselves, protected under international law as a human right of all peoples

**sentience**: the capacity to experience physical sensations such as pain and interpret this as an emotion

**Social Darwinism**: social theory in which natural selection is applied to human persons and groups, and understood as a "survival of the fittest" process through which nature rewards strength and punishes weakness

**soft power**: interventions designed to persuade or shape preferences without coercion

*stare decisis* **doctrine**: legal principle of deciding cases in accordance with precedent (the Latin means "to stand by things decided")

**sufficiency**: idea that users of a resource are entitled to enough of some resource, but not necessarily equal shares of it (related to distributive principle of sufficientarianism, which defines a just distribution in terms of this sufficient quantity)

**sustainable degrowth**: social movement objective for equitable reductions of production and consumption in the global North, with eventual stabilization at sustainable levels (based on critique of growth as inequitable and unsustainable)

**technocracy**: rule by an elite comprised of technical experts, insulated from democratic/political pressures

**trophic diversity**: biodiversity at the various levels of the food web

**virtual water**: amount of water used to produce some good such as a commodity crop, viewed as consumed when the crop is consumed

# 1 Introduction and Approach

By the end of January in 2020, 1,333 local governments, in 26 countries and representing 814 million people, had declared climate emergencies, as have 16 national governments and the European Union, calling upon themselves and others for a more urgent response to climate change than had yet been taken. The Climate Mobilization, which advocates and tracks such declarations, describes them as "a critical first step" in an effort to "rescue and rebuild civilization."[1] A similarly dire assessment and urgent call to action is expressed by the Extinction Rebellion movement, which proclaims "an unprecedented global emergency" in which humanity is "in the midst of a mass extinction of our own making."[2] In May 2019, *The Guardian* Editor-in-Chief Katherine Viner (following a call to do so by teenage climate activist Greta Thunberg earlier that month) issued new language guidelines, advising her staff to use "climate emergency, crisis, or breakdown" rather than "climate change," in order to convey the requisite urgency "when what scientists are talking about is a catastrophe for humanity."[3]

While such apocalyptic rhetoric is hardly new to the environmental movement, its recent coalescing around a discourse of crisis or emergency reflects not only what scientists describe as a closing window of opportunity to avoid catastrophic climate change, but also the recognition that the scope and scale of human-caused environmental change on the planet over the past half-century represents a multidimensional crisis. It will likely involve social, economic, and political crises for those affected by it, intensified as meaningful action to mitigate its various threats is postponed or otherwise avoided. "Ecological crisis" is probably an understatement for the expected period of mass extinctions that threatens to irreparably harm the planet's biodiversity and ecological stability. Many will experience personal crises, whether from loss of places and livelihoods or through the anxiety that psychologists link to the awareness of increasing environmental insecurity. For our purposes here, however, the crisis is also one of ideas about what matters in the organization of politics and society.

## Ideas and environmental politics

At a time in which Australian bushfires have killed over a billion nonhuman animals in a single season (potentially driving the iconic koala to extinction in the wild), collapse of pollinator colonies from exposure to neonicotinoids used in agriculture threatens the planet's food systems, ocean acidification from climate change and plastic wastes are combining to devastate marine life, and water supplies to major world cities are being shut off due to chronic drought, it may seem naïve or self-serving to fault ideas rather than more palpable sources of power for the environmental crisis. Ideas are in our heads, and perhaps books and other texts, but they have no material power of their own and seem benign next to instruments of power such as weapons or political authority. They are not what is starting bushfires or killing bees, and will not in themselves extinguish those fires or save those bees. As a professional political theorist who studies ideas for a living, it may seem particularly disingenuous for me to claim that ours is a crisis of ideas. Those holding hammers may often mistake many things in the world for nails, and the political theorist's interest in abstract ideas is a pretty esoteric hammer.

But ideas matter. They can orient us in the world and to each other, link causes and effects and explain complex phenomena, and provide meaning for our individual lives. In the form of social and political ideals that inform and direct our collective existence, they can articulate our aspirations and can direct our energies in maintaining or reforming public institutions in an effort to realize them. When our imaginations are impoverished of fruitful ideas or are trapped in conventional ones, our possibilities likewise become limited. As William Blake characterizes the self-imposed limitations of the imagination, our "mind-forged manacles" can imprison us in despair.[4] But ideas can also be emancipatory, freeing us from such limitations. They can contribute to ocean pollution or climate change in manifold ways to be explored in upcoming chapters, or prevent our realization that we're doing so. They can also bring recognition of these problems or inform constructive solutions to them.

Our ideas can and do also change, either in response to changes in the world or in our understanding of or relationship to it. In this sense, they comprise what Sheldon Wolin calls "a continuously evolving grammar and vocabulary to facilitate communication and to orient the understanding."[5] They can effect change, particularly when they have normative content that identifies a gap between what we observe or experience and that toward which we aspire. Ideas and events therefore exist in a dynamic relationship with each other, reacting to and causing reaction in the other as ideas change the world and changes in the world disrupt and transform our ideas. They exist in dialectic with other ideas, disrupting and being disrupted by new or competing ideas. Theorists seek to understand these dynamics – political theorists do so with important social and political ideals, and environmental political theorists direct their attention to the shared space between politics and collective social life, on the one hand, and the ecosystems that can provide the material bases for their flourishing, or render this more difficult.

Events in the world have shaped the ideas and ideals through which we understand our world and orient ourselves within it. The execution of Socrates by democratic Athens and its fall to militaristic Sparta surely influenced Plato's understanding and evaluation of democracy. The English Civil War shaped Hobbes' views of human nature and political authority, while the Glorious Revolution led Locke to view these somewhat differently. But the emergence of new ideas and ideals has also been formative in Western political thought, as Tocqueville and Mill – in their own ways – sought to accommodate a new ethos of democratic equality with what they saw as its potential and its pathologies. Such disruptive ideas can also be scientific ones, as with Copernican heliocentrism denying that humans were at the center of the universe, or Darwin's theory of natural selection and its influence on politics and religion. When disruptive events occur or new ideas emerge, existing systems of ideas must accommodate them.

Ideas and ideals exist in time and can evolve or be transformed over time without the full erasure of previous incarnations, like a modern city built on an ancient footprint, with layers of foundations associated with earlier generations to be found beneath the surface. Like toxic chemicals emanating from barrels of industrial waste decades after being shortsightedly stored in underground chambers incapable of containing them, toxic ideas and ideals associated with race and gender hierarchies or authoritarian politics can return to democratic polities that had previously rejected them. But, like a forest ecosystem devastated by fire, nurturing ideas and ideals can return over time to those places and **peoples** that repudiated them, giving new life to the aspirations that they enable.

As climatic changes shift disease vectors and induce species migration through changes to habitats, creating new assemblages of species that allow some to prosper, others to die off, and new hybrids or adaptations to appear, so also with ideas and ideals that are shifted by environmental change. Species adapt to changes in their environment, whether through developing productive forms of resilience or through decline and extinction, but do so without the mediation of disruption to and transformation of their ideas about the world and ideals that orient them to it. Humans also adapt – whether successfully or not in developing resilience against environmental change – through their ideas and ideals, and only then through their institutions, material relationships, and social practices.

Understanding the planet that we inhabit and the changes that we have brought about, and must therefore adapt to, requires our catching a glimpse of the world in deep or geologic time. The natural scientist learns to see the world in this way, then – like the philosopher returning to the cave in Plato's *Republic* – helps the rest of us see a bit of what this perspective offers. Empirical social scientists sometimes view the world in what Stephen Skowronek calls political time,[6] understanding change scaled to decades or centuries of human history rather than millennia of earth systems history, and gleaning insights that would not be available to those of us experiencing a world of more limited time horizons.

Normative political theorists seek a perspective that is wider than political time – as this is necessarily contained within the period occupied by a single political community or regime, in order to follow how it changes and in order to observe patterns that emerge over time – so that they can trace the emergence and evolution of formative ideas and ideals across political communities and regime types, as well as through major world events and the appearance of disruptive and transformative ideas. In conversation with those viewing the world in geologic time and those viewing it in political time, the political theorist is thus well equipped to understand how changes at the earth system level interact with those in formative ideas and ideals, in turn shaping social and political institutions and practices. A disposition toward ideas, or a critical method of seeking to understand forces in the world through the ideas that animate it, political theory is less a collection of texts than an activity or quest. Our goal in this book will therefore be focused upon theorizing environmental politics in ways that assist in understanding the crisis of ideas described above. While this may involve some engagement with canonical texts in the history of Western political thought or contemporary political theory, its objective is to motivate and inform students seeking to understand how ideas may be complicit in the environmental crisis or constructive in addressing it.

## Sustainability as emergent and disruptive ideal

With the emergence of the environmental crisis (discussed further in chapter 2), many of our received social and political ideals face profound challenges in accommodating new facts such as ecological limits to growth, or new kinds of transnational and intergenerational threats such as climate change. The existence of ecological limits to growth, along with the real possibility of approaching or transgressing such limits within our lifetimes, appeared as the kind of event or scientific discovery that would disrupt many of our received ideas and ideals. Not only could economic growth no longer feasibly be taken as an indicator of social progress (as discussed in chapter 5), but the crisis associated with the planet's finite ability to generate the ecological goods and services upon which human societies and their normative aspirations depend now requires a broader reassessment of the role that social and political ideals, such as liberty and equality or democracy, play in orienting collective life. Long-settled norms of sovereignty are challenged as the system of states or resistance to international cooperation in protecting the global environment is viewed as a possible contributor to the environmental crisis. Conventional assumptions about agency and responsibility appear ill equipped to grapple with some drivers of environmental degradation or frustrate some promising environmental solutions. Attachments of community are likewise challenged as complicit, with new constructions of community offered as potential remedies. The crisis has required a rethinking of conventional theories of justice, with new conceptions and novel hybrids between existing ones allowing us to conceive of and articulate environment-mediated injuries and construct solutions in creative new ways. Examination of each of these ideals and its role in intensifying or diffusing the crisis forms the basis of this book's eight substantive chapters.

Sustainability can be regarded as a kind of social or political ideal, growing out of the events and discoveries of the environmental crisis and ecological limits, to be added to the list of the eight treated within this book. Whatever else is constitutive of the good society, it must be a sustainable one if it is to persist over time, with impacts of increasing scarcity threatening to undermine or destabilize the other eight ideals. As we shall see, impacts of unsustainable institutions and practices often disproportionately affect the disadvantaged, undermining ideals of equality and justice, while also potentially threatening democracy and sovereignty. We may in this sense view sustainability as essential for other social or political ideals, as well as an ideal in its own right. Insofar as personal virtues describe character traits that tend toward the common good, it may comprise an essential aspect of the good life for individual persons, as well as having value for collectivities.

Since societies must soon transition to becoming ecologically sustainable, as we shall consider in more detail in chapter 2, sustainability captures a set of objectives for social institutions and practices, with the ideal orienting the present toward a future that is possible, necessary, and desirable. While few may find attractive the sustainable society that does not also embrace other ideals like justice and democracy, in many ways the sustainable serves as a vital complement to these other ideals, seeking to maintain the material preconditions for society to perform its most basic provisioning functions, as well as realizing the other aspirations that we see expressed in its various ideals. The other ideals thus also serve as important constraints upon sustainability – for example, in maintaining its humanitarian aspirations.

## Sustainability as transformational ideal

But we must not overstate the compatibility between sustainability and other social and political ideals. As we shall see in the chapters that follow, critics have called for restrictions on important liberties in the interest of sustainability, have suggested that democracy is complicit in the environmental crisis and so must be limited or replaced, and have called for an end to the sovereign state in the interest of more effectively governing earth systems. Some visions of the sustainable society threaten ideals of equality and justice, or dramatically restrict individual agency. Were sustainability the only social and political ideal, or one that was universally viewed as taking priority over all other such ideals when they conflicted, it would be relatively easy to advance. Resources that would otherwise be used to advance other ideals could be devoted toward sustainable energy or transportation infrastructure. Powers that are constrained by ideals of democracy or sovereignty, or by consideration of the rights of persons or peoples, could be mobilized on behalf of rapid technological development or change. An environmental leviathan (to borrow an image from Hobbes) could identify and address the many obstacles that now prevent our transition to a sustainable society, working single-mindedly and purposefully.

Where we recognize multiple and (sometimes) incommensurable ideals, the pursuit of any one of them can be constrained by the existence and imperative nature of the others. We want our political system to be democratic, but also to be able to take actions necessary to avoid catastrophic climate change. We want to create resilient cities, but must respect the rights and liberties of their residents. We want to protect biodiversity, but struggle to do so in the face of a view of progress for which it gets in the way. As we shall explore in these pages, these can take the form of a dilemma: suggesting that we must choose between democracy and sustainability, or between a free society and a sustainable one. Since these ideals and the values they represent are not commensurable, we lack a clear method for prioritizing one over another. Both are important, and indeed neither could be sacrificed for the sake of the other without generating serious objections. How are we to move forward, though, when such conflicts arise (or appear to arise)?

The need to balance competing imperatives is hardly unique to contemporary politics, even if the appearance of sustainability as a new imperative has introduced new conflicts with older ideals. To consider only one of many such examples, liberty and equality are often seen as competing with one another. We know that allowing a kind of market freedom will lead to significant economic inequality over time, which in turn can undermine legal and political equality as those with more income and wealth translate these into forms of power that confer advantages with legislatures and in courts. Conversely, maintaining a strict economic equality would conflict with influential conceptions of freedom. Constructively resolving a dilemma like this one requires a normative theoretical method that allows us to appreciate the value of both horns of the dilemma, to understand the historical origins and evolution of the relevant concepts, to propose balancing points in areas of unavoidable tension, while identifying means of reducing those tensions where they are unnecessary.

These powers of political theory – combined with an orientation that counsels epistemological humility in understanding such ideals as constructions that cannot readily be reconstructed at will, but instead call for critical challenges that can only come through collective and political action, rather than words in a book – enable this method of political inquiry to generate insights into the historical trajectory of environmental politics that would not be available to scholars or students of other disciplinary perspectives.

Must we choose to confer absolute priority to one ideal over the other whenever they conflict? Few libertarians are prepared to scrap legal equality (or equality before the law) in pursuit of the variety of liberty that they otherwise favor, and few strict egalitarians would so restrict individual freedom that voluntary simplicity (or the voluntary choice of leisure over more material possessions) would be banned as an affront to material equality. We seek to resolve such conflicts by balancing competing ideals, rather than granting one absolute priority over the others, and, while the libertarian and strict egalitarian may each identify a quite different balance, they both aim to do what will be our goal in the chapters of this book: to strike some balance between ostensibly competing ideals (sometimes by reinterpreting one or both to minimize the tension between them), and then to defend these interpretations and this balancing point. This art of balancing, along with the associated arts of appreciating points of tension in ideas as well as understanding the historical origins and normative force of each source of tension, allows the mode of inquiry used in this book to assist our comprehension of what is needed to usher in the kinds of changes that will allow us to maintain our noblest and most considered aspirations.

Canonical texts in political theory reveal the origins of and major developments in the prevailing social and political ideals, as visionary historical thinkers wrestled with value conflicts or to accommodate important events or changes in the world. Understanding how various and often competing conceptions of key social and political ideals emerge, exert influence, and either become institutionalized or give way to new conceptions can assist our understanding of how an ideal like sustainability, an event like the environmental crisis, or a discovery like ecological limits has shaped our received ideals as well as been shaped by them, and how their evolution in adaptation to the constraints of ecological limits or imperatives of sustainability might occur. In understanding human history and environmental change through environmental political theory, we can gain a unique perspective on how and why we as a species organized into societies and, influenced by their constitutive ideas and ideals, got to where we are today, and can better appreciate our possible human and social futures, what they hold for those residing in them, and how social and political ideas and institutions can in some sense help to determine those futures. It is to this task that we now turn, following a chapter on the idea of ecological limits, and the several possible reactions to it in shaping the sustainability ideal and generating its imperatives.

# 2 Environmental Change and the Sustainability Imperative

"In the beginning all the world was America," John Locke wrote in his seminal 1689 *Second Treatise of Government*. Locke, who owned thousands of acres of undeveloped land in the Carolinas through his patronage with the first Earl of Shaftesbury, developed perhaps the most influential modern political text with this image of an abundant and largely uninhabited continent in mind. Nature was, for Locke, inert matter or raw materials awaiting human exploitation and transformation. Unless and until humans appropriate land as private property by fencing it off from the commons and laboring upon it – perhaps the quintessential expression of human nature in Lockean liberalism – nature is devoid of value and humans are without purpose or direction. Upon the foundation of this theory of nature, Locke's canonical text constructs much of the edifice of Western liberalism, profoundly influencing the design and self-image of liberal democracies in Europe, North America, and beyond.

As will be explored further in our examination of Lockean ideals of freedom, equality, and progress, many of our received ideas about politics originated in a text that denied the relevance to politics or society of ecological scarcity, and which consequently viewed nature and its life-support systems as of little value to humans. A key premise for Locke – and, by extension, for many other seminal texts in Western political thought, and consequently in the political cultures of Western liberal democracies – held that finite natural resources were in fact perfectly abundant and so could not be depleted by human activities. Humans as a result need not care for them or design institutions to protect them. Such a premise might have seemed plausible to many at the time insofar as relocation to European colonies like those in America was a feasible option, as much of the English land that Locke describes in his treatise had already been privately appropriated by then, and only colonization of the New World would dispel this fiction of cornucopian abundance on both sides of the Atlantic. It can no longer be seen as plausible.

Indeed, ecological scarcity is the sort of idea that is *disruptive* of established views about the relationships between humans and their territorial environments, as well as their relationships with each other, and is *transformational* of their ideas in requiring existing social and political concepts and ideals to accommodate the facts of ecological limits. As historical ideas such as **popular sovereignty**, the nation-state, and colonial oppression had disruptive and trans-formational impacts on law, politics, and society, sustainability imperatives have challenged and will continue to challenge our social and political institutions and the ideas and ideals in which they are embedded. They disrupt previously settled conflicts, challenge worldviews that cannot account for their rise or force, and demand to be accommodated within the penumbra of existing social ideals and organizing principles. To the extent that existing ideas, ideals, and institutions cannot do so, the new ideas require the old ones to be transformed, often against the resistance of those invested in the older ideological order.

Popular sovereignty, for example, claimed that state power derives from the consent of the governed, challenging the patriarchal authority of kings who had previously been regarded as ruling by divine right, in hereditary succession. Once the idea gained traction, older accounts of political authority could not accom-modate its demand for popular consent, which required attention to the many, and ultimately to their participation. Associated ideas and institutions had to adapt or be displaced. Some, like the British monarchy, adapted to its challenge and managed to persist, albeit through significant transformation. Others, like the monarchy in France, could not adapt and ended. The idea of the nation-state forged new identities, redrew old borders, and required entirely new sets of institutions. With the idea of colonial oppression, insti-tutions and practices organized around the "white man's burden" view of benign imperialism were challenged (a challenge that is still resisted), ushering in a period of decolonization and shifting the patterns and practices of economic globalization.

Ecological scarcity has, over the past half-century, begun to exhibit this disruptive and transformational potential. As we shall explore further, many of our norms, ideals, and institutions depend upon maintaining the conditions of merely moderate scarcity in which they were established (indeed, this condition is among what David Hume called the "circumstances of justice" that allow for relationships of justice to order politics and society). Conflict would not arise without some scarcity, obviating the need for governments to resolve such conflicts and otherwise allocate social resources, but many of the norms, ideals, and institutions that have developed over time to more peacefully and fairly resolve conflicts and allocate resources (including those ideals to be examined in later chapters of this book) come under strain and may collapse with intensifying scarcity. As episodes of more severe scarcity of food, water, or other critical goods around the world have demonstrated, characteristics of a well-ordered society – such as freedom of movement, due process, democratic governance, and the rule of law – can erode and disappear under such conditions.

We must, of course, be attentive to maintaining those necessary conditions of merely moderate scarcity for manifold reasons, among which is the ongoing viability of our most cherished and considered ideals. To the extent that our existing ideals fail to accommodate sustainability imperatives (or, worse, actively contribute toward exacerbating scarcity), they may contribute to their own erosion and eventual irrelevance. Insofar as a society's ideal of freedom is construed as allowing for unlimited exploitation of finite resources or the prerogative to undermine the planet's life-support systems, for example, the idea of ecological limits requires that the ideal either evolve to accommodate the facts of scarcity or risk undermining the material conditions of its continued possibility. Likewise with its prevailing view of the democratic ideal: if it (as some critics allege) cannot accommodate sustainability imperatives or allow for their successful pursuit, then democratic governments and societies will be guided by an ideal that risks contributing to its own undoing.

The overarching thesis of this book holds that the eight social and political ideals to be examined in this book now exist in some tension with the idea of ecological limits and its associated sustainability imperatives, but that it is at least conceptually possible for each of these ideals to accommodate that idea and those imperatives. Put another way, the environmental crisis is, among other things, a crisis of ideas and ideals, and the challenge of sustainable transition includes the sustainable transformation of those ideals. In this time of increasing scarcity of ecological goods and services, a window of opportunity for transformed conceptions of freedom, equality, democracy, and sovereignty remains open, but at some point it will close. Whether we, as members of societies whose attitudes and institutions are founded upon or informed by ideals that cannot accommodate to ecological scarcity, will recognize this in time remains to be seen. With recognition should come a sense of urgency, along with the opening-up of previously settled convictions and conventions that accompanies the disruptive force of an idea such as ecological limits.

Some of this disruption is already evident, with the urgency implied in the contemporary discourse of a climate "crisis" or "emergency" observed above. But many have not yet noticed it, and the entrenched resistance to its disruptive force must not be underestimated. Nor must we assume that successful disruption necessarily leads to successful transformation; ideals such as freedom or democracy could well be abandoned if viewed as incompatible with sustainability imperatives, or they could be replaced with different but equally dysfunctional alternative conceptions. Transformation of these ideals, if it occurs, may need to happen within the next generation, so many alive now may be witnesses to either the successful sustainable transition of our social and political ideals (and with this, of our societies and politics) or the impacts of a failed transition. They may, in those ways that we either reinforce or challenge prevailing ideals in our everyday lives or through concerted political efforts – and with or without realizing that they are doing so – become participants in this process. Developing an appreciation for this fact among students of environmental political theory is therefore among the primary objectives of this text.

## Ecological limits and sustainability imperatives

While well grounded in the physical sciences, the idea of ecological limits is abstract and defies sensory observation. We can observe a rising price for gasoline at the pump, from which we might infer decreasing market availability, but such observational data are several steps removed from resource scarcity itself. Planned production decreases designed to raise the price of crude oil, geopolitical conflicts in oil-producing regions, or overseas economic expansion are more likely explanations for oil price increases than is diminishing supply (as a nonrenewable resource, oil supplies can *only* decrease, albeit at varying rates, whereas market prices fluctuate in both directions). Likewise, we might observe diminished snowpack in the mountains or reduced water levels in our reservoirs (key indicators of future water availability where I live), but the climatic changes that lie behind these indicators can only be grasped conceptually, utilizing theory and abstraction, not observed empirically.[1]

The concept, in turn, arises to explain observable phenomena, and then alongside competing explanations. Ecological limits and scarcity may contribute to a lot of bad outcomes, but they are never their *only* cause. As the case studies in Jared Diamond's *Collapse* (2005) illustrate, several historical instances of relatively small and isolated societies contributing to and then experiencing severe resource scarcity (Easter Island, the Anasazi of the American southwest, etc.) underscore the importance of accommodating ecological limits in the ideals that inform the organization of those societies. However, settler colonial societies tend to exploit distant sources of such resources to counter any domestic shortages, in so doing preventing (with a few notable exceptions) the concept's appearance in the social and political thought of such societies, as Locke's treatise illustrates. Biophysical limits and sustainability imperatives remain abstract and contested, not urgent and serious.

Now, in what John McNeill has aptly termed the "great acceleration of the Anthropocene"[2] (itself in reference to the dominance of human impacts on the environment within the geologic epoch), whereby the past half-century has, according to natural scientists, "without doubt seen the most rapid transformation of the human relationship with the natural world in the history of humankind,"[3] the observable indicators of increasing ecological scarcity cannot so easily be ignored. Nor can their human causes or impacts, as these become increasingly evident and linked in the public imagination to our failed planetary stewardship. The effects of this failure cannot readily be mitigated through resource colonialism – where affluent countries plunder ecological goods and services within poor ones to make up for their domestic overuse – as the impact of the **Anthropocene** and transgression of ecological limits transcends borders; nor can they be entirely transferred onto distant and powerless others: put out of sight and mind.

The good news is that humans have historically shown a remarkable ability to adapt to change and may yet be able to successfully adapt to anthropogenic environmental change and the increasing scarcity that it involves. In addition to our infrastructure and institutions, our norms and ideals must also find a way to accommodate ecological limits if humans are to successfully adapt to the environmental changes that we (through our existing infrastructure and institutions, as well as norms and ideals) have brought about. This book explores what that latter form of adaptation might look like, with the attendant urgency that these paragraphs suggest is appropriate. We cannot continue to deny the facts of scarcity or their relevance to our social and political ideals, as Locke could and did; nor can we continue to uncritically accept, as what John Stuart Mill called "dead dogma,"[4] the many received ideas and ideals that have been constructed upon such a faulty foundation. So long as it remains possible to aspire toward enlightened or informed versions of those social and political ideals that have admirably guided human struggles against injustice in the past, we must subject them to critical examination in light of these facts, preserving what we can of them.

In doing so, we must remain cognizant of the importance of such a project, but also of its limits. With abstract ideas like ecological limits, there can often be a significant lag between our recognition of the implications and force of an idea and its full incorporation into many of our other received ideas that were shaped by its absence. For many years, the aphorism "the solution to pollution is dilution" was repeated and internalized by those managing water resources, and was also routinely acted upon. Because ecological limits (in this case, the capacity of lakes or streams to assimilate waste) seemed sufficiently distant, those dumping their wastes in water might for decades have believed this convenient claim about cornucopian abundance. At some point, sensory evidence would belie the fiction as sewage and other waste began to harm the nonhuman users of polluted surface waters and then did the same to humans, with the resulting dissonance calling for some explanation.

Abundance is a powerful myth, however. Long after we intellectually acknowledge that dilution isn't really a "solution" to pollution created through human activity, human societies continue to act as if it is. The continued existence of an atmospheric commons that is almost entirely open to nearly unlimited greenhouse gas pollution, despite the ample observable indicators of dangerous climate change, attests to that power. Intellectual acknowledgment is one thing, but accommodating the ideas within our system of related ideas and practices is another and more daunting challenge. Ideas such as resource abundance, which allows for unlimited growth, can create a kind of path dependence through which they continue to exert influence long after they have been formally discredited, acting (to preview a term from chapter 5) as a kind of zombie, dead in some technical sense and yet still able to cause a zombie apocalypse alongside other ideas.

## Ecological limits: origins and possible responses

In this chapter, we shall examine how the idea of ecological limits arose; how it came into conflict with other received ideas – initially slowing its wider acceptance but later disrupting, and in some cases forcing a transformation of, those older ideas in order to accommodate it; and then consider three possible kinds of response to it (recommending one of those three). First articulated by Thomas Malthus in his 1798 *Essay on the Principles of Population*, the idea of ecological limits to growth has long been associated with class-based equity conflicts, albeit in various and opposing ways. Malthus, who cast the "population problem" in terms of a crisis that would eventually arise as exponential increases in population growth exceeded an arithmetically increasing food supply, described the "actual distresses" of England's poor, in being "disabled from giving the proper food and attention to their children" (with the avoidable suffering and death that resulted), as providing a "positive check to the natural increase in population." Rejecting the egalitarian social policies advocated by William Godwin, which he devoted a quarter of his book to refuting, Malthus adopted a form of **Social Darwinism** in which state interference in these "positive checks" on population from starvation and disease were to be understood as contributing toward this population crisis, and claiming that poor laws "create the poor which they maintain." From his point of view, it would be preferable to allow those poor to starve rather than to interfere in the natural processes that had previously kept the English population size in check.

Revived in the late 1960s by Garrett Hardin and Paul Ehrlich, among other neo-Malthusians (so-called because they were influenced by Malthus), the focus on the bivariate relationship between population and food supply would give way to the five-variable (adding resource depletion, industrial output, and pollution) analysis of the Club of Rome's influential 1972 *The Limits to Growth* report. Formed in 1968 as an "invisible college" of scientists, political elites, and philanthropists "to rebel against the suicidal ignorance of the human condition,"[5] the Club (based on the computer modeling work in system dynamics by Jay Forrester at MIT) popularized the idea of ecological limits, selling 30 million copies of their report and galvanizing a generation of ecologically minded population control advocates as well as popularizing related ideas such as **carrying capacity** and **overshoot**. While the report's methodology and predictions have been the subject of heated debates, it is properly credited with bringing the idea of limits into public consciousness and calling for urgent and ambitious action. Wide shifts in elite opinion and the sort of action that the report recommends have largely remained elusive, however, with the Club's *30-Year Update* report (published in 2004) lamenting that "humanity has largely squandered the past 30 years in futile debates and well-intentioned, but halfhearted, responses to the global ecological challenge."[6]

## Ecological limits and their discontents

An indirect legacy of this revival of the Malthusian tradition was a rift opened between the global North and South about who or what was most damaging to the global environment, with neo-Malthusians typically blaming rapid population growth in the global South (with what Hardin characterized as their "under-equipped lifeboats," in reference to their high poverty rates and chronic food insecurity), while others faulted the high impacts of the global North's patterns of industrialization and consumption. Its race and class dimensions added to the perception that environmentalism was an upper-middle-class white movement for affluent societies only, and the xenophobic pronouncements of neo-Malthusians calling for the withholding of famine aid and closed borders suggested a concern with the safeguarding of privilege rather than planetary stewardship. This image would persist for decades, with the idea of ecological limits motivating some misogynistic social views and heightening conflict and division within and between countries. Resource scarcity, that is, was held by some to vindicate or require wide and growing environmental inequality as the zero-sum nature of allocating finite resources forced uncomfortable choices about which claims to deny. As Hardin casts the dilemma through his lifeboat metaphor, to spare the global poor from deprivation by admitting them into one of the well-equipped boats of the global North would lead to global ecological ruin rather than confining this to the poor countries where it was, in his view, inevitable (as he writes: "The boat swamps, everyone drowns. Complete justice, complete catastrophe").[7]

Limits to growth make scarcity more palpable, and intensify conflict over increasingly scarce resources, awakening avarice and often leading to the abandonment of aspirations toward a more equitable society or world. Treating the world's poor as drivers of overpopulation and ecological degradation, while denying them the agency needed to escape their fate without northern intervention, simultaneously patronized and infantilized entire peoples. Then, when the death toll fell short of the hundreds of millions over two decades that Ehrlich had predicted would starve in his 1968 *The Population Bomb*, charges of alarmism and intentional exaggeration became narratives for what still were (and continue to be) real and preventable humanitarian atrocities, with real ecological drivers.

Denial of the idea of ecological limits comprises another response, whether by persons associating it with despair and resignation or those (like industry-sponsored climate science deniers) spreading false information to influence public opinion for economic gain. In this context of a disruptive idea being actively contested and members of the lay public seeking to rationalize its dismissal, mis-steps by advocates of the idea can have the opposite effect from what they intend. By impugning their own credibility, advocates may embolden deniers.

When Ehrlich's apocalyptic prediction about famine deaths didn't come to pass, skepticism about the idea, rather than urgency in meeting its challenges, was a common reaction. Ehrlich's confidence about future mineral prices rising as the result of their increasing scarcity led him to accept a public wager with the **Promethean** economist Julian Simon, pitting Ehrlich's Malthusianism against Simon's contrarian view that such resources would remain abundant into the indefinite future.[8] When those resource prices declined, owing to quirks of the particular ten-year period over which the bet was made rather than longer-term trends, Ehrlich's credibility was again called into question, sowing further doubt about limits. The seeds of public doubt about human causes of the environmental crisis were planted well before those industries most responsible for intensifying global resource scarcity and ecological degradation had grown savvy to the threat to corporate profits from an emerging environmental concern among the public (which would later lead them to finance what Naomi Oreskes and Erik Conway call "merchants of doubt" to shape public opinion through industry-sponsored science denial campaigns[9]), but have in the decades since been magnified by campaigns of misinformation.

## International responses to ecological limits

International reactions to the revival of ecological limits were several and varied. Its influence on the development of international environmental law and governance can be seen in the role of such limits at the 1972 UN Conference on the Human Environment, which issued the Stockholm Declaration, calling for international cooperation on environmental protection. Persuaded by the reality and urgency of ecological limits, signatories to the Declaration pledged to cooperate in sustainably managing the planet's natural resources and guarding against pollution threats, but also linked environmental protection to social and economic development and condemned South African apartheid and the history of colonialism as related to environmental inequality. In this sense, the conference revealed tensions between the global North and South over their inequitable prior exploitation of the global environment, with criticism aimed at the US for its ongoing war in Vietnam as well as its colonial history. It set the stage for later multilateral engagement around environmental equity issues, including the Brundtland Report's vision for sustainable development (discussed in chapter 5) in 1987, and the two landmark conventions on biodiversity and climate change from the 1992 Earth Summit (discussed in chapter 9), both of which would also revive key international tensions and dynamics from this conference while embracing global equity among their guiding principles.

Delegates from the global South approached the issue of limits with skepticism – not about their scientific validity, but from a concern about limits on development being imposed on poor countries that might impede development opportunities that had been afforded to affluent countries. Since the developed North had benefitted from over a century of unconstrained exploitation of territorial resources, as well as those within the oceanic and atmospheric commons, representatives from the poor South objected to sustainability constraints that would curtail growth, and called for equitable burden-sharing in protecting the global environment (in what would later emerge as the "common but differentiated responsibilities" principle). Later, this tension would give rise to claims to a right to development: the idea that ecological limits should not prevent the least developed countries (or LDCs) from developing, and, in so doing, addressing their poverty, hunger, and economic insecurity. The idea of *sustainable development* would later come to name this attempt to balance sustainability and development imperatives in a manner consistent with their early expression in the Stockholm Declaration. As defined by the Brundtland Report, "development that meets the needs of the present without compromising the ability of future generations to meet their own needs" requires sustainability in order to protect those future interests.

Another tension emerged from the 1972 conference and its attempt to promote cooperation around the environment and development. Noting the interests of "the great international corporations which operate in the developing countries" in ensuring that "environmental controls should be weak in the Third World," one scholarly observer of the international dynamics at the Stockholm conference suggested that it was also "in their interests that Third World governments should have good arguments to justify that weakness" so that "poor countries" can "agree to be dirt havens for the rich."[10] Here, concern for development rights was alleged to merely be a pretext to justify the continued exploitation of the global South by the North, as necessary for development, on the basis of the pernicious claim (described as "a polluter's gambit") that environmental values would not emerge among the global poor until they had experienced higher levels of economic development. Associating development with exploitation of the territorial environments and resources of poor countries was, according to this critique, more about defending profits for multinational corporations than about the global poor.

Other critics have observed a similar dynamic. Thomas Pogge identifies the "resource privilege"[11] (the right to control, and thereby profit from, territorial resource extraction, leading to stunted development for some resource-rich LDCs in what has come to be known as the "resource curse"[12]) as serving the interests of multinational corporations and the governments of the LDCs, with the former getting cheap access to valuable mineral resources and the latter getting revenue from their sale (funds which, as research on the resource curse suggests, are often used to arm states against the people, feed corruption, and thereby hinder development). In the interest of development, designed to benefit the peoples of poor countries, the privilege was in some cases hindering that development, while, in most, hindering its sustainable potential by polluting and rapidly depleting local LDC environments. The cruel irony was that at least a putative concern for global equity in development, along with ecological limits, would result in additional pressures to export pollution and resource depletion from the North to the South, doing little to promote a sustainable transition while worsening environmental inequality.

## Ecological limits and US politics

Within the United States, the reception of ecological limits would lead to changes in the partisan alignment around environmental protection. The conservation movement that preceded the environmental movement as the dominant vision for reforming the relationship between humans and their environment largely appealed to (with its main nongovernmental organizations mostly led by) white, male, and upper-middle-class resource users. The landmark environmental laws adopted in the late 1960s and early 1970s (the National Environmental Policy Act, Clean Water Act, Endangered Species Act, etc.) enjoyed bipartisan support in the US Congress and were championed by the Republican President Richard Nixon, who also presided over the founding of the Environmental Protection Agency. California Republican House member Pete McCloskey served as the co-chair of the first Earth Day in 1970, with numerous members of both parties in the House

and Senate claiming strong environmental credentials. For generations, protection of the environment enjoyed bipartisan support,
which would begin to erode after 1972, in part due to the way in
which the idea of ecological limits had been received and translated
into policy.

By the 1980s, changes within the US Republican Party led to
an abandonment of Nixon's environmental leadership and its
replacement with the deregulatory and obstructionist politics of
the Reagan administration, with the widening of partisan polarization on environmental issues in Congress beginning with its shift
to the right in the early 1990s. As Dunlap, McCright, and Yarosh
show, this widening partisan gap is reflected in widely disparate
attitudes and beliefs about climate change, with those identifying
as Republicans, in the electorate as well as government, increasingly embracing a particular version of one of the three possible
responses to ecological limits to be considered next: supporting
business as usual (i.e. enacting no new environmental protections
as well as rolling back existing ones) on the basis of climate science
denial, which shows similar patterns of partisan polarization.[13]

The environmental movement, by contrast, increasingly (if
haltingly and inconsistently) moved away from what I shall,
below, call the "eco-fortress" response (characterized by a desire to
maintain exclusive control over scarce resources at the expense of
the disadvantaged) that was characteristic of the early conservation
movement, and toward what I call the "just transition" response,
which aims to protect ecological goods and services for all. In doing
so, it embraced multilateral cooperation and centralized environmental regulation, at the same time that US conservatives were
rejecting these. The idea of ecological limits could not be ignored,
but how the idea was received gave rise to widely disparate
and competing political visions. Some chose science denialism or
other forms of dismissal, while others saw limits as justifying the
exclusion of others from the benefits of development or enjoyment
of increasingly scarce ecological goods and services, and still others
saw the challenge as requiring a new focus on equity in understanding the causes of and solutions to environmental problems.
To those three kinds of response and to their implications we shall
now turn.

## Business as usual

One kind of reaction to the emergence of ecological limits is to deny
that such limits require the reevaluation of any existing ideals or
practices at all. In one form, this response involves the contestation,

attempted suppression, or denial of the science behind such limits in rejecting imperatives for action to mitigate environmental problems. A model for this strategy had been set in the 1960s, with the chemical industry threatening to sue Houghton Mifflin and the *New Yorker* to prevent the 1962 publication of Rachel Carson's *Silent Spring*, then mounting an expensive public relations campaign to discredit it (including the circulation to US media outlets of a parody entitled "The Desolate Year," claiming that Americans would not be able to grow enough food to survive without pesticides), along with vicious *ad hominem* attacks against Carson herself. Half a century later, the Competitive Enterprise Institute (which has also been active in climate science denial) continues to malign Carson by falsely claiming on its rachelwaswrong.org website that her "false alarm" on the dangers of DDT is responsible for the suffering and death of millions from bans on its anti-malarial uses[14] (in fact, the chemical's use to combat malaria was explicitly allowed in the 1996 Stockholm Convention on Persistent Organic Pollutants, and it continues to be used for such purposes in Africa and Asia).

This model was also used in the US tobacco industry's strategy for avoiding smoking-related lawsuits by what the majority opinion in *United States v. Philip Morris* (2006) describes as a conspiracy to defraud the public "with zeal, with deception, with a single-minded focus on their financial success, and without regard for the human tragedy or social costs that success exacted." The industry's regulatory avoidance strategy of contesting the scientific consensus and creating doubt about the scientific basis for the dangers of smoking created a playbook that would later be used to contest the existence of ecological limits or resist pressures for regulatory responses to them. David Michaels notes of this strategy of "manufacturing uncertainty" that "the vilification of threatening research as 'junk science' and the corresponding sanctification of industry-commissioned research as 'sound science' has become nothing less than the standard operating procedure for parts of corporate America."[15] Climate science denial is perhaps the most prominent use of this model, but it has also been used against scientific research on acid rain, biodiversity loss, and animal pain and suffering.

Both uses involve the *politicization of science*, or intentional effort to deceive policymakers or the public about scientific facts in order to promote the narrow financial interests of industry, a strategy that has been central to the US anti-environmental movement and is increasingly being used elsewhere to similar effect. Following the template advocated by then-corporate lawyer (and later Supreme Court Justice) Lewis Powell in his 1971 "Attack on the

American Free Enterprise System" memo, corporations began in the early 1970s to establish contrarian sources of expertise in defense of corporate interests against what Powell characterized as anti-capitalist critique "from the college campus, the pulpit, the media, the intellectual and literary journals." Powell's memo, which was quoted at length in the 1973 establishment of the Pacific Legal Foundation[16] (an industry-sponsored legal advocacy group designed to oppose environmental regulations that would also play a role in the anti-environmental Wise Use movement[17]), describes much of the strategy of anti-environmental foundations (Olin, Coors, Scaife, Koch, Bradley, etc.) and the free-market "think tanks" that they established to obfuscate science on behalf of industry.[18] They pursue their advocacy goals through industry-sponsored contrarian science and other public relations efforts to discredit mainstream scientific research, in a campaign to deceive the public about the scientific bases of environmental problems and thereby to delay calls for stronger regulatory protections against environmental degradation.

Under the Trump administration, this politicization of science has included not only the president's own expressed climate science denialism but also the replacement of scientists with industry advocates on key regulatory bodies, the termination of numerous science advisory posts and commissions, the muzzling of government scientists and scrubbing of their research from agency websites, and even the pressuring of National Oceanic and Atmospheric Administration (NOAA) weather forecasters to corroborate a false claim by the president about whether Hurricane Dorian was expected to threaten Alabama in September of 2019. Its disregard and disdain for science-based decision making became so anomalous and alarming that the bipartisan National Task Force on Rule of Law & Democracy describes Trump administration politicization of government science and research as having reached a "crisis point" in obfuscation and denialism that includes "almost weekly violations of previously respected safeguards" and "undermine[s] the value of objective facts themselves."[19]

While science denialism is perhaps the most prominent version of the business-as-usual response, another version accepts some of the science behind anthropogenic environmental threats but claims that market-driven technological innovation will successfully avoid any adverse human impacts, obviating the need for state regulation or any kind of retooling of prevailing ideas or practices. In the context of peak oil forecasts, for example, such a response would dismiss calls for stricter government efficiency standards or alternative fuel research and development by citing the market incentives available to entrepreneurs in bringing alternative automobile technologies to market (ignoring the sordid history of General Motors' EV-1 in 1997, as well as government subsidies needed to launch Tesla Motors). Its message is one of optimism about markets but skepticism about policy solutions. Ecological limits may be real, but neither government nor the public needs to worry about them or do anything to fix them.

Rejecting the call for governments to proactively anticipate and respond to ecological limits with conservation and efficiency policies, this version acknowledges the need for change but denies that it needs to be directed by states, instead vesting markets and voluntary rather than regulatory efforts with the power to transform production and consumption. An associated view invokes the environmental Kuznets curve (discussed in chapter 5) to suggest that continued promotion of economic growth will eventually rectify any environmental impacts of growth once a tipping point has been reached, again rationalizing business as usual against calls to more proactively address the impacts of ecological limits. Regardless of which form it takes, all versions of this response reject any need to embark upon planned changes to government institutions, economic organizations, or public values or behavior. For our purposes here, they also deny the need to disrupt or transform social and political ideals like the ones to be examined in later chapters, since ideals can neither be complicit in, nor serve as solutions to, nonexistent environmental crises that require no change from the status quo.

## The eco-fortress

A second and quite different response (if one also being advanced by right-wing populists in Europe, America, and Australia, alongside science denial) accepts some threat to human welfare from ecological limits or anthropogenic environmental change unless some kind of action is taken, but seeks to insulate powerful states or groups against the biggest impacts – typically at the expense of the disadvantaged. In Hardin's version, extending his opposition to famine aid on neo-Malthusian ecological grounds from his "The Tragedy of the Commons" (discussed in chapter 3), the international sharing of agricultural surplus from affluent countries in the form of emergency food aid for famine victims would "move food to the people, thus facilitating the exhaustion of the environment of the poor," while allowing refugee status to those fleeing poverty and hunger "moves people to the food, thus speeding up the destruction of the environment in rich countries."[20]

As he casts the problem, which he views from the perspective of the affluent global North only, the populations of poor countries are already in overshoot of their carrying capacity and their ecosystems will inevitably be degraded, so the primary imperative for those in affluent countries ought to be containing the suffering and damage within those countries. Fortifying borders to guard against immigration and withdrawing from international humanitarian aid efforts are here justified in terms of protecting the environments and people that matter against those that do not.

John Dryzek identifies the environmental discourse of "survival" as often countenancing centralized and authoritarian systems of control in response to ecological limits, as with the kind of eco-authoritarian visions discussed in chapter 4. According to Dryzek, the "basic story line" of such responses "is that human demands on the life support capacity of ecosystems threaten to explode out of control, and drastic action needs to be taken in order to curb these demands."[21] In most cases, this "drastic action" and the state of emergency to which it responds is viewed by those embracing this discourse as justifying the suspension of humanitarian ideals, as well as of democratic processes, allowing the powerful to protect themselves at the expense of others. In describing a dystopic response to runaway climate change that he calls "Fortress Climate State" and characterizes as in a permanent state of emergency, Peter Christoff anticipates it "either seeking to protect the welfare of its citizens equally but with little capacity to deal humanely with the world beyond its borders, or by protecting only its political and economic ruling elite."[22] The conscious decision to disregard the welfare of others is justified by the reality and urgency of an environmental threat, coupled with the claim that it requires the abandonment of processes and ideals that would normally apply.

While the eco-fortress response does (unlike business as usual) take seriously the scientific basis for predicted ecological crises, it so prioritizes sustainability within one's own territory above competing ideals like justice and democracy that it practically sets those aside, rather than seeking any kind of balance. Refusing entry to environmental migrants displaced from their home territories by climate change, or refusing to support famine relief where possible on grounds that "positive checks" on population are needed, would constitute serious violations of human rights and international humanitarian law, but follow from a fortress ethos.

As in eco-authoritarianism, which we shall consider in chapter 4, replacing democratic institutions with authoritarian ones would likewise respond to the emergence of the sustainability ideal by entirely displacing the democratic ideal, ignoring the dismal track records of existing authoritarian states in this regard. Perhaps most importantly, the response circumscribes the community ideal (discussed in chapter 8) to a particular people (or subset thereof) in order to forcefully defend that community's privileges at the expense of other communities. The politics of fear and resentment used by right-wing populists to demonize immigrants and the disadvantaged often accompanies this response, and the discourse of emergency often accompanies its call for exclusion of the disadvantaged and the states of political and moral exception this requires. The result of any eco-fortress response would be – and, indeed, is intended to be – highly inequitable.

Milder versions of this response can be seen in efforts at, or proposals for, concentrations of environmental privilege in the midst of increasing scarcity. As discussed in chapter 9, the permanent sovereignty principle grants to states or peoples an entitlement to territorial natural resources, which, for resource-rich states, could be akin to an eco-fortress as the principle guards against competing claims. Proposals to grandfather high rates of per capita greenhouse gas emissions, as was embodied within the Kyoto Protocol, likewise grant legal entitlement to a form of environmental privilege to those states that had polluted more in the recent past, while denying development opportunities to smaller historical polluters. On a local scale, Pellow and Park's *The Slums of Aspen* chronicles how residents of an affluent resort community sought to maintain their environmental privileges while scapegoating local Hispanic service workers, in an eco-fortress of gated communities and exclusionary local regulations.[23] All share in common the desire to maintain or extend environmental inequality for the benefit of the relatively privileged, often through narratives by which the disadvantaged are blamed for their misfortune rather than acknowledging complicity on the part of the privileged, which might give rise to calls for equity in burden-sharing or a corrective-justice response instead.

## The just transition

The third kind of response to the challenge of ecological limits, and the only one that takes seriously the precautionary response called for by the science of environmental change, as well as the social and political ideals upon which modern liberal democracies are founded and toward which they in their best moments continue to aspire, seeks mutual accommodation between the sustainability ideal and those other existing ideals that it disrupts and must transform – but need not necessarily displace. It faults the business-as-usual response for underestimating the disruption posed by sustainability imperatives, and the eco-fortress for overestimating it and thus failing to maintain tenable versions of existing social and political ideals. Recognizing the need for sustainable transition in our institutions, infrastructure, practices, and ideas, this response meets the challenge of ecological limits through constraints imposed by (updated and reimagined) critical social and political ideals, ensuring that the transition it recommends is guided by imperatives of justice as well as sustainability.

Failing to maintain the material conditions necessary for society to treat its members justly and to govern itself democratically makes business as usual self-undermining, as justice and democracy are both threatened by worsening scarcity, while failing to maintain social conditions and institutions necessary to promote respect for, and protect the dignity of, persons and peoples undermines the normative basis for human society itself. Doing both – maintaining defensible versions of key social and political ideals, but making these compatible with the maintenance of those ideals over time – comprises the third response of the just transition. Here, "just" serves as a kind of shorthand for the mix of ideals to be discussed in chapters 3 through 10, with the ideal of justice incorporating the seven others in various ways. For the purposes of the next eight chapters, this response aims to maintain some conceptions of the social and political ideals to be surveyed in those chapters. In the concluding chapter, we shall return to the question of what the just transition might look like, or how sustainability interacts with those other ideals. First, however, we must turn our attention to those eight ideals.

# 3 Freedom

Perhaps no social or political value has been more central to modern political theory than freedom or liberty, as indicated by the fact that many terms in political theory derive from it. Western liberalism is the dominant school of modern political thought in the West, influencing movements for liberation or emancipation and reflected in the institutional design of nearly all contemporary Western democracies. Its political implications are now multiple and even often opposed to one another, with streams within the liberal tradition diverging at different historical junctures, and with both sides retaining identification with the ideal. Social or welfare liberals embrace an extensive welfare state and regulation of markets, while classical liberals or libertarians prefer *laissez faire* economic policies, with both tracing their origins to the same historical texts. As a result, "liberals" are now associated with left-of-center ideology in the United States, but the Liberal Party in Australia identifies with the ideological right (opposed by the Labor Party). "Liberation" refers to the objective of anti-colonial and postcolonial movements, while "neoliberalism" reinforces colonial patterns of oppression (the negation of freedom) by supporting the existing global economic order.

Can a concept with such a capacious meaning, and which is appealed to from across such wide ideological terrain, function as a political ideal? As an "essentially contested concept" with no core meaning, appeals to any one of its meanings may not have the unifying effect of appeal to an ideal with shared meaning across a polity. As William Connolly notes, when controversies arise about the meaning of such concepts – with "freedom" perhaps the most contested term of all – a "definitive resolution of these controversies is usually impossible."[1] Agreement upon which course of action best promotes liberty is complicated by the multiple meanings that liberty has for those advocating different alternatives. **Negative liberty** requires that others refrain from posing external obstacles to some individual's freedom of action, whereas **positive liberty** requires that person to have the power and resources to fulfill their potential.[2] States promote the former by refraining from interfering in the lives of citizens, but promote the latter through interference designed to protect their health and safety or provide them with education. Insofar as political ideals allow for the evaluation of current institutions or conditions and prescribe courses of action in reference to their normative terms, freedom's capaciousness may be a liability in this sense. But its multiple meanings also provide a rich basis for theorizing a wide variety of important social and political problems.

## Concepts and conceptions

In order to move forward with the assessment of various ideals in terms of their potential compatibility with sustainability impera-tives in either their existing or evolved meanings, I shall rely here and elsewhere upon a useful distinction introduced by Ronald Dworkin.[3] *Concepts* are more general normative ideals, he notes, and are typically abstract and encompassing. More specific instan-tiations or realizations of those ideals are *conceptions*, and any singular ideal may contain multiple conceptions. All members of a group may agree that fairness (a concept) should inform the group's procedures, but disagree about what fairness requires in a particular case (a conception). Perhaps all members agree that everyone's food preferences should be considered in selecting a restaurant for a group meal (a concept of fairness), but they disagree as to whether they should always eat where a slim majority of members prefer or alternate this with someplace preferred by the other members (a conception that seeks to operationalize the concept for action). In order to resolve this definitional controversy jurisprudentially, Dworkin suggests, members ought to review "standard cases" within the concept to identify "benchmarks" of agreement by which "more controversial cases" for the concept can be tested. In doing so, the group seeks agreement not on the concept itself, but upon its applicable or most defensible conception.

Here, as elsewhere, our primary attention will be upon particular conceptions of social or political ideals, like freedom, as manifesta-tions of concepts, some of which may be more or less compatible with sustainability imperatives than others. As noted in chapter 1, we assume that political ideals evolve over time and in response to historical events and changing sensibilities, and this evolution can be cast in terms of either relatively small amendments or redirections of emphasis within any conception of the ideal, or relatively larger transformations or instantiations that might best be understood as involving a new conception of the same concept. Our purpose is not to identify one particular conception that is best for all purposes, given the environmental crisis as the kind of event that requires adaptation of existing ideals, but to consider several conceptions as available within environmental political theory as guiding responses to this event.

With this in mind, we shall begin with a conception of freedom that has been implicated as complicit in ecological degradation, considering both its development within political thought and the applicability of this critique to the concept of freedom more generally. Must we impose draconian restrictions upon freedom to realize the demands of sustainability, as the critique suggests, or are there alternate understandings of this conception, or other conceptions, that might allow us to reconcile imperatives of freedom and environmental protection? Our critique manifests in two forms, with one utilizing game theory to impugn reproductive freedom in the degradation of the commons, and the other associating a kind of economic freedom with rampant and ecologically destructive **consumerism**. Both take a conception of freedom (whether they invoke a singular conception or two distinct conceptions will be for the reader to decide) to stand in a fundamentally adversarial relationship with sustainability, arguing in both cases that sustainability takes priority and that freedom must therefore be restricted.

## Freedom as culprit in commons tragedies

How can ecological limits be disruptive of settled ideals like freedom? Does the protection or pursuit of some conception of freedom exacerbate the environmental crises? Garrett Hardin's essay on the "tragedy of the commons" impugns individual freedom as responsible for at least some forms of environmental degradation, claiming that "freedom in a commons brings ruin to all."[4] Calling for restrictions upon reproductive freedoms as necessary for population control, Hardin's article ushered in an illiberal environmentalism that took liberal democratic social and political norms like liberty to be contributors to the environmental crisis and called for restrictions on them. While the eco-authoritarian case against democracy is further discussed in chapter 4, we shall focus here on Hardin's critique of freedom, from which a case for authoritarian solutions to environmental crises can be made.

Writing during a period of great concern about human overpopulation, Hardin's article was one of several that he wrote in defense of US isolationism from a putatively ecological perspective. For context, Paul Ehrlich's *The Population Bomb* was also published in 1968, framing that year's Sahel drought and famine that killed a million people in terms of carrying capacity and ecological overshoot. According to ecologists like Ehrlich, ecological laws governing how large a population can be sustained within a territory apply to humans as well as nonhumans. When populations grow too large for their territorial environments to sustain, they exceed carrying capacity and enter a period of overshoot, during which the ecosystem's capacity to grow food declines through such overuse of natural resources as overgrazing, overfishing, and the depletion of aquifers. These assumptions, which ecologists like Ehrlich had previously applied to limits on nonhuman-species populations, were held to bound human societies to ecological limits that, if exceeded, would lead to rapid population die-off, unless food could be imported from elsewhere.

Ehrlich became a kind of intellectual celebrity, in large part by applying such laws to human population growth, which for many offered a compelling account of the causes of the famine that had captured public attention. His predictions in the book were dire and fatalistic. Declaring "the battle to feed all of humanity" to be over, he claimed that there was nothing to be done to prevent "hundreds of millions of people" from starving to death over the succeeding two decades, given the laws of ecology as he conceived and applied them.[5] For Ehrlich, the real question was whether or not humanity could change course and limit population growth in time to prevent many millions more dying of starvation. The American public at the time, shocked by the images of African famine and craving explanations and solutions, had been primed for grim predictions and unattractive solutions. Hardin didn't disappoint in this regard.

## Hardin on the tragedy of the commons

Hardin upped the ante, with predictions that were as grim and fatalistic as Ehrlich's, but with a diagnosis and prescriptions derived from them that went beyond the voluntary measures endorsed by Ehrlich, through his activism with Zero Population Growth. Faulting reproductive freedoms for the high birth rates in impoverished countries, he advocated for coercive limits on family size in regions beset by rapid population growth. Noting of reproductive freedom that "it is painful to have to deny the validity" of a right that had just been affirmed as among the set of universal human rights the previous December, Hardin nonetheless remarks that "to couple the concept of freedom to breed with the belief that everyone born has an equal right to the commons is to lock the world into a tragic course of action."[6]

Although Hardin's target was human population ethics, his essay draws on a parable of users overgrazing a shared pasture, termed a "commons" because of its lack of restrictions on access. Since the commons has a carrying capacity, it can be overgrazed if livestock numbers exceed this capacity, at which point it will become degraded and that capacity will be reduced. Each user, when facing the decision about adding an additional animal to their herd, considers their own costs and benefits from doing so. Since each animal represents an economic gain to them from its eventual sale, but also a degradation cost to the commons (shared by all users), it lies within their economic interests to keep adding more animals regardless of what other users do, and beyond the point at which the commons is degraded. Herein lies the tragedy, or what game theorists call the "collective action dilemma": each user, guided by the desire to advance their individual interests, overgrazes and thereby degrades the common resource, which it would be in the collective interests of the group of users to protect.

Steeped in economistic assumptions about human behavior, Hardin explains rapid population growth through the overgrazing metaphor, which applies to *common-pool resources* that share the features of being *rivalrous* (i.e. one user's enjoyment detracts from the ability of others to enjoy it) and *non-excludable* (i.e. use of the good cannot be limited to paying or permitted users). According to Hardin's analysis, which is widely influential in understanding natural resource management incentives, all common-pool resources are subject to this *free-rider problem*, which is a type of market failure whereby users degrade or fail to maintain such goods because they can enjoy their benefits without contributing to their provision or protection. From these assumptions, Hardin treats the global environment as a commons into which additional persons are born, subject to the same free-rider problem that led to overgrazing in his parable, but degrading the global environment instead. Reproductive rights that leave family planning decisions to parents make this commons non-excludable, in his view.

Hardin's prescriptions for averting the tragedy involve either privatization or regulatory restrictions on access ("mutual coercion, mutually agreed upon"), which, in the case of human population growth, would involve compulsory family-size limits like China's one-child policy. Voluntary limits, he argues, would fail because they rely upon what he calls conscience, or the moral concern for others. Appeals to conscience, such as those being made at the time by Zero Population Growth to parents to refrain from having more than two children, were "a verbal counterfeit for a substantial *quid pro quo*" and "an attempt to get something for nothing,"[7] as those refraining from having more children would (like those voluntarily declining to add animals to their herds to prevent overgrazing) receive no private gain for their sacrifice. Hardin simply rejected the force of either ethical or social norms in compelling any person "to restrain himself for the general good," going so far as to suggest that "conscience is self-eliminating," in that those parents adhering to sustainable family-size limits would eventually eliminate the cooperative trait from the gene pool (Hardin is also well known as a eugenicist).

Despite impugning freedom as responsible for causing potentially catastrophic ecological degradation, Hardin attributes little agency to those he saw as deterministically reproducing in tandem with increases in available food supplies. His view of freedom leaves little room for moral agency or responsibility, depriving human action of the voluntarism with which it has most commonly been associated. His description of cooperative norms causing anxiety among those deterministically inclined toward free riding likewise offers a dim view of stunted human moral development, with persons unable to cooperate or act collectively. The important work of Elinor Ostrom and her team of researchers demonstrates (against Hardin's dire claims to the contrary) that norms capable of yielding cooperation in the management of common pool resources can and do develop under the right conditions, enabling cooperation.[8]

Hardin's call for restrictions on freedom as necessary for environmental protection failed to imagine how freedom could be reconciled with sustainable population growth. As we now know, freedom-enhancing provisions like the education and the political and economic empowerment of women can effectively lower birth rates, obviating the need for Hardin's preferred solutions in coercive family-size limits and the withholding of famine aid (which he called "misguided charity"). Hardin does, however, identify a conception of freedom – understood in terms of free riding, or using depletable goods without cooperating in pursuit of ongoing provision or sustainable management – that, if allowed and pursued, would be incompatible with ecological limits. We shall consider this below as neoliberal freedom.

Hardin's game-theoretic focus on incentive structures has been influential, and can be instructive of theorizing freedom and its compatibility with such incentives. We know that social norms can help to structure cooperation in many contexts, including many environmental ones, and that in many cases they can be more effective than government coercion in changing behavior. Key to the emergence and operation of such norms are institutions designed to support them, with **choice architecture** arranged to support rather than compete with the norm to be instantiated. One might still object that reliance upon norms is sometimes insufficient, and that coercive regulatory actions are needed, but this conclusion ought to be reached only after consultation with applicable knowledge about the potential limits of approaches rooted in normative change, not on the basis of spurious and pseudoscientific claims.

## Freedom and incentive structures

Hardin's case for draconian limits on reproductive freedom appears to have failed to consider less objectionable means to the same end, and his claims about the incompatibility between freedom and sustainability appear similarly hasty. Changes to economic incentive structures within which land use or other environmental decisions are made remain popular policy options that enjoy wide (if not universal) ideological appeal, with few viewing them as inimical to freedom. Carbon taxes, for example, shift incentives away from reliance on fossil fuels for energy and toward renewable sources like wind and solar, while generating revenue that can be used to assist in the decarbonization of the energy system. Although proposals to privatize public lands and other ecological goods and services in order to alter their incentive structure in favor of conservation are more controversial,[9] objections to such proposals more plausibly turn on maintaining equitable access or the poor conservation records of large private landowners, rather than turning on concerns about liberty.

Norms and incentives are ubiquitous and their presence in the world is not generally seen as averse to maintaining a significant measure of individual freedom. Norms encouraging me to reduce the waste that I send to the landfill or to turn off lights after leaving my classroom are promoted by the campus Environmental Center, and have proven effective while maintaining considerable freedom to throw away garbage or waste electricity. My local grocery charges a nominal sum for grocery bags in order to reduce waste from single-use plastics, but this does not oppress those who prefer to engage in wasteful behavior. Behavioral "nudges" that arrange either economic incentives or "choice architecture" to encourage desirable behaviors being chosen are not viewed as limiting freedom of choice. Indeed, Cass Sunstein and Richard Thaler describe the use of such nudges as embracing "libertarian paternalism," in that they preserve the freedom to engage in undesirable behaviors while legitimately encouraging desirable ones.[10]

Does the use of (positive or negative) incentives reduce freedom in an objectionable way? Positive incentives are frequently used in policy contexts and are commonly regarded as among the least intrusive tools available. Subsidies for conservation behaviors like the purchase of zero emissions vehicles or the installation of grid-connected solar panels do not limit the liberty of those choosing not to engage in such behaviors. Negative incentives like fees for supermarket bags to deter reliance upon single-use plastics, or carbon taxes to deter reliance upon fossil energy, are more controversial, if equally effective in encouraging desirable behaviors. Both do what Hardin implicitly recommends, aligning actions that serve the social good with individual self-interest. Both would also seem to be compatible with a conception of the liberty ideal in an ecologically limited world, even if Hardin's view of freedom as non-cooperative and egoistic free riding would be a challenge to accommodate in it. Unless one takes the view that all such policy tools are illegitimate, and setting aside questions about their objectives and procedures used to adopt them, such incentives do not appear to threaten freedom.

## Neoliberal freedom and scarcity

Some do reject such incentives as illegitimate, however. The charge that freedom is complicit in the environmental crisis remains a serious one but can be detached from Hardin's formulation of it. A conception of freedom that is associated with unfettered economic exchange and consumption might be seen as conflicting with sustainability imperatives in two ways. To the extent that such a conception advocates *laissez faire* policies with respect to environmental protection, viewing pollution-control regulations or sustainable resource-management mandates as restrictions on freedom, it would oppose effective environmental policy solutions. To the extent that it endorses consumerism or gratuitous consumption as compatible with – or even an expression of – freedom, it would contribute toward environmental degradation as well as opposing solutions to it. Indeed, an influential conception of freedom does both of these things. We shall explore each of them in turn.

This conception of liberty focuses upon the economic domain of life, including business activity and individual contracts and economic exchanges. It is thus commonly distinguished from political liberty, which includes civil liberties like freedoms of speech and association, voting rights, and freedom from arbitrary punishment. While it is often called "economic liberty" in reference to this focus, and is embraced by economic libertarians (some but not all of whom also identify as civil libertarians, embracing political liberty), the term "neoliberal freedom" better captures its ideological origins and conceptual features. The more ecumenical term could also include what Franklin Roosevelt (FDR) in his 1941 annual address to Congress called the "freedom from want" (one of "four freedoms" that his New Deal aimed to advance), and the neoliberal conception of freedom embraces only a specific conception of economic liberty, opposing the use of state power to create jobs or redistribute wealth in the way that FDR aimed to do.

The term "neoliberal" references its origins in classic liberalism, but the conception of neoliberal freedom that is popular today owes its development to twentieth-century thinkers, from Austrian economists like Friedrich Hayek (whose 1944 *The Road to Serfdom* condemns centralized state economic planning as inimical to freedom) and Ludwig von Mises (whose *Planning for Freedom* claims that "political freedom is the corollary of economic freedom"[11]) to writers like Ayn Rand (whose "objectivism" is influential among many contemporary right-libertarians). Milton Friedman's 1962 *Capitalism and Freedom* captures the claimed relationship between economic and political freedom characteristic of this view, to which his book's title alludes. He argues that state interference in the economic domain (whether as direct state ownership of production, or indirect control through regulation of production and consumption) would lead to repression of political liberty, such that only free-market capitalism could protect individual liberty.

Neoliberal freedom thus invokes Adam Smith's notion of the market's "invisible hand" as a guarantor of individual welfare and happiness, arguing for *laissez faire* economic policies that cast any state interference in market exchanges – whether in the form of economic regulations like minimum wages or workplace safety standards, welfare state programs like unemployment insurance or state retirement benefits, or environmental regulations like pollution control or biodiversity protection laws – as inimical to freedom itself. As claimed by The Heritage Foundation / *Wall Street Journal Index of Economic Freedom*, which measures 10 variables of "economic freedom" across 162 countries in an effort to promote this conception (see chapter 5's discussion of defining progress in economic terms), Smith's "lesson" in *The Wealth of Nations* (1776) was that "basic institutions that protect the liberty of individuals to pursue their own economic interests result in greater prosperity for the larger society."[12]

This conception is frequently invoked by opponents of state environmental regulations designed to encourage sustainable resource use or reduce pollution, which are cast as restrictions on freedom itself. For example, when Colorado was considering a law requiring new household fixtures like showerheads to meet federal WaterSense conservation standards as part of an effort to reduce residential water consumption, opponents cast the 2014 law as a threat to individual liberty.[13] Among the opponents of similar water-conservation requirements in North Carolina is a conservative "think tank" called the John Locke Foundation,[14] which claims to promote Locke's vision of "individual liberty and limited, constitutional government."[15] Former member of the US House of Representatives and current anti-environmental activist Ernest Istook has called for "a modern-day Boston Tea Party" in which "it would be the low-flow nozzles and toilets that get dumped in the harbor" in opposition to federal water-conservation rules.[16] According to this conception, restrictions on high-flow toilets or showerheads limit individual liberty.

## Classic liberalism and neoliberal freedom

Since this conception claims its basis in canonical texts like Locke's *Second Treatise*, and compares resistance to conservation mandates to emancipatory actions like the Boston Tea Party, we shall examine its origin and relevant normative claims in historical political thought before returning to the question of whether it stands in opposition to sustainability imperatives. Those historical texts articulate a conception of liberty that might be thought to pose an obstacle to the use of regulatory coercion or other incentives on behalf of sustainable transition, but also identify a set of limits on that liberty that are relevant to assessing its application to policy measures designed to reduce the environmental impact of consumption.

Libertarians across the ideological spectrum typically ground their ideological claims in classic liberalism, which developed during the seventeenth and eighteenth centuries through such thinkers as Locke and Smith. David Boaz of the right-libertarian Cato Institute cites Locke, Smith, David Hume, Thomas Jefferson, and Thomas Paine as seminal to the development of contemporary libertarian ideology – for example, locating in this tradition two main elements of the neoliberal conception of freedom (to which left-libertarians do not subscribe): a rejection of egalitarian redistributions of wealth, and the claim that "people will be both freer and more prosperous if government intervention in people's economic choices is minimized."[17] The former undermines efforts to rectify environmental justice, which, as discussed in chapter 10, call for a kind of redistribution that neoliberal freedom opposes. The latter claim impugns the sort of restrictions on consumer choices noted above. In order to understand this conception of freedom and assess its potential compatibility or conflict with environmental protection imperatives, we must examine its foundational texts.

Writing at a time in which a feudal land tenure system reinforced systems of patronage and domination, Locke defended the individual right to acquire property in land as instrumental to freedom. English land was ultimately controlled by the king as lord paramount, but granted to layers of lords in return for loyalty and service to the crown. Lesser lords could in turn grant free tenure to knights in return for military service, or clerics in return for spiritual services, as well as granting unfree tenure to serfs in return for agricultural labor and other services. Even the relatively privileged nobility had little political freedom to criticize the king, as revocation of titles in land could be threatened for such disloyalty. Commoners were subject to often-brutal exploitation by virtue of their economic dependence upon lords, with their inability to possess private property in land preventing their economic mobility, as well as any effective social or political freedom. Land was at the time the most important source of power, which enhanced the freedom of its possessors but, in being highly concentrated among the elite, prevented the masses from experiencing any real freedom. That we still refer to contemporary domains of power as *fiefdoms* is a testament to the importance of land tenure in Locke's early modern England.

These links between land ownership and freedom or power underscore the radicalism of Locke's theory. By claiming property acquisition as a natural right, he opened the door to its wider distribution and more effective personal control, as many more persons would, under the proposal in Locke's *Second Treatise*, be allowed to acquire private property, and their claims to it would be more robust than under the feudal system he sought to replace. By promoting private accumulation of capital in land, rather than the concentration of economic power within the state, he anticipated and advocated for the replacement of mercantilism with capitalism, which would later coincide with the rise of a new middle class to challenge the power of the nobility. Against the webs of economic dependence and domination characteristic of feudal society, Locke argued for the emancipatory value of labor, and called for an end to the economic bases for much of the existing hierarchy within English society. Opposing inherited economic privilege by calling for a prohibition on inheritance in property, Locke required all to acquire it through their own labor. Nonetheless, many contemporary inheritors of the classic liberal tradition emphasize other aspects of Locke's theory, to which we now turn.

## Locke's property theory and provisos

Locke's labor theory of property is often invoked in justification of neoliberal freedom, warranting further examination of its normative argument as well as its faithfulness to Locke's text. It starts with two premises: that "the earth, and all inferior creatures, be common to all men" (i.e. that natural resources are originally unowned); and that each person "has a property in his own person"[18] (or what is known as the "self-ownership" thesis, claiming that persons own themselves and therefore also their labor power). According to Locke, when persons mix their labor (to which they alone are entitled, as owners of themselves) with unowned natural resources (assumed to be without value prior to the mixing of human labor with them), they acquire property rights to the goods that result, which "excludes the common right of other men." For Locke, the labor investment can be minimal – in gathering apples or acorns from the commons, a person "has certainly appropriated them to himself."

The right to property, like the natural rights to life and liberty, is fundamental for Locke. By associating the right with the pre-social state of nature, he implies that no social conventions (like environmental laws) may validly restrict it. Only two restrictions limit how much of the commons any person may appropriate for themselves. First, since God gave the earth to humans in common and for their beneficial use, no person may claim so much of it for themselves that they allow its bounty to go to waste (this, Locke writes, "is more than his share, and belongs to others"[19]). The invention of money, which for Locke also occurs in the state of nature, allows for virtually unlimited acquisition without spoilage, since surplus agricultural produce could be exchanged for something that does not spoil. Notably, Locke recognized that rights to acquire property in this way would lead to unequal holdings, to which he did not object. Although "God gave the world to men in common," Locke writes, "he gave it to them for their benefit." Since only those appropriating land for themselves "improved" the land above its natural condition, he argues, they deserved to claim a disproportionate share of the world as their own. As he notes, God "gave it to the use of the industrious and rational (and *labour* was to be *his title* to it)."[20]

The second restriction (which, following Nozick, is known as "the Lockean proviso") is concerned with a person's appropriation of property from the commons offending other persons rather than God. Locke rhetorically asks: "Was it a robbery thus to assume to himself what belonged to all in common?"[21] Even though the commons belong to all, he argues, removal of land or resources from them is not "robbery" so long as the removal leaves "enough, and as good" for others to use. Since the rivalrous goods that are subject to commons tragedies increase in scarcity as they are used, this condition can only apply to them under conditions of moderate scarcity, when ample stocks of resource remain available to all. Unless one person's appropriation of property adversely affects another's opportunity to do the same for themselves, the proviso suggests, no one is injured by the loss. Given his desire to justify private property ownership against both the conventional Tory claim that kings own all property by divine right,[22] and that of the Levellers that all property is theft, Locke must have believed that few if any actual appropriations from the commons violated the proviso. Since this proviso limits property acquisition within Locke's theory, we can understand it as compatible with the conception of freedom that he developed.

## Nozick's entitlement theory and the proviso

Robert Nozick, whose *entitlement theory* of justice is perhaps the most influential of the recent uses of Locke in support of neoliberal freedom, develops his account of historical entitlement from Locke's theory of property. Any distribution of resources is just, he argues, if it results from either just acquisition (removal from the commons through labor) or just transfer (or consensual exchange, which for Nozick implies that it is also mutually beneficial). Rejecting the egalitarian **distributive justice** theory of John Rawls, whose *A Theory of Justice* was published three years earlier, Nozick argues that "liberty upsets patterns" like resource equality in that neoliberal freedom allows for (and commends as virtuous) capitalist accumulation. Indeed, Nozick places such priority on liberty over competing ideals like equality that he claims that "taxation of earnings from labor is on a par with forced labor," since both involve the state making claims upon some person's justly acquired property.[23]

How does Nozick reconcile his countenancing of virtually unlimited accumulation with the proviso that each must leave "enough, and as good" for others? As with Locke, the proviso sets limits on the legitimate exercise of freedom for Nozick, as it involves harm to others. In a finite world, each appropriation from the commons would increase scarcity in land, leaving less for others. At some point, and certainly by Nozick's lifetime, further appropriation would be impossible, leaving only just transfer as a means of acquisition for those residing in a world without an open-access commons. Indeed, Nozick identifies the proviso as limiting just transfer as well as original acquisition from the commons, constraining how resources can be bought or sold. As he notes, "if the proviso excludes someone's appropriating all the drinkable water in the world, it also excludes his purchasing it all" (provocatively adding that it also "may exclude his charging certain prices for some of his supply").[24] With goods like water that are subject to scarcity, he writes, "this proviso (almost?) never will come into effect" since "the more someone acquires of a scarce substance which others want, the higher the price of the rest will go, and the more difficult it will become for him to acquire it all."

Herein lies the crux of Nozick's analysis. He here embraces what John Dryzek calls a "Promethean" (after the mortal in Greek mythology that stole fire from Zeus, in reference to its "unlimited confidence in the ability of humans and their technologies to overcome any problems"[25]) view about resource scarcity and incentives for substitution. No person will ever own all drinkable water, according to this view, since it would get increasingly expensive as its scarcity increased. It would eventually become prohibitively expensive to acquire more, as those forfeiting it would also be forfeiting their capacity to support life. The Promethean argument concerning technology is similar. As any good becomes increasingly scarce, its price rises with its diminished supply, creating economic incentives for innovations like substitution, or for technologies that allow for more efficient use of the resource. Note that humans have yet to develop a substitute for water, despite pervasive shortages, yet Nozick tendentiously claims that it is possible to exacerbate scarcity for resources like water while leaving "enough, and as good" for others (even though water-scarce areas typically have insufficient supplies and lower water quality). According to Nozick's conception of freedom, the reason that persons should not be limited in their use of natural resources is that the latter are practically unlimited: if ever we were to approach limits like those chronicled in *The Limits to Growth*, market incentives would spur innovation that would generate efficient technologies or substitutes for those resources. The ecological abundance of "enough, and as good" would perpetually obtain.

## Prometheanism and the proviso

Julian Simon (whom Dryzek calls "the leading American Promethean") illustrates the premises involved in this analysis, and what he sees as its implications for policy, by invoking the historical case of coal being developed in nineteenth-century England as a substitute for wood, which had become increasingly scarce as the result of deforestation to fuel early industry. With market forces alone driving this innovation, Simon claims, England's "resource problems become opportunities and turn into the occasions for the advances of knowledge that support and spur economic development. We need more and bigger problems, rather than just have them solved, as conventional economics would have it."[26] Scarcity, according to this view, leaves humans better off than they were before, with resource depletion ironically generating greater abundance. Simon, who claims, in his published rebuttal with Herman Kahn to *Global 2000* (a US government report on societal development in the face of ecological limits), that "stresses involving population, resources, and environment will be *less in the future than now*,"[27] views human ingenuity and capacity for innovation as unlimited, obviating any ecological limits to growth. Nozick subscribes to the same kind of technological optimism.

For a Promethean like Nozick or Simon, low-flow showerheads or toilets represent an innovation of the market when they emerge as a technology available to households, but offend against liberty when they are mandated by building codes. Given their ambivalence about the water scarcity concerns that prompted the legislation, both would likely regard the incursion upon the domain of liberty as unnecessary. (Nozick allows property rights to be "overridden to avoid some catastrophe," like the suffering that occurs when someone appropriates "all the water holes in the desert" and charges exorbitant prices for the water, but only in such extreme cases.) Their confidence in markets and the Pareto improvement[28] of voluntary exchange would allow buyers and sellers of plumbing fixtures, rather than the state, to determine how much water gets used in taking a shower or flushing the toilet. Since the appropriation would be immune from Locke's proviso, compulsory water conservation would infringe upon neoliberal freedom.

Wood is unlike water in that it has multiple substitutes as a fuel source. One might also quibble with Simon's claim that each new fuel source has been socially and environmentally better than what it replaced, given coal's pernicious role in acid rain and climate change, but the inability to develop substitutes for water makes it immune to the effect that Simon describes. If scarcity-driven wood price increases drove the development of coal (a cheaper and better fuel, he claims), will water scarcity also lead to the discovery of an abundant substitute for it? Increasing water scarcity has driven innovations in water efficiency (for example, those low-flow toilets and showerheads), and in some parts of the world chronic water shortages have led to development of large-scale desalination facilities to extract freshwater from the ocean (at high ecological cost, given their massive energy requirements, and through state investment rather than the market forces that Simon commends). However, shortages have mostly led to conflict over increasingly scarce water resources, and deprivation from drought-induced famine, and are expected to continue to do so in the future, increasing human suffering rather than relieving it.[29] While Nozick might be technically correct in his claim that high prices would keep anyone from appropriating *all* of the planet's water resources, the world in which it becomes price-prohibitive to do so would also be a world in which the vast majority of humans would not be able to afford to eat or drink. Most importantly, Nozick's assumptions about its permanent abundance (necessary given the proviso) appear to be empirically false.

## Neoliberal freedom and externalities

Accounting for ecological scarcity brings the neoliberal conception of freedom into uncomfortable conflict with Locke's property theory, driving the evolution of the ideal as it adapts itself to the conditions of the contemporary world. The libertarian claim that low-flow showerheads violate liberty is premised upon a conception of liberty in which any state interference in voluntary transfers violates the freedom of both buyer and seller, but those libertarian claims rest on faulty premises regarding ecological scarcity when grounded in Lockean property theory and the conception of freedom it embodies. In rejecting conservation mandates (or other regulations designed to protect ecological goods or services), those embracing the neoliberal conception of freedom implicitly claim a right to impose the harmful byproducts of exchanges between producers and consumers onto third parties that benefit by neither the production nor the consumption of the exchanged good. In Hardin's analysis, they claim that freedom includes the prerogative to freeride, even if this causes commons tragedies.

Economists call this kind of byproduct an *externality*, or unremunerated cost of economic exchange that is borne by neither buyer nor seller but imposed on society at large. Externalities are a form of market failure, whereby unregulated production and consumption produces less utility than would one that was properly regulated, with mainstream economic theory thus requiring restrictions upon such actions. When economic libertarians reject environmental regulations as an affront to freedom, their argument must therefore not rest upon efficiency or social utility, as externalities undermine both.

To conclude this section, we may make two observations about this neoliberal conception of liberty. First, to the extent that it is taken by advocates to override competing imperatives like sustainability, it would be incompatible with a sustainable transition. Society cannot continue to protect this kind of freedom while also becoming or remaining sustainable. Given that neoliberal freedom is often wielded by advocates against environmental protection and resource-conservation efforts, we may assume that its claimed priority over competing imperatives is an aspect of the conception itself, claiming liberty as a dominant ideal that trumps other ideals (including equality, justice, and democracy). Such a conception would not be compatible with recognizing these other ideals, let alone with sustainability imperatives.

Second, whatever its justification might be, its canonical authority in Locke's *Second Treatise* is dubious, given the way that the environmental scarcity it exacerbates would seem to violate the Lockean proviso to limit our appropriation of scarce environmental goods and services when this fails to leave "enough, and as good" for others (a condition that applies under moderate scarcity and ecological limits). Nor can it rest on claims about efficiency or social utility derived from economic theory, as previously discussed. Rather, this opposition to regulations designed to prevent exacerbated scarcity must involve a dogmatic conception of freedom that is justified by no further normative claim than its own assertion, embracing a conception of freedom that is outmoded for any society constrained by ecological limits.

## Individuality, consumerism, and sovereignty

Let us consider a similar conception of freedom that is sometimes thought to be incompatible with sustainable individual lifestyles or a sustainable society, with a different potential source of canonical authority for neoliberal freedom. We might start by viewing liberty as it is described by John Stuart Mill, perhaps the ideal's most outspoken advocate in the Western canon of political theory. Freedom, according to Mill, consists in living our lives in our own way, as directed not by pressures toward conformity but according to our own unique individuality. Its essence, he writes in "On Liberty," is the "liberty of tastes and pursuits" in our private lives, where we ought to be free from the interference of others (negative liberty, or a conception in which persons are free from impediments posed by others).[30] Mill's defense of an expansive **private sphere** for the purpose of cultivating our own individuality is perhaps the defining feature of what we might call the *expressive* conception of freedom. The purpose of liberty, according to this view, is the development and expression of individuality. In order to use our liberty to cultivate our own individuality, many of our actions must be protected against interference by others, especially through law and the state.

Its domain is the private sphere where, Mill argues, persons ought to be insulated from coercive laws as well as conformist pressures from others, for the purpose "of framing the plan of our life to suit our own character."[31] He contrasts this outward expression of liberty with what he describes as the "inward domain of consciousness," implying that others observe how persons use it to express themselves through a commodity consumption metaphor:

> A man cannot get a coat or a pair of boots to fit him, unless they
> are either made to his measure, or he has a whole warehouseful to
> choose from: and is it easier to fit him with a life than with a coat,
> or are human beings more like one another in their whole physical
> and spiritual conformation than in the shape of their feet?[32]

Only here can persons exercise "the only freedom which deserves the name," which is "that of pursuing our own good in our own way."[33] While Mill certainly did not intend that persons would develop and express their individuality through commodity consumption only, or even primarily, his expressive conception could be invoked on behalf of those choosing to do so.

In this sphere, "self-regarding" actions cannot be restricted by state coercion without infringing upon liberty, Mill argues, but are instead to be guided by each person's vision of the good life. Since democratic societies tend to infringe upon individual liberty in this sphere through what he calls the "despotism of custom" (which he describes as "the standing hindrance to human advancement"), members of such societies must be protected against the oppressive imposition of majority tastes upon the minority. He writes:

> Protection, therefore, against the magistrate is not enough:
> there needs protection also against the tyranny of the prevailing
> opinion and feeling; against the tendency of society to impose,

by other means than civil penalties, its own ideas and practices
as rules of conduct upon those who dissent from them; to fetter
the development, and, if possible, prevent the formation, of
any individuality not in harmony with its ways, and compel all
characters to fashion themselves upon the model of its own.[34]

For Mill, this domain of individual autonomy is essential to ends
of human perfectionism and social progress. Carving out a domain
in which individuals can make choices, free from the interference
of either law or public opinion, is regarded by Mill as a necessary
component for cultivating individuality and advancing the "spirit
of liberty." Given's Mill's use of the boot metaphor to associate
this conception of freedom with the expression of individuality
through consumerism, one might think Mill's libertarianism a
suitable basis for arguing against contemporary campaigns against
commodities from fur coats to high-flow showerheads, or generally
against the politicization (that is, removal from the private sphere)
of consumption.[35]

## Consumerism, consumption, and freedom

*Consumerism* relies upon a similar account of individual self-
expression. Thorstein Veblen's analysis of "conspicuous
consumption" holds that persons use their public-facing
consumption as "the means of showing pecuniary strength, and
so of gaining or retaining a good name."[36] We consume commodities or leisure as a public expression of who we would like
others to see us as being, Veblen suggested over a century before
Instagram made this kind of expressive consumption *de rigueur*.
Since commodity consumption is now the primary way in which
many persons in market societies express their individuality to
others, we might posit (returning to this below) that the domain
or activity through which we are most free is that of the consumer.
Those eschewing mainstream consumption preferences now have
multiple options for expressing their dissent from majority tastes,
including ironic hipster chic fashion as well as anti-consumerist
consumption through which persons can signal their green credentials to like-minded others. As Michael Maniates notes of our
ubiquitous consumer society, even dissent itself has been commod-
ified so that we can express it to others.[37]

We might note that this association between freedom and
consumption is at least partly the product of marketing efforts to
sell us particular things, but also to inculcate consumerist norms
more generally, whereby we associate happiness or success with

consumption. This association is sometimes more subtly drawn, as when advertisers market a class of vehicle that is almost always driven on paved roadways by promising to liberate its owners from such oppressive constructs as roads (or, in a less imaginative campaign, simply naming one of their products in this category the "Liberty").[38] Governments also contribute to this association, as when a former president, worried about the sudden drop in consumer spending after the 9/11 attacks, urged the American public to resume its gratuitous consumption lest they allow the terrorists to win (or when an appointee of the current president sought to loosen export restrictions on natural gas by deeming them to be "molecules of freedom"). For now, we can set these skeptical thoughts aside in order to appreciate how pervasive this association between freedom and consumerism has become.

From this conception, we might see environmental campaigns to reduce consumption generally or to politicize some consumption options as doing exactly what Mill aimed to resist: interfering in a private domain of individual self-expression. If we cannot express ourselves and our individuality through our consumption, one might think, we cannot pursue the individual good life in the way that Mill commended. A free society, full of diverse sizes and shapes of feet, along with different personality types and aspirations, must require a shoe warehouse (or perhaps, now, an online shoe retailer) that has hundreds of styles and colors in every conceivable size and width. Freedom, such a conception claims, is evidenced by a wide variety of commodity options. Mill's freedom-loving nonconformist today might, according to this view, have a closet full of shoes, ready to deploy the right pair for any occasion, signaling to others their refusal to conform. Predicting that some would seek to pressure others in this domain of expressive freedom, Mill notes that it is "the disposition of mankind" to "impose their own opinions and inclinations as a rule of conduct on others," perhaps capturing efforts to alter the consumption of others through campaigns against single-use plastics or conflict diamonds. The relation to neoliberal freedom should be clear: freedom is conceived in terms of buying and selling, with interference in its domain viewed as inimical to liberty.

## Neoliberal freedom and harm

Alas, Mill's expressive conception of liberty cannot be used to defend unbridled consumption when this degrades the environment and exacerbates scarcity for others. The view that individual freedom is best expressed through consumerism remains axiomatic for many libertarians, however. Murray Rothbard, for example, argues that a "free society" is one in which "each individual is sovereign over his own person and property," and in which "no one is 'sovereign' over anyone else's actions or exchanges."[39] His mentor, the Austrian economist Ludwig von Mises, favorably compares individual commodity consumption to democratic citizenship, calling the unregulated market "a democracy in which every penny gives a right to cast a ballot."[40] George Hildebrand adds that the sort of individual autonomy that it allows enables "individual spenders, by their spending" to "reign supreme in controlling both the allocation of resources and the distribution of goods," which uniquely recognizes that "individual choices have intrinsic value."[41] According to Hildebrand, this kind of economic freedom "constitutes the good life and the good society," and its value "is formally a part of the case for individual freedom itself: that such freedom is good, in and of itself."[42]

Insofar as freedom entails this kind of autonomy to cultivate and express individuality through unconstrained consumption, environmental regulations might be construed as oppressive, undermining the freedom of the individual consumer. Hildebrand, however, follows Mill in limiting the scope of this protected sphere by recognizing the need for a *harm principle*. Mill's principle is directed at coercive laws, aiming to protect this domain of liberty:

> The sole end for which mankind are warranted, individually
> or collectively, in interfering with the liberty of action of any of
> their number, is self-protection. That the only purpose for which
> power can be rightfully exercised over any member of a civilized
> community, against his will, is to prevent harm to others. His own
> good, either physical or moral, is not a sufficient warrant.[43]

As Mill notes, "in all things which regard the external relations of the individual, he is *de jure* amenable to those whose interests are concerned, and if need be, to society as their protector."[44] Freedom can and must be limited where it causes harm to others, Mill argues, since this interferes with the freedom of others. While some may well find the highly polluting practice of "rolling coal" to express individual or cultural values of some kind, and while these might otherwise be protected under the neoliberal freedom inherent in Mill's expressive conception, its harmful nature can justify coercive restrictions against it.

Following Mill, Hildebrand argues that consumer sovereignty must be restricted by a harm principle that allows for state restriction of consumer choices under circumstances in which uninhibited choice "may be damaging to the individuals concerned or to others," including when "certain groups – or in some cases the public as a whole – are not always adequately informed regarding the consequences of choice, or are incapable of appraising the consequences of certain acts, or are unwilling or unable to avoid acts having injurious consequences to others."[45] Hildebrand also endorses a second category of valid restrictions in those "functions that the state alone can perform or is better able to perform." The first of these include public goods (he cites "national defense, justice, public order, regulatory activities, and probably resource conservation"), where state provision of the good is required in order to "resolve the conflict of private interest and to provide for the public interest,"[46] as free-rider tendencies undermine the market provision of such goods. Within these categories fall most (if not all) consumer choices that degrade the environment or deplete natural resources, allowing for only a quite narrow domain of expressive consumption, and justifying rather than undermining regulatory restrictions needed to meet sustainability imperatives.

## Conclusions: sustainability and the ideal of freedom

As an essentially contested concept, the ideal of freedom can be conceived in numerous ways, some of which may be in conflict with sustainability imperatives. Where some such conflict exists, we might recall James Madison's discussion about freedom in his *Federalist #10*. Having noted the "mischiefs of faction," and freedom's causal role in allowing these insidious groups to form ("liberty is to faction as air is to fire"), he declined to call for restrictions on the freedom of association, calling this a remedy that would be worse than the disease. Likewise with the role of reproductive freedom in human population growth – even if that freedom is (as Hardin claims) among the causes of unsustainable rates of human population growth, we ought to recognize its value and seek remedies that minimize the imposition on it. As noted above, we now know that more effective population policies are available through the political and economic empowerment of women, ending poverty and food insecurity, and equal access to education and health care. While it may someday become a casualty of environmental decline under conditions of severe scarcity, freedom need not yet be sacrificed to promote sustainability imperatives. Indeed, it may be an essential ingredient of sustainable transition insofar as it facilitates the sort of activism and social cooperation that are needed to bring it about, and remains one of the objectives of a just and sustainable society.

Since there are multiple conceptions of freedom available to serve as a social ideal, we might also take issue with the suggestion that sustainability imperatives require a quantitative reduction in freedom, rather than a qualitative shift from one kind of freedom to another. Here, we might turn to Hobbes, who in *Leviathan* (1651) claims that the unlimited freedom characteristic of the state of nature renders life "solitary, poor, nasty, brutish, and short," but that peace and "commodious living" are possible if we exchange that freedom of the state of nature for one that requires a legal and political authority to which we must thereafter be obedient, but which grants us a more useful kind of freedom.[47] So long as persons adhere to a conception of freedom whereby submission to law stands as an affront to their liberty, they cannot leave behind the anarchy of the state of nature, for unlimited freedom entails anarchy. Hobbes does not describe the social contract as a forfeiture of freedom, whereby persons are quantitatively less free as a result of it, but rather as an exchange of one (not very useful) kind of freedom for another (and superior) kind. Law may limit the freedom of those subjected to it, but it also protects their freedom, as hedgerows grown along roadways in the English countryside serve to keep travelers from veering off the road or colliding with one another. Law coordinates each person's freedom with that of others, improving the opportunities for all to make more effective use of it.

We now face a similar (if somewhat less violent or dramatic) circumstance to the one described by Hobbes. The freedom to engage in unlimited consumption, or to act in ways that cause us to have large ecological footprints, threatens to undermine the environmental conditions necessary for peace and commodious living. Each of us acts to satisfy our appetites, resulting in unsustainable aggregate consumption, or what might be described as a war *on* nature rather than *in* it, where all stand to suffer as nature is damaged. So long as we adhere to a conception of freedom whereby the requirement that we reduce our consumption (e.g. through water-saving toilets or showerheads) stands as an affront to it, we remain free but at war with the environment that sustains us. By exchanging this conception for another that is compatible with ecological limits and sustainability imperatives, we may, through an analogue to the Hobbesian social contract, exchange the freedom associated with unlimited personal consumption for a kind of freedom that is compatible with the ecological steady-state. Especially given the potential threat to many of our freedoms that would result from heightened environmental scarcity, it behooves us to adopt such a new conception, lest our pursuit of freedom undermine the material conditions for maintaining that freedom over time.

# 4 Democracy

Perhaps no social and political ideal developed over the past two centuries enjoys the unrivaled status of democracy, which is so commonly accepted as the superior form of decision making and social organization that it has been invoked to refer to an entire social epoch. Revolutions during the late eighteenth century in the United States and France ushered in the Democratic Age, this account often claims, vanquishing alternative forms of social and political organization. So dominant are its imperatives that it has long enjoyed a bipartisan consensus throughout the West, even coming to represent progress itself. Freedom House democracy scores, which evaluate countries in terms of the presence of democratic elements and institutions, are now widely assumed to be a valid measure of national progress, with "democratization" and "political development" often used synonymously.[1]

While this superficial consensus about the superiority of democratic forms of government may have obscured significant disagreement as to what particular elements of democracy contending groups sought to pursue, governing principles like universal suffrage and political equality bind together diverse forms that differently assign and utilize representation, grant ordinary citizens varying degrees of political power, and seek to establish various mechanisms of responsiveness of state institutions to the popular will, as well as popular means for holding state actors accountable. Despite ongoing disagreement over what kind of democracy is best, there remains little doubt for many that the future of governments in the West (and perhaps beyond) ought to be democratic in some sense. Democracy's triumph over its rivals has been heralded as an "end of history" and an "end of ideology" during the latter half of the twentieth century, despite its shortcomings in existing liberal democracies and the social unrest that often accompanied it.[2] To paraphrase Winston Churchill, it has come to be regarded as the worst form of government, except for all the others that have been tried.

## Democracy and the environment

In many ways, it was the democratic culture of the 1960s that gave rise to what we now refer to as the US environmental movement, which emerged as an oppositional and progressive social movement in an oppositional and progressive decade. While environmental historians often trace its origins to the schism between preservationists like John Muir and conservationists like Gifford Pinchot (discussed in chapter 5), it was not until emerging concerns about pollution exposure, following the 1962 publication of Rachel Carson's *Silent Spring*, galvanized the public against threats to public health, that the movement assumed its current form. Rather than focusing upon far-off landscapes, as preservationists had up to that point largely done, activists began during this period to mobilize the public against a host of threats to its wellbeing, transforming environmentalism from a special interest held by a niche of elites to a genuinely public interest, and possibly into a full political ideology.[3]

The dozen years that followed were formative for US environmental policy. With high-profile focusing events like the Cuyahoga River catching fire, and oil spills on Santa Barbara's pristine beaches, the movement sought to challenge a complacent national government to better protect its people by protecting their environment. The grassroots democratic organizing of early environmental groups can be credited for pressuring Congress into action, creating most of the nation's important environmental legislation in this period: the Wilderness Act in 1964, the National Environmental Policy Act in 1968, the Clean Air Acts in 1970 and Clean Water Act in 1972, and the Endangered Species Act in 1973. All were, in an important sense, products of a democratic culture, democratic institutions, and a democratic form of social change, with popular social movements pressuring government to respond to their demands. Born of democracy, the US environmental movement has long embraced and continues to rely upon it.

European environmentalism has a similar historical association with the democratic ideal. The German Green Party ("Die Grünen") formed in 1980 from strands of anti-nuclear, peace, New Left, environmental, and new social movements, embracing grassroots democracy as one of its four pillars, along with social justice, ecological wisdom, and nonviolence. As the first green party to participate in a parliamentary government, which it held in coalition with the Social Democratic Party of Germany from 1998 to 2005, the Greens continued to emphasize the role of grassroots democratic engagement in social change while governing, as have green parties in other European countries. This embrace of the democratic ideal led Robert Goodin to cast what he calls the "green theory of agency" (or theory of political actors and action behind green politics, as discussed further in chapter 7) as committed to "the importance of full, free, active participation by everyone in democratically shaping their personal and social circumstances."[4]

Failure to prevent serious environmental impacts can also threaten democracy, especially those impacts associated with climate change. Many thousands of people are expected to be displaced by climate-related impacts over upcoming decades, from coastal or river flooding to persistent drought or changes in disease vectors, with the resulting climate-induced migration threatening the territorial integrity of some states and the border security of others. Widespread climate-related displacement would overwhelm the world's humanitarian refugee resettlement programs with forced movements of people much larger than those that the current system struggles to handle.[5] Several of these drivers are expected to increase violent conflict, which in turn can lead democratic regimes to suspend or end democratic protections.[6] For fledgling democracies that may not yet have developed the capacity to respond to such emergencies, democratic government itself might be threatened.[7] Even established democracies can fail when faced with conditions of severe scarcity,[8] or when their legitimacy is called into question upon failure to respond to emergencies such as those threatened by climate change. Democracies cannot afford to allow such impacts to manifest, lest the future be a post-democratic one.

## Democracy as incompatible with sustainability?

Given this longstanding association between environmentalism and democracy, it may be surprising to see environmental movement leaders identify democracy as a culprit or obstacle, rather than an enabler of progressive social change. But physicist and Gaia-hypothesis originator James Lovelock did just this in a March 2010 interview with the *Guardian*, claiming that "even the best democracies agree that when a major war approaches, democracy must be put on hold for the time being."[9] Comparing climate change to wartime emergency, Lovelock argued that the urgency of climate change, combined with the apparent inability of existing democratic institutions to adequately address it, warranted a suspension of democratic principles or shift of authority away from its institutions.

Lovelock's concern with the slow pace of progress toward reaching an effective treaty agreement, as well as with the domestic commitments by the UK government that are necessary for its implementation, echoes that of many critics. Whether in criticism of the consensus rule of the United Nations Framework Convention on Climate Change (UNFCCC) governance processes, the popular mobilization of climate science denial by fossil-fuel interests, or other participatory or popular responsiveness deficits, some critics now identify democratic qualities that fostered the growth and early impact of the environmental movement as undermining its efficacy. Lovelock's sentiments, while perhaps remarkable for their frankness, reflect a growing critical current in Western environmental politics that can also be seen in "green" challenges to democracy emerging from environmental political theory.

## Environment and democracy

Is democracy up to the task of facilitating the transition to a sustainable society, or even preventing ecological collapse? At issue is the alleged incompatibility between environmental protection and democracy, or whether a robust commitment to one might undermine an equally strong commitment to the other. Brian Barry captures this dilemma by asking his reader to imagine a circumstance in which a local polity is asked to democratically determine whether to build a dam that would bring needed jobs and hydroelectric power, or protect an endangered species whose habitat would be destroyed by its construction. Where the democratic process prioritizes the dam over biodiversity protection, the committed environmentalist and democrat must choose between her competing loyalties. Does her commitment to democratic decision-making processes vindicate the outcome, which her commitment to ecological integrity opposes, or do her environmental values cause her to question and perhaps reject democracy?

From Barry's point of view, one can distinguish between a commitment to political right or justice, on the one hand, and one's substantive conception of the good on the other. He suggests that the committed biodiversity advocate would be torn if the majority supported the dam's construction, but would accept the outcome as democratically legitimate. As he writes, this "outcome is, as far as you are concerned, legitimate but bad – bad in the precise sense that it offends against your conception of the good."[10] Where fair democratic procedures result in bad environmental outcomes, **procedural legitimacy** conflicts with the environmentalist's substantive values, putting her commitment to democracy to the test. Accepting democratic outcomes that lead to serious environmental degradation would require strong commitment to democracy, at least in the present (even if, as we shall consider, such degradation imperils democracy in the long run). Barry's example highlights how the values supporting democracy are distinct from (and can conflict with) those endorsing sustainability.

## Reconciling democracy and sustainability

While this potential for conflict between values inherent in substantive outcomes like environmental protection and those of democratic processes is not unique to environmental politics, it does raise the issue of their compatibility and priority. Environmental protection is a substantive outcome of political decision making, and its value is not reducible to any set of procedures by which it was selected. As Goodin notes, "to advocate democracy is to advocate proceduralism," whereas "to advocate environmentalism is to advocate substantive outcomes."[11] It would be naïve to expect that every putatively democratic decision would necessarily support sustainable outcomes, such that no conflict between them would ever arise. The relationship between the two is contingent, rather than necessary: democratic decisions sometimes result in strong environmental protections, but won't always do so. In order to reduce this potential conflict and thus to avoid deciding between them, political theorists have asked how democracy might be rendered more likely to endorse sustainable policy outcomes.

One might pause here and ask whether there is anything untoward in posing the question in this way. After all, commitments to democracy are to the inherent fairness of a decision-making process, and with it the legitimacy of its outcome, *whatever* that outcome might turn out to be. From this point of view, seeking to render such processes more likely to adopt any particular substantive outcome seems disingenuous and manipulative, and against democratic values of responsiveness to majority will. Selecting among institutions or decision rules on the basis of the outcomes that they are likely to endorse (or "venue shopping"), rather than on the basis of their intrinsic qualities, may seem like cheating – using democracy merely to confer legitimacy upon a decision that was made in some nondemocratic way. This concern is most plausible insofar as democracy is understood primarily as a procedural ideal, or set of rules for arriving at legitimate collective decisions.

But the democratic ideal is not merely a commitment to certain kinds of decision-making procedures. Rather, it entails several important substantive commitments, as well. Democratic societies are open and inclusive beyond the narrowly political domain of voting, maintain systems of equal opportunity in areas like employment and education, allow for social and economic mobility without discrimination, and insist upon transparency and account-ability for public officials. Democracy is not merely a means of aggregating preferences to reach collective decisions, but involves a set of virtues, habits, and attitudes about how to relate to one's fellow citizens. Perhaps most importantly for our purposes here, liberal democracies strive to balance the will of the majority with the protection of vulnerable minorities, often through the institution of legal rights. Many of these substantive commit-ments could be jeopardized by a strictly procedural conception of democracy, especially where majorities in democratic societies are not themselves committed to democracy despite being empowered by it. While some procedural elements of democracy reinforce some of its substantive commitments – for example, with political equality tending toward decisions that serve the interests of the many rather than only a powerful elite – we must be mindful of those tensions between substantive and procedural democratic values.

## Two kinds of democratic legitimacy

At issue is whether *legitimacy*, which is a perceived quality of political institutions and their outcomes when they adhere to the democratic ideal, has substantive or only procedural dimensions. A *purely procedural* theory of legitimacy would endorse any outcome of a properly constituted democratic process, yielding the dilemma above if the democratic outcome opposes the core values of some of its participants. Since there would be no independent standard for assessing outcomes other than their legitimacy, the "legitimate but bad" verdict would force the committed democratic environ-mentalist to choose between incommensurate values. Aiming to design procedures for the express purpose of generating particular outcomes may here undermine the legitimacy-imparting value of the procedures. But theories that define legitimacy partly or wholly in terms of substantive outcomes exist, easing this dilemma. *Democratic instrumentalism* allows for an independent standard for identifying ideal outcomes but holds that democracy is usually the best procedure for generating that outcome. Where it fails to do so, democracy would not be necessary for a legitimate outcome to be reached. Lovelock's call for nondemocratic decision making to deal with the climate crisis is likely a form of such instrumentalism.

One way to contrast these two kinds of legitimacy theories is in terms of input and output legitimacy.[12] A pure proceduralist would derive all legitimacy from the inputs to a decision: its inclusiveness, its commitment to political equality, its identification of the majority will, and so on. A pure instrumentalist would derive all legitimacy from its outputs: whether the process that was used generated some ideal outcome (or perhaps an outcome within a tolerable range), defined in terms not reducible to the process itself. Pure proceduralists endorse any outcome that results from proper process, while pure instrumentalists would be happy with any process that generated their ideal outcome. Both have their problems – the former exhibits an unfounded confidence in democracy, against historical evidence of its occasional failure; and the latter treats democracy as only contingently useful and, in so doing, undermines the democratic ethos itself (not to mention that there are practical difficulties in determining what to do in the face of disagreement). Mixed theories of legitimacy, such as a deliberative account of democracy, attribute value and derive legitimacy from both inputs and outputs. Later in the chapter, we shall consider how a deliberative account of democracy might help us to escape Barry's dilemma.

Insofar as the democratic ideal is concerned in part with both inputs and outputs, with an element of legitimacy attaching to each, the necessary task involves aligning procedures with the independently defined outcomes that we want, or need, them to yield. Good environmental outcomes are not constituted by fair democratic processes, nor do they always result from them. But fair processes have value apart from their outcomes, often understood in terms of procedural or input legitimacy, providing reasons to maintain them where possible. Democracy is neither a singular nor a perfect process, and its imperfection in yielding outcomes that are substantively democratic, or which otherwise satisfy output legitimacy, gives rise to the need for construction of legitimate democratic processes that are likely to yield legitimate outcomes, combined with mechanisms for identifying and correcting their failures to do so. We do the same for other kinds of imperfect procedures – through due process protections for those accused of criminal acts, for example, since we define the ideal outcome by an independent standard (punishing of the guilty), but rely on processes that occasionally fail to bring it about. Where we can revise procedures that regularly lead to bad outcomes (for example, indigent defendants being disproportionately convicted because of absent or incompetent counsel), we try to align our inputs and outputs.

## Democracy and doughnuts

In seeking to reconcile democracy and sustainability, there may not be a single best outcome that democratic procedures must be tooled to reliably yield, but rather a range of acceptable outcomes that allow the environmental impact of human activities to remain within planetary boundaries. Kate Raworth's image of the "doughnut" of social and planetary boundaries captures this range of socially and environmentally acceptable outcomes. The doughnut's inner ring is formed by the 12 human development goals that represent social objectives that humanity must not fall short of meeting. Inside of that ring is empty space where the doughnut's hole has been cut out, representing failure to meet justice objectives. It sets the social boundary of acceptable outcomes. The outer ring is formed by the eight planetary boundaries[13] that represent ecological limits that must not be exceeded, defining the outer, ecological boundary.[14]

Since it often takes additional resources to meet human development goals like ending poverty or hunger, these can interact with the ecological limits of planetary boundaries. We could feed more people by turning over more undeveloped lands to agricultural use, or through more intensive agriculture, but at the cost of pressure on boundaries like biodiversity loss, depletion of freshwater resources, or chemical pollution from pesticides. Too little use of resources toward such goals shrinks the interior ring of the doughnut, limiting their attainment, and would thus be unacceptable for humanitarian reasons. Between these two rings lies the range of legitimate options (constraints defined in terms of output legitimacy). According to Raworth's image, this "doughnut" defines the "safe and just operating space for humanity" by simultaneously satisfying imperatives of justice and sustainability, conceived in this way.

A similar image might guide the relationship between democracy and sustainability. The inner boundary might represent governance procedures that are minimally democratic, with decisions inside that ring representing authoritarian or otherwise illegitimate forms of collective decision making. With ecological limits defining the outer ring, we might imagine otherwise-democratic processes that fail to maintain environmental conditions necessary for democracy's ongoing maintenance falling outside of the outer ring, as well as outcomes that violate democratic norms falling inside the inner one. Within the range of environmentally acceptable outcomes that are also democratically legitimate, spatially defined in terms of this doughnut, polities may decide on the basis of procedural or substantive democratic commitments (following majority rule, for example, or protecting rights) or commitments to other social ideals. A range of democratic forms or processes may be compatible with remaining inside the ecological boundary, even if not all would. The conception of democracy that informs them would not determine such outcomes, but it could limit them. The tendency to yield outcomes that fall beyond the outer boundary would identify those conceptions or forms that are incompatible with sustainability imperatives.

Allowing for a range of "democratic and sustainable" options, rather than seeking to more specifically identify one ideal outcome and then reverse-engineer decision-making processes in order to reliably yield it, has another advantage. Among democracy's core commitments is that to contingency and revisability: democratic institutions always contain mechanisms through which they can be improved, even if these often require supermajority support that makes their revision difficult, and thus uncommon. Rules and procedures that cannot be revised risk becoming ossified and dogmatic, violating the ethos of democratic **self-determination** by allowing the past to exercise too much influence over the present. It is for such reasons that Michael Saward argues that democracy might yet be vindicated (embracing what he describes as "politics as a substitute for certainty"), despite its noted anti-environmental tendencies.[15] Given its malleability as a social ideal or organizing principle, seeking to balance democracy with sustainability imperatives in this manner offers a way around the dilemma suggested above and allows us to explore how environmental politics and problems have driven some evolutionary development of the ideal.

## Rights as democratic constraints on democracy

Constraints upon democracy typically take the form of rights, which protect interests that are vulnerable to majority tyranny. Insofar as environmentally sustainable outcomes are needed to maintain justice, for example, we might look to rights as protections against majoritarian decisions that imperil a marginalized minority or otherwise violate the rights of an affected group. As noted above, the mere fact that some decision reflects political equality and majority-rule principles (those most commonly associated with democratic procedures) does not vindicate that decision for any but a purely procedural theory of legitimacy. A given decision might be procedurally democratic but, in its treatment of a numerical minority, be substantively undemocratic, since democracy requires equal respect for all and a tyrannical majority would fail to confer such respect. Here, one aspect of democracy (a set of procedures) contradicts and is constrained by another part (its substantive commitments).

Formal protection of individual liberties through legal or constitutional rights would model how a sustainability constraint upon democratic outcomes might be institutionalized. Civil liberties, in which persons are protected by legal rights against interference in their domain of liberty, offer an exemplary form for such a constraint. Rights to free speech or free association have over time become closely associated with democratic forms of government, despite their constraints upon what democratic majorities can legislate. They protect key democratic values while imposing constraints upon democratic processes, in that majorities are disallowed from using their power to restrict the rights or liberties of others. We might view a sustainability constraint as imposing a similar rights-based limit on acceptable outcomes of democratic processes. Several alternatives for such a sustainability right are discussed further in chapter 6, including the legal right to a safe environment, which would provide recourse to those endangered by majority decisions that imposed significant environmental risk.

Where individual rights are at stake, liberal democracies that seek to balance the ideals of freedom and democracy protect those rights against infringement, even where it is a democratic process or legitimate institution that threatens them. Sustainability imperatives might seek a comparable right-based protection against democratic outcomes that threaten them. As Henry Shue notes, "the purpose of a right is to provide protection for human beings against a threat to which they are vulnerable and against which they may be powerless without such protective action."[16] Protection against many forms of environmental degradation would be exemplary in this regard. While self-determination is a collective right of peoples to democratically order their societies, individual rights protect against majority decisions that adversely affect the interests of the vulnerable, limiting what majorities can decide. The development of democratic procedures for the governance of modern societies is necessarily a challenge of balancing responsiveness to majority will with protection of the vulnerable and maintenance of conditions under which democracy can continue to flourish. Environmental constraints on democratic procedures merely add to the set of outcomes that we should want our democratic institutions to protect against, without which the future of our democratic institutions and society would be in jeopardy.

Rights limiting democratic outcomes in order to protect against environmental harm may take several forms. Whether in the form of "equal protection" rights (which serve as the legal basis for US anti-discrimination law) that prevent powerful majorities from concentrating society's environmental hazards and vulnerabilities upon a minority group, or as procedural rights that seek to inform affected parties of environmental hazards or give them a say in decisions that affect them, or through specifically environmental rights like the right to a safe or adequate environment, the use of such rights to safeguard against bad environmental outcomes of otherwise-legitimate democratic processes might help to reconcile the potential conflict between democracy and sustainability noted above. For now, we should note that the reliance upon such rights to constrain the actions or decisions of a majority, while procedurally counter-majoritarian, is not necessarily undemocratic (or, at least, is no less democratic than is any system of government limited by legal or constitutional rights).

## Alternatives to democracy

In the preceding section, we considered limits to or constraints on democracy designed to avoid potentially harmful scarcity or the imposition of environmental risks, aiming to reconcile majority-rule democratic procedures with substantive environmental protection imperatives. Such a project may be viewed as realistic about anti-environmental tendencies inherent in existing democratic institutions, but optimistic about the prospects for reform that reconciles these different values within the range of the doughnut discussed above. Some, however, are not so optimistic. Rather than seeking to constrain democracy or develop versions of it that are more compatible with such imperatives, some critics view the various incompatibilities between democracy and sustainable environmental policies as requiring that democracy be supplanted by undemocratic institutions or decision-making processes. Lovelock's suggestion that democracy be put "on hold for a while" illustrates this call for alternatives to democracy, rather than alternative democratic forms.

### Technocracy as alternative to democracy

We might briefly distinguish several versions of nondemocratic alternatives that promise to rectify some of the shortcomings of democracy in the context of environmental decision making. Along a continuum of increasing opposition to the democratic ideal, the first is best described as supplementing rather than supplanting democracy, drawing upon what Mark Brown calls the "liberal-rationalist" conception of democracy. Government advisory committees or science advisors to legislative bodies rely upon expertise to represent public interests, Brown suggests, on the assumption that they do so most effectively when they remain "epistemologically and institutionally insulated from popular expression of those interests."[17] Authorizing politically insulated experts to make policy decisions (or *technocracy*) would be a nondemocratic alternative (and likely one that Lovelock had in mind), but utilizing them in an advisory capacity is compatible with maintaining democratic control over those issue areas.

Nonetheless, even reliance on expert advisory bodies may be in tension with aspects of the democratic ideal. One problem with the liberal-rationalist conception, as we shall explore further below, lies in the artificial boundary that it seeks to draw between facts and values, or between the expert and the citizen. As Brown argues, scientists cannot study nature without engaging with and transforming it in the process, and scientific research cannot be insulated from values in the way that the liberal-rationalist view demands. Insofar as experts draw their authority from claims to have access to pure and impartial facts, which might guide the selection among policy options without any interference by values, the conception is untenable. Values influence the work that experts do in manifold ways, and facts cannot determine policy choices without the intervention of values in some form.

## Technocracy as compatible with democracy

Expert advisory bodies working in tandem with democratic institutions, when properly constructed as having access to valuable knowledge but not viewed as operating in a domain that is devoid of values, are more of a form of democracy than an alternative to it. Wildlife biologists may validly utilize their expertise to determine how human activities have affected the habitats of other species, drawing upon their privileged access to facts that results from their training, but cannot, without invoking values (to which they lack such privileged access), determine when those activities should be curtailed in order to protect remaining habitat, and thus prioritize endangered species protection over other imperatives. Technical expertise can be one input to a democratic decision-making process, while allowing for other inputs and for decision-making authority to be vested in democratic institutions. Likewise, it can be called upon by democratic bodies (as it has been in the US Endangered Species Act) to make fact-based decisions (such as when a species has become threatened or endangered, as defined by that statute), in order to prevent those decisions from becoming politicized. Technocracy thus represents a nondemocratic (but not anti-democratic) alternative to more democratic forms of representation, in that it represents expert knowledge of, rather than popular experience in, the natural world in decision-making processes and institutions.

Many expert advisory committees are already embedded within democratic states, and few regard these as undemocratic. The Congressional Budget Office (CBO) prepares economic forecasts and budget impact assessments of bills under consideration. Environmental Protection Agency (EPA) scientists conduct environmental impact analyses of proposed federal government actions. While both mobilize a kind of authority that can be regarded as hostile to democracy in that it makes claims to facts gleaned through expertise held only by specialists, neither is vested with legislative power. CBO economists and EPA scientists can only advise decision makers through these roles, and government officials are free to ignore that advice (and often avail themselves of this freedom). Expertise does have some **epistemic authority**[18] that can threaten the political authority of elected officials (hence the Trump administration's purging of experts from some standing advisory bodies, and its termination of other bodies), but in an advisory role such bodies lack formal powers to oppose or override decisions made by political authorities.

Some expert bodies are empowered with decision-making authority, and this introduces some tensions with procedural versions of the democratic ideal in that those experts are not held accountable to the electorate in the way that legislators are. For example, US Fish and Wildlife Service scientists determine whether a species should be listed as threatened or endangered under the Endangered Species Act, triggering protections against destruction of their critical habitats. Some critics of US biodiversity policy cast this power as undemocratic – despite the fact that its authorizing statute was adopted by Congress – because of the power that it delegates to unelected experts. As we shall consider further below, this kind of insulation from political pressures can be beneficial to the integrity of certain kinds of decisions. Delegation of administrative powers to executive branch experts can also serve the electoral interests of legislators, but this does not stop legislators from occasionally seeking to influence such administrative discretion through their criticism or budgetary power, or prevent them from trying to permanently revoke it.

Whether expertise is called upon to supplement democracy in an advisory role or to supplant democratic authority by vesting it in empowered bodies of experts, technocracy offers a competing ideal for governance, limiting the responsiveness of institutions to the public and increasing their responsiveness to expert knowledge. All contemporary democracies contain democratic and technocratic bodies that are set up to balance each other – with members of the public sometimes contributing toward knowledge production through activities like citizen science; and experts, either in an advisory role or entrusted with authority that requires insulation from electoral or other political pressures. Few would characterize this as anti-democratic, but in their ideal form democracy and technocracy co-exist in some tension with one another over the kind of authority that each wields and the qualifications necessary for wielding it.

## Reconciling technocracy with democracy

Competing models for the proper role of expertise within democratic politics suggest the challenges involved in reconciling the desire for greater command of the technicalities involved in many issues, and the importance of evidence-based decision-making, with the democratic imperative of constructing the public good through popular participation, rather than domination by elites. One model, coined the "honest broker" by Roger Pielke, Jr., would limit scientists and other experts to a policy advisory and evaluation role, but expressly prohibit their participation in policy advocacy.[19] Given the widespread politicization of science in recent US politics, Pielke argues, the mere appearance of bias among those charged with providing their assessments as experts threatens to undermine the credibility of science as an evaluative tool. When scientific experts become policy advocates, Pielke claims, they abandon the impartiality with which science is vested and take on the appearance of political actors. This, he argues, unnecessarily jeopardizes the potentially constructive role that scientists might otherwise play, should they instead opt to remain within their domain of expertise (in facts) rather than sliding into a domain in which they have no special claims to a comparable authority (in values).

One example of this honest broker that has been imperfectly realized in practice is the Intergovernmental Panel on Climate Change (IPCC). Created in 1988 by the World Meteorological Organization and the UN Environment Programme, the IPCC was charged with reviewing all peer-reviewed scientific research on the causes and effects of climate change, and publishing periodic assessment reports summarizing the consensus of the scientific community on what is known about the phenomenon and what remains uncertain. Employing a democratic process of its own, the panel (which is split into three working groups on different substantive areas of climate research) works by consensus toward text that all members endorse, sometimes spending hours contesting single summary statements or debating whether language conveying findings or uncertainty has been accurately phrased. Importantly, the panel is charged with advising governments on the scientific bases of the causes and likely effects of climate change, which are reported through a single summary for policymakers that combines the three working group reports. Importantly, the IPCC summarizes the science but does not advocate any policy.

For those, like Pielke, who fear that allowing IPCC scientists to engage in climate policy advocacy would politicize its scientific findings, this kind of strictly enforced restriction may help to preserve the panel's credibility and epistemic authority. Among the rhetorical tools of climate denial is a conspiracy theory about politicized scientists falsifying data and issuing exaggerated or erroneous warnings to the public in order to maintain the existing social order and frighten government officials into providing them with more research funding (the plot of Michael Crichton's fictional denialist narrative *State of Fear*). Maintaining a strict separation between the reporting of facts and policy advocacy may help to avoid this denialist narrative.

Others are more skeptical about either the need for this prohibition upon advocacy or its putative benefit. Unlike Pielke's honest broker, which would evaluate the merits of various policy proposals without endorsing any particular option, the IPCC does not evaluate policies themselves, but instead tracks various future emissions scenarios, which turn on policy as well as other drivers. If it was to evaluate particular policies, it would be only one step removed from advocacy of the one deemed most effective. But opting out of evaluating various policy options comes at a cost to the potential for more informed public debates about those options.

Public-opinion research suggests that the US public is badly misinformed about what consensus exists among climate scientists, with respondents consistently and significantly overestimating the amount of reported uncertainty and the proportion of credentialed scientists opposing the consensus statements of the IPCC. While it is possible that policy advocacy by the IPCC would further undermine the credibility of science among those misinformed about its findings, this pervasive misinformation is likely a product of the organized effort by the climate denial industry. Its narrative impugning the credibility of climate science and scientists does not depend upon their participation in policy advocacy, as it portrays them as self-interested alarmists, overstating climate impacts in order to frighten a gullible public into supporting more government-funded scientific research, as well as pushing governments into forfeiting their sovereignty to a multilateral climate regime bent on curbing US power.

The upshot is that critics find Pielke's strict separation between domains of facts and those of value – with his identification of scientists as couriers of the former, to be contained in a role where their values are to remain publicly opaque and noncommittal in order to keep up the appearance of neutrality – to be untenable. Many of those most opposed are scientists who are themselves passionate advocates for action on climate change, and who resent being muzzled on an issue on which they are experts and in which they have vested value commitments as well as factual knowledge. Advocates like former NASA Goddard Institute of Space Studies Director James Hanson, who has become an outspoken advocate for strong climate action, are now arguably among the most effective policy advocates, and yet are able to navigate the challenge of not conflating the epistemic authority associated with their expertise with tendentious claims to normative authority issuing from it. Hansen's appeal to intergenerational justice as his central motive for activism is evident in most of his public appearances in an advocacy role, as well as in his advocacy-oriented book *Storms of My Grandchildren* (2009).

This second model of the engaged expert/activist comes with risks of its own, which ought not to be taken lightly. Some fear that the power vested in scientific authority threatens the democratic character of politics by creating another group of elites and by further removing the public from issues deemed too complex for their limited competence. Others criticize the claims to a putatively value-free science, noting that values infuse and guide multiple stages of the knowledge-production process – from decisions about what research to fund to ideological disposi-tions within the community of inquirers – and thus seek to limit the influence of what is taken to be a political actor regardless of whether it formally participates in policy advocacy. Still others find science and expertise generally to be inherently patriarchal, and are generally skeptical of its truth claims as mere exercise of power, viewing science as a manifestation of the desire to dominate and control nature. Ultimately, the choice between models for including science in democracy is likely to turn on one's impression of the influence that science has on political decision making. In the present environment of government suppression of scientific research and the purging of scientists from expert advisory boards, it is perhaps a low point in the ebb and flow of expertise run amok, with the narrative about excessive influence by experts less plausible than in recent decades – but that cannot by itself settle the question.

## Eco-authoritarianism as alternative to democracy

*Eco-authoritarianism*, or strong centralized government that rejects democratic oversight and accountability as well as individual rights, but takes environmental protection as a core state imperative, represents the biggest challenge to and departure from the democratic ideal. Viewing democracy itself as complicit in causing or failing to prevent environmental crises, eco-authoritarians endorse anti-democratic alternatives to democratic institutions. Unlike technocratic bodies such as expert advisory commissions, or government scientists who are granted administrative discretion to implement democratically enacted statutes within a state and society that is otherwise democratic, authoritarian alternatives to democracy would wield power without electoral accountability of any kind and could do so against interests that would otherwise be protected by individual rights. Insofar as Hardin's solution to the overpopulation dilemma (discussed in chapter 3) restricts reproductive freedom, but does so in the putative interest of protecting the environment, it could be construed as eco-authoritarian.

As Dan Shahar notes, the kind of eco-authoritarianism that flourished in the late 1960s and early 1970s, which embraced a vision of centralized planning by a cadre of ecologically minded elites (modeled on the Soviet Union, despite its poor environmental performance), had largely disappeared by the 1990s with the collapse of communism. But Shahar warns of a new version, modeled on contemporary China, that is enjoying resurgence. This version, he suggests, denounces centralized planning but calls for suspension of democratic procedures, and for state power to override individual rights. As he notes of this revival of the eco-authoritarian ideal, "impatience with the glacial pace of environmental reforms appears to have led some western commentators to look ruefully eastward and wish that their own nations would act with more impunity."[20] Shahar cites a column by Thomas Friedman praising China's "one-party autocracy" as uniquely able to "just impose the politically difficult but critically important policies needed to move a society forward in the 21st century."[21] Like Lovelock's call for alternatives to democracy that promise greater responsiveness to looming ecological challenges like climate change, both the old and new versions of eco-authoritarianism start with a critique of Western market liberalism, identifying this as fatally flawed, as well as synonymous with democracy itself.

*Eco-fascism*, which uses totalitarian government to subordinate individual interests to those of an "organic whole" of nature, and draws upon the militarism and expansionism of twentieth-century European fascism, offers another variation on the eco-authoritarian ideal which is emerging from alt-right ideology and is overtly hostile to procedural as well as substantive democratic norms. Rooted in white supremacist ideology, and taking Nazi Germany as its model regime, eco-fascism embraces violence and exclusion in pursuit of a view of nature in which "Blood-and-Soil" ecological purity requires racial purity, with non-whites viewed as a kind of pollution.[22] White supremacist agitator Richard Spencer, for example, declared in his August 2017 manifesto (inaugurating that month's "Unite the Right" rally in Charlottesville, Virginia, at which protester Heather Heyer was killed by a Nazi sympathizer) that "European countries" should "invest in national parks, wilderness preserves, and wildlife refuges, as well as productive and sustainable farms and ranches" because "the natural world – and our experience of it – is an end in itself."[23] Perpetrators of 2019 terrorist attacks in Christchurch and El Paso also cited eco-fascist ideologies as motives for their attacks in rambling manifestos.

The case for eco-authoritarianism is sometimes expressed in terms of a regrettable necessity, given democracy's alleged inability to cope with increasing scarcity. While he does not specify what should replace the democratic processes that would be put "on hold for a while," Lovelock's criticism of democracy expresses this regret. Often cast as an eco-authoritarian, William Ophuls conveys a similar lament that democratic societies may be unable to prevent the exacerbated scarcity that will be their undoing, but never actually endorses authoritarian alternatives to democracy. Indeed, he suggests that "the personal and civil rights" in the US Constitution "could be largely retained in an appropriately-designed steady-state society," with only "the right to use private property in ecologically destructive ways" requiring new restrictions. As he notes, "authority in the steady state need not be remote, arbitrary, and capricious," but could instead be "made constitutional and limited."[24] Ophuls does not so much advocate eco-authoritarianism as warn against its possibility, much as Plato in the *Republic* condemns democracy for its tendency to collapse into tyranny. Unless we tend to the drivers of ecological scarcity now, we may find our democratic governments unable to respond to the crisis that results, paving the way for an authoritarian leader to seize power.

Unlike **technocracy**, which can harmoniously co-exist with the democratic ideal, all forms of eco-authoritarianism fundamentally reject and oppose democracy, and in this sense represent a genuine alternative (and threat) to it. Ophuls is more coherently read as advocating technocracy, since he suggests that (again invoking Plato) "the ecologically-complex steady-state society may therefore require, if not a class of ecological guardians, then at least a class of ecological mandarins who possess the esoteric knowledge needed to run it well."[25] Platonic guardians are characterized by their philosophical dispositions, which Plato thought sufficient to orient them to the public good and allow them to detect threats to it. By contrast, the contemporary version of the philosopher-king calls for scientific and technical rather than philosophical knowledge as its relevant credential, but commends a similar rule by the wise few, supplanting rather than supplementing democracy.

## Technocracy as antidote to democracy's failings

A technocratic government by ecologist-kings oriented toward the public good, along timescales that also serve future generations, offers what advocates of technocracy find to be a tempting antidote to some of the pathologies of contemporary democracy, including the scientific ignorance of the mass public, the short time horizons of elected officials, and the insidious influence of campaign finance on government. Rather than seeking to treat these pathologies with a view toward improving the quality of democratic decision making, those advocating technocracy as a remedy view these as endemic to democracy and thus seek to contain their insidious influence by shifting power to politically insulated technocrats.

To the extent that democracy's faults lie in its slowness, and other difficulties in making decisions with such large numbers of constituents as in large contemporary nation-states, the small size of eco-authoritarian or technocratic institutions likewise becomes attractive. To the extent that those faults lie in the wide breadth of interests that must be accommodated in popular democratic institutions, and the related difficulties in representing or consulting a wide variety of groups or perspectives, the narrower set of perspectives and more homogeneous interests of technocratic institutions hold some allure. To the extent that democratic publics struggle with the scientific or technical competence to understand complex science policy issues like climate change or biodiversity – and empirical evidence on scientific competence among electorates in advanced industrial democracies like the United States is not encouraging in this regard – the turn toward rule by elites selected on the basis of this competence may be compelling. Observation of faults in familiar regimes or forms of governance often lead those seeking better performance to consider alternative regime types rather than internal reform.

Few go as far as Ophuls in seeking to vest all political authority in technocratic bodies that operate as a panel of scientific mandarins. More commonly, political theorists call for a shift away from electoral institutions staffed – as they tend to be – by non-experts, and toward some more empowered and politically insulated decision making by expert bodies (insulated from political pressures by their absence of electoral accountability, as with US Fish and Wildlife Service [FWS] biologists, rather than elected politicians, making listing decisions under the Endangered Species Act), whether in administrative branches of government or originating outside the state but consti-tuted for the purpose of applying expertise to a particular policy challenge. Mainstream political science provides the rationale for moderate delegation to experts in cases of technically difficult or politically sensitive decision making in many science policy fields. Elected officials lack the expertise and time needed to understand the finer details of many science policy decisions, and have electoral incentives to delegate these to executive branch administrators that members of the public can hold responsible when they take contro-versial regulatory actions.

The *politicization of science* – episodes in which political actors interfere in decisions that had been delegated to technocratic bodies – illustrates the challenge involved in maintaining a healthy balance between technocracy and democracy, but underscores the urgency of maintaining the integrity of the arrangement. The convening of a politicized "God Squad" to oversee listing decisions for endan-gered species during the Pacific Northwest "timber wars" of the early 1990s, and the Trump administration's current efforts to scrub references to climate change from agency websites and extirpate it from governmental research reports, both suggest the dangers of politicizing science. Determining the proper balance between electoral accountability and political insulation in science policy decision making is difficult enough. Establishing and maintaining that balance can be even more challenging in practice, but is no less essential to the maintenance of democracy than are mechanisms of popular responsiveness.

## Reforming environmental democracy

One might endorse the critique of many existing democratic institutions as inadequate in the face of environmental crises, but challenge the critique as applicable to only some forms of democratic decision making. Perhaps the problem is not, as Lovelock suggests, that existing institutions are too democratic to respond to challenges like climate change, but rather that they are not democratic enough. Several proposals for reformed democratic institutions or practices, as well as alternative conceptions of democracy, seek to preserve the essence of democracy but provide greater responsiveness to those environmental crises for which conventional conceptions of democracy (and the institutions constructed from them) commonly fail. Some of the proposed reforms to be considered below aim to treat more general pathologies that have developed within contemporary democratic institutions, but which are not uniquely applicable to environmental challenges, while others take their cues from unique features of the environmental issues to which they are designed to more adequately respond. Together, they suggest that democracy's resources for protecting the environment have yet to be exhausted.

To begin with a rather mundane and general, but nonetheless important, pathology of democracies like that of the US government, proposals for campaign finance reform aim to reduce the insidious influence of industry upon the selection of candidates and over campaigns. Given the massive and escalating costs of waging a competitive campaign for the US Congress, viable candidates must be either extremely wealthy and willing to use their personal wealth for campaign purposes, or else adept at raising the funds needed from donors. Neither bodes well for the election of candidates who are concerned by, and willing to act on behalf of, sustainability imperatives, even where such positions reflect public opinion. Reform of the campaign finance system designed to enhance public responsiveness by diminishing the sway of campaign donors or independent spending campaigns would likely contribute toward more ecologically minded legislators being selected, and legislative bodies being more responsive to environmental imperatives, while at the same time enhancing rather than diminishing the democratic qualities of the institution. For a "green democracy" to be possible, the state must embrace the ideal of equal citizenship, rather than allowing a small donor class a voice that is able to "roar with a clarity and consistency that policymakers readily hear and routinely follow."[26]

In another general pathology of existing representative institutions – but one that is clearly detrimental to their environmental performance – most tend to do a poor job in representing all those affected by many of the decisions that they make. Impacts of US climate policies, for example, are likely to be primarily borne by those residing outside of the country's territorial borders, as well as those not yet born or below voting age. Neither group is represented under the current system, which is designed to be responsive only to adult citizens. Potential reforms include either schemes to replace the geographic representation system upon which US Congressional seats are based with a demographic or interest-based scheme that would allow for ecologically focused third parties, or the addition of alternative forms of representation to institutions already organized around geographic representation. Terence Ball, for example, impugns geographic representation for its inability to account for the interests of nonresidents, future generations, and nonhuman animals. Since many environmental protection initiatives aim to protect the global environment, benefitting these three groups of nonvoters, but would involve costs to be borne by voters in Congressional elections, electoral incentives prevent stronger environmental protection measures. If the interests of these currently disenfranchised parties could be included – as, for example, through proxy representation of nonresidents, future people, or nonhumans, alongside those seats representing voters in states – those affected interests could be properly represented.[27]

## Greening democracy

Theories of *deliberative democracy* posit that democratic processes organized around reason-giving, and directed by lay citizens rather than experts or governmental elites, have the power to transform preferences in a more informed and empathetic direction, and as a result to reduce conflict, develop consensus, and contribute greater legitimacy to decision outcomes. Moreover, evidence suggests that incorporating deliberative elements into democratic decision making can improve environmental outcomes. James Fishkin, who is perhaps the leading empirical theorist of deliberative democracy, has found from deliberative polling experiments that participants, after deliberation, consistently and significantly increase their support for stronger state regulatory action on climate change, as well as state investment in renewable energy, suggesting that the enhanced democratic capacity resulting from deliberation is likely to yield greater public support for environmental protection. More deliberative decision making, from participatory public fora like issues conventions to reason-giving requirements for legislative bodies, might diminish tensions between democracy and environmental protection by enhancing both at once.

Others have incorporated insights from other applications of deliberative democracy into environmental politics. Walter Baber and Robert Bartlett propose a "juristic democracy" based on deliberative norm construction through rule-making by citizen juries. These juries would be tasked with constructing democratic norms for international environmental law and policy, with the outcomes of various empaneled juries compiled for the purpose of deliberative democratic will formation. Jurors would listen to the presentation of opposing sides of current controversies in environmental law and policy, then deliberate among themselves and report back decisions that reflect informed public opinion. While not authorized to make decisions themselves, jurors would contribute toward a democratic voice of the people that could be used to enhance the democratic qualities of decisions made elsewhere as well as state environmental performance.[28]

More direct citizen participation in environmental decision making may likewise yield better environmental policy outcomes, strengthening direct democracy while also enhancing the environmental responsiveness of states. In order to facilitate the transformation of the state from its present liberal form to a postliberal "green state" capable of leading the sustainable transition, Robyn Eckersley calls for facilitation of a "green public sphere" in which a critical form of democracy could be exercised outside the state, characterized by "fulsome environmental information and the mechanisms for contestation, participation, and access to environmental justice – especially for those groups that have hitherto been excluded from, or under-represented in, policy-making and legislative processes."[29] Conceiving of democracy primarily through the lens of political action in civil society, and prioritizing values of inclusiveness and participation over those of majority rule, Eckersley views the "key to such transformation" as being found in "deepening the democratic accountability and responsiveness of states to their citizens' environmental concerns while also extending democratic accountability to the environmental concerns of transnational civil society, intergovernmental organizations, and the society of states in general."[30]

## Democracy and global governance

As with enhancing popular participation and deliberation within domestic political institutions, so also can institutions of global governance be made more responsive to environmental problems through such democratic reform. Perhaps the most pernicious weakness of existing schemes for global governance of an international and intergenerational threat like climate change lies in its absence of a sufficiently strong form of accountability for decision makers within the polity (a key part of their "democratic deficit"). States are democratically accountable only to their own citizens, whereas their decisions affect many beyond those able to hold any state actors to account. Private actors like multinational corporations exert significant influence over such decisions with even less accountability to the global public. Similar to Ball's case for representing the currently disenfranchised, which is also informed by the **all-affected principle**, accountability binds decision makers to those affected by them by allowing the latter to hold the former to account in their decisions.

The most common form is electoral accountability, by which citizens can either approve or reject incumbent decision makers on the basis of their performance between elections, but other accountability mechanisms exist where electoral ones do not apply. This includes reputational accountability, whereby states or decision makers suffer loss of standing or credibility when those affected by their decisions hold them to account, often by publicizing the bad environmental behavior or performance of those decision makers. Neither provides recourse for those vulnerable to the international climate policy actions of powerful countries like the United States, which indeed often denies any accountability to the global public.

Representative institutions are characterized by internal accountability – that is, they are accountable to the polity from which representatives are elected – but the people to which any state actor in international politics is accountable in this sense comprises only a small subset of the people affected by its decisions. Likewise with multinational corporations, which are internally accountable to their shareholders but not to the broader public. As a result, powerful interests within powerful states are typically overrepresented in international politics, while less powerful groups in such states and nearly all those residing in less powerful states have little voice, undermining the democratic accountability of global governance institutions. External forms of accountability (i.e. accountability to those affected by some actor's decisions) that are capable of holding states or multinational corporations accountable for their climate policies are weak – limited to a form of reputational accountability[31] that has proven to be inadequate for motivating strong climate policies or actions. When combined with the democratic deficits that critics have identified in international climate policy development bodies like the UNFCCC,[32] inadequate mechanisms exist for effective democratic control over the decision-making processes that are capable of mitigating climate-related harm.

The real or perceived impotence of democratic forms of governance in mitigating global climate change has led several critics to call for less inclusive or even nondemocratic procedures, through which decision-making authority over climate policies would be concentrated rather than dispersed. Lovelock's call for an alternative to democracy may do this, although it is vague about the alternatives to democracy. David Victor has denounced the inclusive and consensus-based UNFCCC process as unworkable, calling instead for smaller "climate clubs" of major emitters (e.g. the US, EU, China, and other major economies) to work toward a limited agreement outside of the UNFCCC, thus avoiding the objections and veto powers of smaller states that might exert pressure for more ambitious actions.[33] In reply to Victor's concern, but committed to ensuring that the interests of the most vulnerable are not silenced in favor of the powerful, Robyn Eckersley endorses what she terms a form of "inclusive minilateralism," which would seek to reduce the number of participants in climate policy negotiations, while remaining attentive to their interests.[34]

Daniel Bodansky attributes the end-run around UNFCCC processes at the Copenhagen Conference of the Parties (COP) in 2009, along with the more recent retreat from legally binding commitments in the Paris Agreement, to the consensus rule, through which a single dissenter can potentially block any action and thus derail the climate policy development process.[35] Others have proposed institutional bodies in which control over some aspects of climate policy-making would be vested in nondemocratic bodies as a counter to what are perceived as the weaknesses of democratic decision-making procedures, as in the Earth Atmospheric Trust proposal,[36] or cast climate politics as prototypical of what Colin Crouch terms the emerging "post-democratic" world.[37] Frustration with the performance of international climate policy-making bodies such as the UNFCCC has driven critics like these to call for less democracy as a remedy to their shortcomings.

One must not conclude that international climate policy processes cannot be beneficially democratized, however. Key to the development of environmentally sustainable democracy is its form, with models of democracy that stress stakeholder participation and deliberation offering more promise than those focusing upon national or multinational institutions alone. John Dryzek and Hayley Stevenson argue for the inclusion of elements of deliberation within UNFCCC processes, demonstrating that improved environmental performance results from the presence of deliberative elements in governance.[38] A key element of such deliberation is discursive transmission from the active transnational civil society movements that follow COP meetings to the forum in which policies are made.[39] Similarly, Karin Bäckstrand calls for attention to be paid to stakeholder participation in climate policy-making processes, which she casts as a form of "democracy from below," in contrast to the centralized and hierarchical forms within formal UNFCCC processes.[40]

New forms of democratic governance arise to fill gaps where democratic deficits appear, whether at the domestic or international level. Even if these new democratic forms are rarely authorized to make meaningful policy decisions, they are able to provide some measure of oversight and accountability for the elite-led institutions that dominate decision-making fora, contributing some legitimacy to them in the process.

## Conclusions: environmental change and the democratic ideal

Frustration with the slow pace of democratic change, along with the poor records of several existing democratic states, may prompt critics to conclude that democratic forms of social and political organizations are incompatible with sustainability imperatives. As we've seen, however, the problem with the poor adaptability by states to environmental change may not be *too much* democracy, necessitating a shift to some alternative like the ones discussed above. Rather, the problem may be the *kind* of democracy that such states rely upon to make (or fail to make) environmental decisions. State institutions may be made more responsive to environmental problems without becoming less democratic. Indeed, the problem may be that states (or the international system of states) need to become *more* democratic.

Because reform proposals engage democracy as a political concept at the normative level, arguing about what democracy requires and how it ought to be institutionally embedded, they engage in environmental political theorizing rather than simply govern-mental or policy reform advocacy. They seek to recover from the canon of more contemporary works a compelling account of what democracy requires, as well as an assessment of how institutions organized around the concept might perform, and then to bring together the normative dimension of what justifies democracy or makes it legitimate with the specific needs of a particular appli-cation. Because this approach must simultaneously attend to what is normatively defensible and what might be effective in addressing a shortcoming in extant institutions, it can lead to the evolution of existing theories of democracy or the development of new ones. Theory informs practice, but the relationship also works in the other direction. Both kinds of theorizing are instructive in considering relationships between democracy and sustainability.

# 5 Progress

Conceptions of progress locate present conditions within a changing world, orienting us toward both the past and the future. To the extent that actions in the past have contributed toward the meeting of some important social objective, those actions can be identified as *progressive* and justified as such. Expansion of the franchise toward universal suffrage was regarded as progressive in this sense, even if opponents rejected the conception of progress with which it was associated. We seek to identify those among our present options that will guide us toward a progressive future, evaluating and justifying those options in light of their assumed tendency to advance or forestall progress. In doing so, we must identify compelling conceptions or defend them against alternatives. While conceptions of social progress allow our evaluation and justification of alternative actions in terms of desirable outcomes or future worlds, they can also help to bring those worlds about, defining intermediate success and failure in their terms and often aligning incentives accordingly. Furnishing the motivation for social change and providing its direction, progress is defined by conceptions of the good society while also acting to direct actions toward realizing the objectives that constitute it.

Insofar as a society maintains a clearly defined and consistent conception of progress that is ethically defensible and commands universal assent, that conception can provide its members with a powerful normative compass capable of evaluating and directing a wide range of actions and choices, by public institutions and private actors alike. It can define social identity and orient members to each other, constructing a people where common ethnicity does not. Such unifying conceptions are rare, especially in modern social and political life. Instead, modern societies are typically constituted by multiple and competing conceptions of progress, resulting in disagreement about future destinations, as well as present actions that correspond with them. Social objectives that many find progressive, such as racial integration or increasing participation by women in the workforce, are associated with social decline by opponents.

Some conceptions exert a powerful hold on the social imaginary for a period, often having their imprint built into social institutions as a result, only to be amended or discarded later, as conditions or sensibilities change. Cheap plastics were once thought a progressive technology but are now viewed as an environmental menace, and the private automobile may see a similar dissociation from prevailing conceptions of progress when the social costs of urban sprawl and air pollution are considered. When they are instantiated into social institutions while enjoying social support, conceptions of progress continue to exert influence over actions long after support for them has waned or even vanished, functioning as a kind of zombie objective that can obstruct the new conceptions that replace it.

## Conceptions of progress within a contested social compass

As we shall consider further below, the equation of economic growth with social progress in most Western liberal democracies has become a zombie objective in this sense, living on in its pervasive influence on both public and private actions and choices, despite repeated attempts to dislodge or at least refine it. With the recognition of ecological limits, we now know that society cannot continue upon its current path of exponentially increasing economic production and consumption without profoundly harming the planet and future people. The continuing and pervasive influence of this conception of progress, despite the widespread recognition of its ecological impossibility and associated undesirability, is attributable in part to its being built into our minds as well as our institutions. Like the addict that continues to be drawn to their substance or activity of addiction, growth continues to exert a pull on society even while being recognized for its destructive tendencies. Dismantling its structure and influence has been complicated in significant part by our inability to identify a replacement for it in prevailing conceptions of social progress, as well as by those contesting the necessity of doing so.

We often disagree about several dimensions of progress. We can and do often differ about its content, or what constitutes progress, because we disagree about the nature of the good society that serves as its compass. We can disagree on empirical and causal grounds, sharing a vision of the future good but contesting which actions are needed in order to realize it. We can – as Burke did in his 1790 *Reflections on the Revolution in France* – reject the capacity of bounded societies, or humanity in general, to pursue the objectives associated with progress through more than an incremental pace that many are likely to find frustratingly slow, without necessarily rejecting the objectives themselves. We can even reject progress altogether, viewing change without the normative lens that is involved in a historical sense of progress toward or regress from some ideal.

Progress functions as a second-order ideal, guiding or confirming the advancement or retreat of first-order ideals like freedom, equality, justice, or democracy, but is dependent upon these other ideals for its content and normativity. Social progress could in this sense refer to the expansion of full citizenship rights for formerly marginalized persons (building on an ideal of freedom), to the development of democratic institutions (thus dependent upon a democratic ideal), or improvements in life prospects for members of a political community (requiring an ideal of equality). It therefore must be defined in terms of these first-order ideals, even if it, as an action-guiding conception, is mediated by instrumental goods or resources that correspond with the realization of them, like increases in income and wealth, the appearance of new technologies, or development of just institutions. Insofar as economic growth defines progress, it must be linked in some way to the advancement of one or more first-order ideals for its conception to function as an ideal toward which society may aspire. First-order ideals provide a map to a destination, with instrumental social resources and relationships furnishing locomotion, and indicators of progress marking distance travelled over a given period. To the development of such indicators we shall now turn.

## Progress in Western political thought

Economic resources and social relationships of production have long served as the focus of progress in Western political thought, although the myopic reliance upon economic growth as an all-purpose indicator of social welfare has a more recent origin. At the social level, a society that is able to produce sufficient goods to meet the needs and satisfy many of the wants of its members has long been regarded as better than one that cannot, so identifying economic productivity as among the indicators of progress has long enjoyed wide appeal. Other objectives, like those associated with human development, depend in part on having the economic resources available to fund them, as well as agreement on what such development entails and which persons ought to enjoy it. Improved health and better education have costs and tend to correlate with affluence, as well as potentially being controversial in measurement and when extended to formerly excluded groups. Increases in economic productivity, or changes in economic organization that enhance this productivity, have thus long been recognized as instrumentally related to progress – as they enable many first-order ideals if gains are directed toward other social objectives – if not constitutive of it. How progress came to serve as a social ideal, and how economic growth was transformed from one of several means to realizing other progressive goals into the primary objective of progress, will be explored below.

Progress has not always served as an ideal in Western political thought, even if economic organization defined the good or just society. In the *Republic*, for example, Plato defined the just city in terms of the assignment of guardians, auxiliaries, and artisans to their natural roles within a social division of labor, with the city's economic production and consumption a primary focus of the dialogue. Plato, however, was more concerned with corruption and decay than with progress, describing a historical process in which the just city could regress through five inferior stages, eventually ending in tyranny. Since he did not believe that the utopian city that he described in the dialogue could be built on earth, his purpose was to commend his audience to live justly in an unjust world, rather than to use his template as a guide to future social progress.

## Ancient and medieval conceptions of progress

We might nonetheless glean some important components of modern ideals of progress from the ancients. Plato's just city was what Herman Daly describes as an **ecological steady-state**, avoiding population or economic growth,[1] with increases in production or consumption of material goods viewed as antithetical to the justice-enhancing aspects of the economy in this older and wider sense. Guardians and auxiliaries were socialized to avoid consumerist desires, being prohibited from owning private property and specifically insulated against developing desires for luxury goods.[2] Indeed, Daly develops his vision of the steady-state with reference to Aristotle's notion of economics (*oikonomia*), or management of a household, on which management of a society or community could be based, sustainably increasing use values over time. Both of these components might now be identified as central to the ideal of ecological progress, which might ironically involve recovering ideals from the past rather than being oriented only to the future.

Indeed, since modern conceptions of progress oriented around economic growth and the mastery of nature have been faulted for contributing to the environmental crisis, the development of ecologically sustainable conceptions of progress has involved looking to the past for sources of inspiration. Aristotelean virtue ethics are now also viewed as a potential source of virtues or character traits associated with sustainability, as are other Presocratics such as Empedocles and the Stoics.[3] Contemporary scholars now look to indigenous and traditional culture, philosophy, and resource management practices for guidance in recovering elements of sustainable relationships with the land. The Transition Town movement seeks to inform its efforts for sustainable transition partly by "building on the wisdom of the past" in seeking bygone practices that can be recovered for contemporary purposes. Finally, those now rejecting any ideal of progress as complicit in the environmental crisis look to the ancient ideal of stasis for normative guidance.

As Jacobus Du Pisani notes, the notion of progress as a social ideal did not emerge until medieval theologians gave "expression to the linear conception of time as a directed succession of events" – for example, in the progressive human history portrayed in Augustine's *City of God*. The two formative elements for modern Western conceptions of progress were not established until the thirteenth century, Du Pisani observes, with "awareness of the cumulative advancement of culture and a belief in a future golden age of morality on this earth" arising from Christian theological foundations.[4] In Western modernity, from the Reformation in the sixteenth century through the Enlightenment in the eighteenth, a strong belief in progressive human history took hold, first – and perhaps best – articulated in Fontenelle's 1683 *Great Idea of Progress*: that "mankind with the new science and improved technology had entered on a road of necessary and unlimited progress."[5] From Francis Bacon's claim in his 1620 *Novum organum* that "human knowledge and human power meet in one," to Immanuel Kant's 1784 call in his essay "What is Enlightenment?" for "freedom to make public use of one's reason in all matters," modern conceptions of progress came to involve the harnessing of knowledge for the purpose of social improvement and human emancipation. Prior to this modern embrace of progress as directed human improvement, the future was commonly viewed as largely beyond human control, and change as something to fear or regret – but not to eagerly anticipate.

In order to understand how economic growth came to be associated with social progress, we must look to a parallel and occasionally overlapping strain of thought in Western liberalism, through which growth first emerged as an engine and indicator of social progress. First in the form of rising private property ownership, and later as increasing production and consumption of goods, economic growth would compete with and eventually displace scientific advancement and human emancipation as a conception of progress (or growth-as-progress), becoming reified in the process as the target, rather than a correlate or driver, of social improvement.

## Growth-as-progress in early liberalism

The ideal of progress has been essential to liberal political thought since their common origin in early modernity, providing its critical orientation and distinguishing it from rival ideologies. Historically, its association with gains in economic productivity, whether from social or technological factors in production, can be traced back to its seventeenth-century origins. While liberals have historically associated other objectives with social progress, including universal literacy and education, racial and gender equality, and democratization, these other objectives were never rivals to economic growth in defining progress, as they have commonly been assumed to correlate, rather than compete, with it. Growth – whether conceived in terms of increases in production and consumption, growing wealth or per capita income, or the accumulation of private property – has over time become a surrogate for these other objectives. In order to understand how growth had emerged as the dominant indicator of progress by the late twentieth century, we must examine its origins in early modern political thought.

As a political ideology, liberalism celebrates individual freedom and embraces progressive change. John Locke is credited with founding the tradition, with his *Second Treatise* reshaping the social contract approach that Thomas Hobbes began half a century earlier with his *Leviathan*. Locke's version stresses popular sovereignty and limited government that is bound by contract to protect natural rights to life, liberty, and property. Most importantly for purposes here, liberty and property ownership were for Locke the inexorably intertwined ends and means of social progress. Locke saw property acquisition as the quintessential expression of liberty, declaring its appropriation from the commons through labor to be fundamental to human nature, and property ownership as a key protection for liberty. The conception of freedom that C. B. Macpherson calls "possessive individualism," and that is discussed in chapter 3 as seminal to the development of neoliberal freedom, construes liberty in economic terms – as the freedom to buy and sell through voluntary contract – and society itself as little more than "a lot of free equal individuals related to each other as proprietors of their own capacities and of what they have acquired by their exercise."[6] Social progress is for Locke, thus, a function of these individual capacities being put to productive economic use, with growth in production and consumption a reliable indicator of that progress, if not constitutive of it.

As Locke declares in his *Second Treatise*, labor and industry are the drivers of social progress as well as individual improvement, "for whatever *bread* is more worth than acorns, wine than water, and *cloth* or *silk*, than leaves, skins or moss, that is wholly *owing to labour and industry*."[7] It is through labor and industry that value is added to what nature yields, and from this value comes progress. Here, Locke refers to productivity gains from the legal recognition of private property appropriated from formerly common pastures through enclosure, soil tillage technologies and regional crop specialization, and a shift from livestock grazing to agricultural cultivation, which he celebrates as furnishing "the far greatest part of the value of things we enjoy in this world." Labor and industry were, for Locke, valuable for the material goods that they yielded, but also a mark of personal virtue. "God gave the world to men in common," Locke claims, but for "the use of the industrious and rational, (and *labour* was to be *his title* to it)."[8] Thus, for Locke, a growing economy would indicate not only an advancing society, harnessing nature for productive human use, but also personal virtue, as humans honored God through their labor.

Private property in land promised to reduce the economic dependence of affluent subjects upon the monarch – as feudal ownership allowed kings to reallocate land to reward loyalty and punish dissent – as well as reducing the economic dependence of serfs upon feudal lords, both of which in Locke's time served as limits to liberty. Improvement in material conditions from the increase in agricultural productivity and nascent industry could likewise relieve want, making possible the emergence of a new middle class that would later claim political power and status and help to produce a new social order. Increasing property ownership, and with that incentives for labor and industry, were not irrelevant to liberty, as they played an important instrumental role in challenging several key obstacles and providing the material conditions for liberty, but most view Locke as defending property rights as intrinsically valuable, not instrumentally so.

With this early reification of growth in property ownership and industry as providing the basis for social progress, the natural environment was devalued. Locke describes "unassisted nature" as providing "but a very small part" of "the value of things we enjoy in this world," with land "that hath no improvement of pasturage, tillage, or planting" in a state of "waste," and with its benefits to humans amounting to "little more than nothing." Labor combined with private property rights promised the emancipation of a class of landed and self-made citizens through economic growth. At the same time as he praised this growth as emancipatory and progressive, Locke denied that the land with which that labor was mixed in economic production was itself valuable, setting up the opposition between economic growth and sustainability that animates this chapter. In order to manifest individual freedom, and thus to achieve economic growth, forests had to be cleared and fields converted to agricultural use. Environmental preservation was in this sense inimical to Lockean progress.

Productivity gains from nascent capitalism defined liberal progress in the seventeenth and eighteenth centuries, as the economic growth in production and consumption that it drove promised a more comfortable life for the new middle class that it created. Compared with the land and other natural resources that would feed this emerging industrialism, the labor-extending powers of technologies and social arrangements of production, such as the privatization of capital and the assembly line, were relatively scarce, leading observers from Locke to Adam Smith to cast the latter as more valuable instruments of social progress, with little regard for the former. Indeed, the environment in its natural condition, unimproved by human labor, was taken during this period as dormant matter awaiting appropriation and improvement, and as the very antithesis of social progress. Where it existed in large proportions, relative to the land under agricultural cultivation or used in industry (as in America for Locke), progress had not yet visited.

## Scarcity and modern conceptions of progress

As Herman Daly explains (with the benefit of hindsight), Locke's relative valuation of human capital and labor over natural resources in land was largely a product of their respective scarcity at the time. Although the English enclosure movement had been well under way before the *Second Treatise* was published in 1689, Locke writes from the perspective of its beginning, where open land was so abundant that anyone could appropriate as much as they could put to productive use while leaving "enough, and as good" for everyone else. As Daly notes:

> Historically, in the "empty world" economy, manmade capital was limiting and natural capital superabundant. We have now, due to demographic and economic growth, entered the era of the "full world" economy, in which the roles are reversed. More and more it is remaining natural capital that now plays the role of limiting factor. The fish catch is not limited by fishing boats, but by remaining populations of fish in the sea.[9]

With a global population that has increased by more than an order of magnitude since Locke's lifetime, and with ecological limits to growth all the more pressing, we might find Locke to have undervalued land and natural resources. But Daly's message has for the most part still not been received, as we, in most official estimates, still regard GDP growth as an indicator of progress, but take no account of declines in natural capital as counting against it.

The conception of growth-as-progress from Locke's classic liberalism can be traced through the *laissez faire* economic liberalism of the seventeenth century (with Smith's notion of the "invisible hand" of the market guiding the lot of free proprietors that comprise society toward their own separate goods) and into the market liberalism of the late twentieth and early twenty-first centuries. While market liberals no longer seek private accumulation only in land, and few acknowledge the scarcity implicit in Locke's "enough, and as good" proviso (discussed further in chapters 3 and 6), they continue to believe in economic growth as instrumental for (and perhaps constitutive of) freedom. As Robert Antonio explains, they "hold that growth raises living standards, reduces poverty, drives scientific/technological advances, enhances cultural capacities, and provides resources to overcome its negative externalities," and leads to "growing profits, productive powers and population [which] increase demand, goods and services, and quality of life."[10]

## Growth as core state imperative

Within classic liberalism, promoting core ideals like freedom and private property acquisition yielded economic growth as a byproduct, but growth was not itself an objective or constitutive of progress. It was not until the twentieth century that it would assume this status. According to John Barry, the emergence of growth as a core state imperative occurred after World War I, as "the promotion of GDP growth became a neoclassical Keynesian policy, presented as the panacea to a whole host of problems from unemployment to welfare and securing the political legitimacy of capitalist regimes." It was during the US Great Depression that GNP was invented, assisting political leaders in better deploying economic resources toward the war effort against Germany and Japan – this acquiring strategic importance. After the war, he notes, acceptance of trade liberalization and GDP growth as a measure of economic progress became conditions for receipt of American aid. During the Cold War, Barry explains, Western capitalist states "being able to reach and sustain high rates of economic growth" served the ideological goal of demonstrating "the superiority of capitalism over its communist alternative, and buttressing popular support for capitalism within western countries."[11]

Understanding the growth imperative as part of what Barry calls an "elite ideology" accounts for its resilience against critique, including that coming from concern about ecological limits. GDP growth serves the interests of elites, while the ability to promote it justifies the rule of the same elites, whether or not it contributes to the "progress" or general welfare of the larger society. Its status as a core state imperative entails that the state provide support for capital accumulation, whether in order to maintain flows of revenues into its treasury or to secure the reelection of governments by voters conditioned to regard growth as success and stagnation or economic decline as failures. As Charles Lindblom noted a generation ago, the "privileged position of business" in contemporary democracies gives industry an effective veto power over legislation that restricts growth, given the growth imperative and the disproportionate power over society's productive capacities exercised by the business sector.[12] Owners of capital, in turn, are likewise dependent upon the growth imperative, as economic recession erodes the value of accumulated capital (e.g. through declining asset prices from reduced consumer demand) while also increasing calls for its redistribution. These forces combine to render liberal democratic states unable to effectively address problems like climate change, given not only the interests of fossil-fuel companies that oppose carbon regulation as averse to their profits, but also the force of the growth imperative imposing a veto on any program that restrains economic growth. As we shall see below, this commitment may also account for the popularity of "green growth" conceptions that promise continued economic growth while also acknowledging ecological limits and sustainability imperatives.

## Progress reoriented

Hunter and Amory Lovins, who, along with Paul Hawken, have popularized the "natural capitalism" business discourse, follow Daly in suggesting that the "logic of economizing on the scarcest resources, because that is what limits human progress" remains as valid today as in Locke's lifetime, with the relative scarcity of human and natural capital having reversed.[13] All three endorse a friendly amendment to the growth-as-progress conception in seeking recognition of the value of its inputs based on their relative scarcity, imploring business elites to recognize the **instrumental value** of the environment in order to maintain growth in the face of increasing ecological scarcity. Through resource productivity and efficient practices, "green growth" is still possible, they maintain, and progress may still be understood in terms of this kind of growth. So long as we conserve our scarce natural resources – reducing usage, reusing, and recycling them where possible, and harnessing sustainable design and technology to more efficiently utilize them in economic production – we as a society can continue to grow and progress. This conception of *ecological modernization* embraces the power of science and technology from early modern conceptions of progress and fuses these with some recognition of ecological limits, in offering a vision for continued growth-as-progress if only it can be structured in the right way.

Similarly, the US conservation movement emerged from this recognition about the increasing relative scarcity of land and natural resources in fueling growth, a century and a half before its insights were being taught in business schools. Like the eco-modernization vision described above, conservationism remained fully within the growth-as-progress value conception (hence the need to more effectively "conserve" its "limiting factors" in order to secure "the greatest good of the greatest number in the long run"[14]). Noting impacts of rapid deforestation and overgrazing in the American West and seeking to accommodate ongoing population growth in water-scarce regions, the era of "scientific management" began during the nineteenth century, and extended into the twentieth through creation of resource management agencies like the US Forest Service and large-scale water management policies through the Bureau of Reclamation, which sought to reduce the waste of resources that were presciently identified as valuable long before market signals agreed. Samuel Hays captures the ethos of progressive conservation in its claim that "social and economic problems should be solved, not through power politics, but by experts who would undertake scientific investigations and devise workable solutions."[15]

Like the call by contemporary ecological modernizers for resource productivity through environmental design and efficient technology, the invocation of scientific management by early conservationists declines to fundamentally challenge growth-as-progress, even as both aim to restructure the path by which that growth is pursued, whether by business or the state. In this formative period for what would later evolve into the US environmental movement, growth came to be viewed as contingent upon sustainable resource management practices, understood in terms of impartial technocratic authority, but not at odds with sustainability imperatives. No new vision of the good society was needed, nor did new environmental values need to be added to the first-order ideals by which progress was defined. Viewed as a source of resources for human consumption, to be valued instrumentally rather than in itself – albeit one with limits that could threaten continued human progress – nature did not acquire a sense of intrinsic value in nineteenth-century conservationist thinking, or in its late twentieth- and early twenty-first-century inheritors of its technocratic and managerial – but ultimately anthropocentric and growth-oriented – ethos.

## Challenging the growth imperative

The emergence of the US environmental movement would disrupt this embrace of the growth-as-progress conception. Originating in the 1960s, the US movement evolved from the confluence of several related concerns, some in reaction to the earlier conservation movement and some responding to new environmental issues. At the time, the focus of advocacy groups such as the Sierra Club and Wilderness Society was upon protecting wilderness, not built environments, with both working toward the establishment of the 1964 Wilderness Act. In the process of defending wilderness, founders of these two groups gave voice to important critiques of growth, as well as affirmative conceptions of environmental value that have been seminal to the environmental movement's effort to develop alternative visions of progress for a post-growth society. Our interest here will be with those conceptions.

The preservationist sensibility that informed the Sierra Club's wilderness protection advocacy largely reflected that of its founder, John Muir, who viewed wilderness as offering a respite from modern civilization and an unrivaled experience of sublime nature, enabling a primitive kind of freedom that supplements or even replaces the first-order ideals assumed by conservationists. Only by protecting wilderness from development pressures could the human experience of wild nature be preserved for future generations, even if only a relative few were fortunate enough to experience it. Against the conservationist tendency to view nature's value instrumentally, as a generator of natural resources for human consumption, Muir and the environmental groups that his preservationist ethic inspired viewed nature as intrinsically valuable, and best enjoyed through non-extractive experiences of it in protected wilderness.

Echoing Henry David Thoreau's Romantic conception of nature,[16] Muir writes that "in God's wildness lies the hope of the world – the great fresh unblighted, unredeemed wilderness. The galling harness of civilization drops off, and wounds heal ere we are aware."[17] Development pressures from the growth-as-progress ethos had led to what Muir regarded as an ill-conceived plan to dam the Hetch Hetchy valley outside of Yosemite National Park (a "reclamation" project designed to furnish water for the growing population in San Francisco, hotly contested during a seven-year environmental struggle led by Muir's Sierra Club). Rejecting that ethos and blaming it for the threat posed by the dam, Muir savaged the president and former conservationist ally Theodore Roosevelt, whose administration approved the dam project in 1908: "These temple destroyers, devotees of ravaging commercialism, seem to have a perfect contempt for Nature, and, instead of lifting their eyes to the God of the mountains, lift them to the Almighty Dollar."

Far from a vision of progress, growth for Muir represented an ideological and material threat to wilderness and a false promise of human welfare provision. Wilderness, he thought, offers an antidote for ecologically and psychologically damaging impacts of modern life, and its protection provided Muir with an alternative conception of progress. "The making of gardens and parks goes on with civilization all over the world, and they increase both in size and number as their value is recognized," he writes in his essay on the Hetch Hetchy; "Everybody needs beauty as well as bread, places to play in and pray in, where Nature may heal and cheer and give strength to body and soul alike."[18] Turning the growth-as-progress ethos on its head, Muir's conception of progress involves a widening appreciation of the value of wild nature, along with its formal protection as wilderness, viewing growth as an adversary of this progressive vision. His critique of the growth imperative and preservationist conception continued to guide the Sierra Club, which Muir founded in 1892 – as when David Brower in 1966 (then executive director of the Club) compared the Grand Canyon to the Sistine Chapel in full-page ads taken out in the *Washington Post* and *New York Times*, condemning another dam project.

Implicating the growth imperative and its underlying materialism as responsible for destroying wilderness, and seeking to instill new environmental values rather than merely accommodate existing values within a social construction of progress, Muir's preservationist ethos would later inspire the US environmental movement. Like Plato's view of stasis in the *Republic*, its primary focus was upon preserving something valuable against loss, rather than viewing the future with hopeful anticipation. In contrast to Plato, hope for progress was not to be abandoned as necessarily tantamount to decay, but could instead be vested in the spread of environmental values and increasing legal protection of wilderness. The US environmental movement was born at a time in which hope for emancipatory social change through ongoing movements for civil rights and radical democracy was mingled with existential dread from worries about nuclear Armageddon and ecological catastrophe. It retained the guarded optimism of the former, on display in its vision of a just transition, while also embracing the pessimistic outlook of eco-catastrophism and decline narratives, which furnish visions of regress to avoid.

## Wilderness, ecology, and the land ethic

Wilderness Society co-founder Aldo Leopold provided another critique of growth and alternative conception of progress that informed the ethos of the environmental movement. In rejecting the dominant conception of growth-as-progress, he accuses it of embracing a merely instrumental and extractive view of natural value, which "tends to ignore, and thus eventually to eliminate, many elements in the land community that lack commercial value, but that are (as far as we know) essential to its healthy functioning."[19] Protection of those elements requires laws like the Wilderness Act, which defines wilderness as "land retaining its primeval character and influence, without permanent improvements or human habitation," in which "the imprint of man's work" is "substantially unnoticeable" and there exist "outstanding opportunities for solitude or a primitive and unconfined type of recreation." Against the conservationist ethos of Pinchot and others who saw nature for its economic value, Leopold asserts that "a system of conservation based solely on economic self-interest is hopelessly lopsided." Environmental value must be conceived holistically, as Leopold does through his **land ethic**, which he frames in terms of the progressive expansion of the moral community to eventually encompass the land.

Leopold's land ethic gleans an appreciation for nature from Muir but transforms it into more than an aesthetic appreciation of sublime beauty. Insisting that humans view themselves as "plain citizens" – rather than conquerors – of nature, Leopold's ethic adopts an egalitarian character that might potentially serve as a more authentically democratic source of value. As Jedediah Purdy observes, it challenged Muir's focus upon "the intermingled beauty and sublimity of extraordinary places" in favor of "apprehending the complex, interdependent character of natural systems and seeing oneself as integrated within them."[20] The upshot of this construct of nature and natural value was, according to Purdy "a new category, *the environment*, as an organizing concept for a set of problems and demands; the valence of this idea as a moral account of the perceived failures of democratic society and technocratic mastery, which could now be cast as departures from ecological principles." Humans reside in the environment – unlike the remote and wild places that Muir defended – and might potentially live as "plain citizens" on the land.

This idea of the environment was, Purdy suggests, what Wilderness Society advocates drew from Leopold's work as "a language for the value of nature as such." Drafted by Society Executive Director William Zahniser in 1956, the Wilderness Act embraces an environment that is a complex system of interdependent parts, rather than an idealized landscape of the kind that Muir celebrated (and which would later prove relatively easy to protect under the Act, derisively referred to as "rock and ice"). In locating humans within the environment during the course of our ordinary lives, rather than associating its value with far-off places that most would never visit, and avoiding a dualism that William Cronon would later cast as "an epic struggle between malign civilization and benign nature,"[21] Leopold's conception would provide crucial linkages with other elements of the emerging movement – perhaps most notably anti-toxics activists.

## Toxic chemicals and the war on nature

Rachel Carson's *Silent Spring* was published in 1962, in the midst of this campaign to protect wilderness. Its focus, however, was very different. Calling into question the historical and material processes that thinkers from Locke to Marx had commended for their productive power, Carson revealed these to have been poisoning the environment. With mankind having "acquired significant power to alter the nature of his world," the influence of human productive power was revealed to have been pernicious all along, bringing with it terrible consequences for all living things. In short, she warned, growth-as-progress had endangered life itself.

> During the past quarter century this power has not only increased to one of disturbing magnitude but it has changed in character. The most alarming of all man's assaults upon the environment is the contamination of air, earth, rivers, and sea with dangerous and even lethal materials. This pollution is for the most part irrecoverable; the chain of evil it initiates not only in the world that must support life but in living tissues is for the most part irreversible. In this now universal contamination of the environment, chemicals are the sinister and little-recognized partners of radiation in changing the very nature of the world – the very nature of its life.[22]

Carson's influential reversal of the narrative of human innovation and progress called into question not only whether growth in production and consumption could serve as the instrument for improving human well-being, but whether unequivocal progress was even possible. Industrial chemicals that had facilitated what was taken to be a form of mastery of nature were revealed to have accomplished the opposite – increasing human vulnerability to, rather than control over, the environment. Progress had been illusory – the result of counting benefits but not costs.

Bill McKibben would later cast this ubiquitous human influence as marking the "end of nature," in which "the awesome power of Mother Nature as altered by the awesome power of man" has "overpowered in a century the processes that have been slowly evolving and changing of their own accord since the earth was born."[23] Following Paul Crutzen's identification of this power as marking a new geologic epoch (the Anthropocene), a cottage industry of critique of the growth-as-progress conception has emerged, none more poignant than the genre of catastrophism. In a 2017 essay provocatively entitled "The Uninhabitable Earth," David Wallace-Wells describes in stark but palpable terms the planet's future under some business-as-usual climate change projections. "In a six-degree-warmer world," he writes, "the Earth's ecosystem will boil with so many natural disasters that we will just start calling them 'weather': a constant swarm of out-of-control typhoons and tornadoes and floods and droughts, the planet assaulted regularly with climate events that not so long ago destroyed whole civilizations."

Like the scenarios of ecological collapse in the Club of Rome's landmark 1972 *Limits to Growth* report urging recognition of and action on ecological limits, or Jared Diamond's cautionary tales in *Collapse: How Societies Choose to Fail or Succeed* (2004), Wallace-Wells enlists the prospect of disaster as a motivating force for the critique of dominant models of progress that fail to account for sustainability concerns. The combination of economic and human population growth has, according to this eco-catastrophism, undermined the life-support capacities of some ecological systems to the detriment of peoples that resided in them (as Diamond details in studies of Easter Island and the Anasazi peoples), and now threatens the human future on earth. Without specifying an alternative source of value that could replace growth as a vision for sustainable progress, catastrophism has powerfully impugned the growth imperative as untenable. As David Wells suggests, the message of catastrophism was clear: that "the limits to material growth have been reached, and any sustainable future society must exist within these constraints."[24] Any view of progress that fails to recognize the force of these limits could no longer be tenable.

## Rethinking links between growth and progress

The relationship between economic growth and social progress or human emancipation has long been contested, with distinct categories of criticism often forming the bases for social movements (and later becoming focal areas for political theorists). Those concerned about the increasingly narrow concentrations of wealth and widening gaps between rich and poor resulting from the private accumulation of capital, from early protesters against enclosure of the commons to contemporary social movements such as Occupy Wall Street, have long decried its distributional outcomes without fundamentally challenging the progressive potential of growth itself. Here, critics question the causal links between growth and a more inclusive prosperity, but not the normative justification for growth-as-progress itself. If only its material benefits could be more widely shared or justly distributed, they suggest, increased production and consumption could at last genuinely lead to social progress.

Such an account of this posited instrumental relationship is described by Ophuls as the crux of a "politics of scarcity," through which the approach of ecological limits threatens the very foundations of Western liberal ideals of progress.[25] Casting most of "American political history" as "but the record of a more or less amicable squabble over the division of the spoils of a growing economy," Ophuls describes several progressive social movements as settling for a substitution of "economic growth for political principle," epitomized by the labor movement's "abandonment of uncompromising demands for socialism" in return for the state's legitimization of "its status as a bargaining unit in the division of the spoils." Similarly, he suggests, radical social movements on behalf of immigrants and other formerly marginalized groups "were bought off by the opportunity to share in the fruits of economic growth." Here, economic growth serves as a social lubricant for partially accommodating wider claims to equality, and a sedative against more radical economic demands, in the face of recognition that economic growth alone does not (and indeed cannot) serve the first-order ideals with which it is associated, in the absence of just distribution of its benefits among society's members.

## Toward a post-growth conception of progress

It is one thing to question whether growth must necessarily result in inclusive progress, but it is quite another to reject growth as inimical to progress. Concerns about the ecological limits to growth, as discussed in chapter 2, impugned the desirability of continued growth in production and consumption, in part by noting its ecological impossibility as we approach such limits and partly by calling attention to the environmental impacts of unsustainable growth, many of which humans have begun to experience. Ecological limits make evident the need for a new, *post-growth* conception of progress, but what could replace growth as an indicator of social advancement? A viable candidate would need to be compatible with sustainability imperatives as well as conceptions of other first-order ideals that constitute it. While "greener" versions of such ideals are the focus of this book's other chapters, we might identify several other features and make several remarks regarding the development of a suitable conception here.

One might, of course, reject the ideal of progress altogether, perhaps returning to an ideal of stasis in which societies seek to preserve existing sources of value, rather than seeking improvement through change. Discourses of necessary sacrifice and "managed retreat" involve this imperative to minimize loss rather than to seek social advancement through progress. Insofar as progress itself has been complicit in human degradation of the environment, especially if it has become inextricably intertwined with the growth imperative or the desire for mastery or domination of nature, such an abandonment of the ideal may be necessary. Likewise, ecological limits prevent any feasible conception by which we might imagine a better world arising in the future through our concerted efforts to bring it about. Adopting a kind of classic conservatism about the human future on earth not unlike Edmund Burke's skepticism about progressive change in his *Reflections on the Revolution in France*, one might embrace stability and continuity rather than future-oriented optimism about human improvement in one version of this approach. The term "bioconservatism" has come to refer to such skepticism about utilizing technology to modify or enhance the human condition (as advocated by transhumanists), and a similar rejection of the "technoprogressivism" of ecological modernization – also implicit in climate geoengineering – may likewise impugn ideals of progress as requiring untenably optimistic assessments of the emancipatory potential of technology.[26]

However, stasis rather than progress would offer a more attractive ideal were societies not already on a trajectory to cause catastrophic planetary warming and trigger another mass extinction, as stasis or resistance to change presupposes a stable and morally acceptable status quo. Leaving aside the numerous other social injustices toward which ideals of progress are now currently directed, abandoning the ideal of progress altogether would forfeit the critical power implicit in the exercise of imagining a better future for society and the planet. Given the motivational power in supporting beneficial social change that ideals of progress have generated in the past, the outright rejection rather than redirection of progress may also undermine efforts at avoiding significant social regress, such as scarcity-driven rejections of democracy in favor of authoritarian or technocratic rule, or selfish and insular attempts to minimize the impact of climate change upon the affluent, rather than cooperative efforts to mitigate it for all. An orientation toward the human future led by hope (for Hobbes, "appetite, with an opinion of attaining") rather than despair ("the same, without such opinion") may avoid the kind of fatalism and resistance to change that all but guarantees the worse outcome occurring. Particularly given the scope of change needed for a sustainable social transition, the willingness to accept current costs in exchange for future benefits (even if these involve avoiding further losses) may be vital.

To serve as an effective substitute, a replacement for growth-as-progress may need to mimic its form as well as its content. Contributing to growth's original appeal and resistance to change has been its ready quantitative measurement. Defined in terms of GDP, economic growth took advantage of readily accessible data that could be used to track progress over time, as well as compare nations and peoples in their relative rates of GDP growth or decline.

Critics of GDP as a progress indicator have thus proposed alternative indices of social progress that can also be quantitatively measured and subjected to similar kinds of comparisons.

The aptly named environmental economics think tank Redefining Progress, for example, developed the Genuine Progress Indicator (GPI) as an alternative to GDP, combining 26 indicators in categories of economic, environmental, and social welfare. Noting that many economic activities involve social costs that are not recognized within GDP – costs of pollution and resource depletion, for example, or costs associated with commuting to work or loss of leisure time – the GPI includes components that track such social and environmental costs to account for the negative impacts of increasing economic activity. The results paint a very different picture from GDP. Historical data show a period of positive correlation between economic growth and GPI up to a point in national development, followed by a decoupling of these indicators (around 1960 in the US), with GDP continuing to rise but GPI stagnating or even declining. While this observation should also provide additional force to the critique of the growth conception of progress, the development of indicators such as GPI also recognizes the value of replicating the quantitative form of the earlier conception, if they are to serve as a replacement in the manifold contexts in which growth is seen as a vision of progress.

Despite its appealing form and compelling critique, GPI has yet to replace GDP as an indicator (nor have other proposed alternative indices). Resistance to its use is likely the result of several related factors, one of which is the more complicated and time-consuming project of collecting and aggregating 26 different indicators. For this reason, one might instead look to more ecumenical quantitative indices of social progress to replace economic growth. One such candidate is the Human Development Index (HDI), which combines indices for health (infant mortality and life expectancy), education (mean and expected years of schooling), and a decent standard of living (per capita income) to track progress in a development context. According to the UN Development Programme, which has (unlike the GPI, which has not) been institutionally embraced, "the HDI was created to emphasize that people and their capabilities should be the ultimate criteria for assessing the development of a country, not economic growth alone."[27]

## The HDI as progress index

Built upon the conceptual foundations of Amartya Sen's capabilities theory of justice[28] and its manifestation in welfare economics as human development, the HDI improves upon the limitations of GDP as an indicator of social welfare and operationalization of progress, but its simplicity is also its weakness as a candidate to replace growth-as-progress. Unlike the GPI, the HDI contains no indicator to capture environmental impacts of growth, such as social impacts of pollution or resource degradation. Instead, it aims to measure the extent to which persons are able (or have the capability, which is a kind of latent potential based on their access to certain resources or opportunities) to lead flourishing lives. Noting that GDP increases alone do not necessarily improve the prospects, the HDI combines three variables in order to better account for changes in human development: per capita income (capturing the increased consumption opportunities made possible through economic growth), educational access (which facilitates political as well as economic empowerment), and life expectancy (capturing reductions in external impediments to health). According to the UN Development Programme, which tracks HDI across countries and over time in order to assess the efficacy of development efforts, HDI "was created to emphasize that expanding human choices should be the ultimate criteria for assessing development results." Noting some of the shortcomings of relying upon GDP alone as an indicator of development – as under the conception of economic development that had previously guided international development efforts – it notes that "economic growth is a means to that process but is not an end in itself."[29]

Although a clear improvement upon GDP alone as a development index, HDI is not without its shortcomings. By utilizing per capita income as a proxy for decent living standards, it is insensitive to economic inequalities that mask welfare impacts of poverty. If economic gains are concentrated upon an affluent subset of any population, increasing per capita income may do little for those left behind. Its redirection of development aid toward projects that enhance health and education should not be underestimated, but its conceptual adequacy in offering a reformed vision of "development" (much less a conception of progress itself) to replace GDP growth is limited. Lacking any accounting for the environmental costs of development, as are found in the GPI, it cannot by itself serve as the post-growth conception of progress called for above. Key threats to human welfare – from violent conflict and the rise of authoritarian governments to climate-related flooding and desertification – may overwhelm residents of developing countries without these showing up in HDI scores in time to avert crises. Finally, although HDI data is collected for developed as well as developing countries, as a measure of improving human welfare opportunities it more effectively serves developing country contexts, where increases in per capita income are more directly correlated with improved life prospects. Researchers have shown that, once income has reached the level where material needs (for food, shelter, and so on) can be met, income is decoupled from welfare or happiness, such that further increases in per capita income within a population no longer necessarily result in greater social welfare or happiness. Beyond this threshold, as Ronald Inglehart has shown,[30] **postmaterial values** such as self-expression, political autonomy, and environmental protection manifest more strongly within industrial societies, thus requiring a conception of progress that recognizes their importance.

A more fleshed-out capabilities-based metric than the HDI might serve as a replacement ideal for the growth imperative, insofar as it is better able to capture the ideal of progress as leading to improvements in human and social welfare, while avoiding associated social and environmental costs of growth. Martha Nussbaum's proposed set of ten human capabilities is one such version, specifying ten core human capabilities that give substance to the otherwise-abstract concept of human flourishing.[31] Including the ability to live with and show concern for nonhuman animals and the natural world on her list of capabilities, along with exercising control over one's environment, might better capture the importance of environmental sustainability to human welfare than does the HDI. Neither these two nor Nussbaum's other eight identified capabilities can be readily measured, undermining their utility as in a development metric to replace the HDI. However, Nussbaum intends her capabilities approach as a conceptual metric of justice, which as a first-order ideal can help to redefine second-order ideals like progress by aligning such a conception with it. While her list of capabilities does little to recognize ecological limits and has been criticized for its instrumental and anthropocentric view of nature and the nonhuman, engagement with it by scholars like Breena Holland suggest that it might be steered toward maintaining the ecological bases for human flourishing by including ecological capacity as kind of meta-capability.[32]

## Sustainable development goals

Perhaps the best-known such capabilities-based metric of progress available for replacing growth can be seen in the Sustainable Development Goals (SDGs) – a set of 17 global objectives set by the UN General Assembly in 2015, for achievement by 2030. Replacing the Millennium Development Goals (MDGs) that were informed by Sen's work on capabilities in human development, and which guided international development efforts from 2000 to 2015, the SDGs together call for what Jeffrey Sachs terms "socially inclusive and environmentally sustainable economic growth."[33] Ranging from basic humanitarian goals like ending poverty and hunger to social goals of inclusion and equality, and environmental protection objectives for water quality, sustainable cities, and climate action, the SDGs aim to steep development aid toward a more holistic conception of progress, while retaining the capabilities approach of the HDI. Unlike Nussbaum's more philo-sophical capabilities approach, the SDGs offer quantifiable targets that can be readily measured, allowing for clear assessment of progress toward specified 2030 targets. The Oxford-based online SDG Tracker provides data to track progress toward realization of SDGs over time, providing for an index that can be used in a similar way to reliance upon GDP.[34]

The concept of *sustainable development* upon which the SDGs are based originally promised to decouple growth from the environ-mental impacts that are normally associated with it. Since the HDI lacks any formal sustainability objectives and the MDGs were criticized for specifying only limited sustainability objec-tives, the formal adoption of the SDGs in 2015 (nearly four decades after the appearance of sustainable development within UN development policy discourses) operationalizes the concept of sustainable development within a framework that is capable of informing and assessing international development efforts. While the SDGs improve upon the oversight up to that point of omitting any metric of environmental sustainability in UN processes for measuring development, by including five distinct environmental protection goals, their continued reliance upon economic growth as an engine of development, their limited application to indus-trialized countries, and their somewhat mixed record of success have attracted criticism by scholars. In order to better assess their potential to reorient progress in a more environmentally sustainable direction – at least within their defined scope – a brief history of their core concept is warranted.

Brought into public consciousness by the 1987 report of the World Commission on Environment and Development (WCED) entitled *Our Common Future* (more commonly referred to as the Brundtland Report, after its Chair, former Norwegian Prime Minister Gro Harlem Brundtland), the report defines sustainable development as "development that meets the needs of the present without compromising the ability of future generations to meet their own needs." As the product of a political effort to bridge the concerns of developing countries seeking to fight poverty and hunger while promoting economic opportunity and those of developed countries to accommodate ecological limits within the existing global order, the report's proposal for environmentally sustainable growth (or the decoupling of growth and its usual environmental impacts) was more rhetorical than practical. While acknowledging ecological limits and taking pains to link poverty alleviation objectives with environmental protection, the conception of progress for developing countries that the report proposes continued to rely upon economic growth for the development aid that it required from affluent countries, and included it among its objectives for developing ones. As it notes, the "problems of poverty and underdevelopment cannot be solved unless we have a new era of growth in which developing countries play a large role and reap large benefits."[35]

Noting its call for a seven-fold increase in global consumption in order to address global poverty without fundamentally changing global North consumption expectations, Herman Daly calls its vision of sustainable growth "a bad oxymoron."[36] With humans already appropriating a quarter of the planet's net primary product of photosynthesis, he argues, ecological limits would prevent any such expansion of the human economy. Many still question how sustainable the sustainable development agenda really is, or whether it is possible to decouple GDP growth from growth in use of materials and energy.[37] Three decades after the Brundtland Report, Robert Fletcher and Crelis Rammelt argue that the global movement it began can be understood "as a grand effort to deny the reality of environmental limits" and "to prove that sustainability is in fact compatible with indefinite economic growth," with current efforts at decoupling growth from its usual environmental impacts a "fantasy" that "sustains this faith in the face of increasing documentation of the dramatic environmental consequences of economic growth to date."[38]

Even while its ability to direct the global economy toward a sustainable transition is dubious, the operationalization of sustainable development in terms of the SDGs does improve upon the older conception of progress inherent in economic development as measured by GDP growth. Insofar as it seeks more equitable benefits from growth, sustainable development might be viewed as advocating global justice imperatives such as those discussed in chapter 10. Its inclusion of a wide array of measurable environmental protection goals within 9 of the 17 SDGs improves upon the MDGs, which combined biodiversity loss with threats to drinking water and lack of sanitation within a single goal (Goal 7: Ensure Environmental Sustainability). As a product of the neoliberal global order, the UN Development Programme (like the UNFCCC) has limited leverage to seriously question (much less to fundamentally transform) that order, and so must instead seek to subtly redirect it through modest reform at the margins. Viewed in this way, the SDGs represent an effort to slightly change the trajectory of a large ship that will eventually need to continue veering much further from its present course.

## Green growth vs. post-growth conceptions

Whether humanity can afford to pursue change in this incremental manner is another question. As Petter Næss and Karl Georg Høyer note of the reformist decoupling efforts of the MDGs, these may "change the quality of growth" but "are thus only able to postpone the collision between ecological limits and economic growth. They cannot enable humanity to trespass such limits."[39] To use a different ship metaphor, relying upon MDGs to make growth more sustainable is akin to rearranging deck chairs as the *Titanic* careens toward the iceberg. Naomi Klein, in explaining how climate change "changes everything" about how humans need to start relating to our environment, claims that sustainable transition will "require rethinking the very nature of humanity's power – our right to extract ever more without facing consequences, our capacity to bend complex natural systems to our will. This is a shift that challenges not only capitalism, but also the building blocks of materialism that preceded modern capitalism, a mentality some call 'extractivism.'"[40]

Klein's call for a radical shift away from extractivism parallels Andrew Dobson's critique of both *industrialism* (which is attached to the growth imperative and implicit in modern political systems from capitalism to communism) and *environmentalism* ("a managerial approach to environmental problems, secure in the belief that they can be solved without fundamental changes in present values or patterns of production and consumption") in favor of what he calls *ecologism* (which "holds that a sustainable and fulfilling existence presupposes radical changes in our relationship with the non-human natural world, and in our mode of social and political life").[41] Both Klein and Dobson are critical of the notion that reformist rather than radical approaches are sufficient, given the scale of environmental problems.

Such a radical transition would require a similarly radical transformation of social ideals of progress, rather than the sort of reformist vision inherent in sustainable development. While Dobson points to radical green politics as leading the development of an ideology of ecologism, a contemporary manifestation of its challenge to the status quo is on display in the movement for **sustainable degrowth**, defined by Giorgos Kallis in terms of "a socially sustainable and equitable reduction (and eventually stabilisation) of society's throughput."[42] Degrowth – or the intentional transformation of the growth economy and its associated normative support within culture and society into one that meets social needs while undergoing a planned reduction in production and consumption – challenges the growth imperative in a way that sustainable development does not.

As Kallis notes, degrowth differs from "negative GDP growth in a growth economy" in that it also aims to supersede the growth economy; negative GDP growth without such radical transformation already has the name of "recession, or if prolonged, depression." Following an international conference on degrowth (or *la décroissance* in French) in 2008, an international movement urged rejection of the growth imperatives and embrace of degrowth as an alternative conception of progress. As *Farewell to Growth* author Serge Latouche argues, "growth is now a profitable business only if the costs are borne by nature, future generations, consumers' health, wage earners' working conditions and, above all, the countries of the South."[43] Consolidating critiques of consumerism and capitalism while rejecting the "green growth" ambitions of sustainable development and ecological modernization advocates, the degrowth movement represents an ambitious agenda for social and economic change. As Kallis notes, "this will only be possible with such a radical change in the basic institutions of property, work, credit and allocation, that the system that will result will no longer be identifiable as capitalism."[44]

## Conclusions: redefining progress to account for ecological limits

As we've seen, the growth-as-progress ideal continues to exert considerable influence over the way that society defines success or improvement, particularly at the elite level. Periods of growth yield electoral rewards for the regimes that preside over them, regardless of whether or not their policies actually contribute toward that growth, and politicians and parties are routinely punished at elections during economic recessions. This occurs despite the recognition that ecological limits cannot accommodate unlimited growth, that growth exacerbates many of the impacts that are associated with production and consumption, and that growth decouples with happiness above a threshold that most industrialized countries have already reached. For this reason, it might be viewed as a kind of zombie ideal, continuing to exert its influence from beyond the grave and contaminating many of the things that it comes into contact with.

Efforts to redefine or reorient progress in light of ecological limits or the environmental crisis share several features of the growth critique, and many of them share a common reticence to challenge a central feature of the existing social and global orders. Most aim to decouple the environmental impacts of growth from society's ideal of progress. To the extent that growth continues to form a part of that ideal, critics embrace "green growth" as a vision for a growth economy built around sustainable processes of production and consumption, including efficient technologies, streamlined processes, and reuse and recycling of materials. While such measures have considerable potential for reducing the environmental impacts of economic production and consumption, critics are rightly skeptical about the possibility of sustainable growth in an economy that has already well exceeded its sustainable limits. Others aim to decouple a view of progress from growth itself, redefining progress in qualitative terms associated with happiness or well-being, rather than in terms of quantitatively increasing consumption expectations. Despite the promise of this latter approach, as seen for example in the adoption of the HDI or MDGs in international development politics, its ability to steer state economic policies away from growth has been limited. The degrowth movement, while offering perhaps the most feasible vision for progress in an ecologically limited world, also faces the greatest challenge in gaining adherents, given its many conflicts with remnants of the growth culture and ideology that remain.

So embedded within existing social orders of advanced industrialized economies and in the existing global order is the growth imperative that those orders may need to be significantly transformed for us to accommodate a feasible conception of sustainable progress. A tenable global ideal must call for development to address chronic drivers of human misery such as poverty and hunger, with political and economic empowerment of the disadvantaged possible at lower environmental cost through "green growth" and efficient technology efforts. For this kind of development to be sustainable at the global level, it must be committed to equity in the way that global North and global South countries share the planet's resources, as well as how the rich and poor within all countries allocate the earth. Unless it is to be a vision of progress for some that comes at the cost of increased ecological disruption for many, that is, a conception of sustainable and inclusive progress must couple a global equity focus with its sustainability imperatives, lest it risk decoupling the imperatives of justice and sustainability that the Brundtland Report sought to bring together.

# 6 Equality

As with ideals of liberty and community, scholars often distinguish ancient from modern by contrasting the status of equality as an ideal in each. In the *Republic*, for example, Plato asserts that humans are naturally unequal, justifying his separation of the utopian city into three distinct classes of guardians, auxiliaries, and artisans on the basis of natural differences. So important is the belief in this natural inequality for maintaining the stability of this society that Plato insists upon promulgating the myth of the metals, which claims that essential differences in character and capacity in society have an origin in different metals being mixed in the blood of persons born into it. This myth justifies and maintains the power of the guardian class, making facts and beliefs about equality highly relevant to arrangements of power and authority within society. An inegalitarian society such as the one that Plato defends rests upon the premise of natural inequality among humans: that rulers are naturally superior to subjects, and that social stability depends upon social divisions that track natural ones. This natural inequality was taken as a fact by ancients like Plato, to be accommodated by other ideals like that of justice, rather than equality serving as an ideal in itself, as it does in much modern political thought.

Modern political thought typically embraces it as a positive ideal, to be reflected in social and political institutions, rather than rejecting it as Plato did. Modern conceptions of equality are therefore not so much incompatible with sustainability imperatives as they are related to some efforts to meet such imperatives, as well as some obstacles to meeting them. As we shall see below, contestation of the moral equality of species engages this ideal in a manner that is reminiscent of past struggles for equality, potentially playing a positive role in a just transition. Equality also features in environmental rights, which rely upon an important conception (legal equality) and aim to mitigate environmental inequality. Debates over the nature of equality and its implication for policy and values also arise in the context of **carbon offsets**, which are an important policy tool for mitigating climate change, as well as in those over the respective normative implications of equality and **sufficiency**, which we also consider.

## Equality as ideal

Equality now functions as a foundational ideal, serving as the basis for other ideals, including those of justice and democracy. If we accept that humans are by nature unequal and that only some possess the capacity to exercise political authority, democracy appears to be inappropriate for political decision making, and a core concern for justice will be ensuring that social goods such as power are allocated in accordance with natural differences. On the other hand, concentrating political power or other privileges in the hands of a small elite appears deeply unjust if persons are relatively equal by nature and if the many are capable of exercising political authority. In this sense, premises about human nature are foundational in political theory insofar as they serve as starting points for identifying various ideals around which social and political institutions can be constructed. For this reason, contestation of existing institutions often takes the form of a dispute about human nature, including human equality. Those seeking to exclude others from full participation in politics and society on the basis of their race or gender often invoke pseudoscientific claims about their capacities or pathologies in an attempt to dislodge settled premises upon which egalitarian society is founded.

Modern conceptions of equality maintain its status as a foundational ideal, but reverse claims about facts, as well as social assumptions about those facts, compared to ancients like Plato. Persons are assumed to be naturally equal in some sense as a matter of fact, as well as meriting equal treatment (a conferred status rather than a natural fact) for social, political, and ethical purposes. As they did for ancients like Plato, claims about equality today justify arrangements of power in society, and so play crucial ideological roles. Questioning or disputing those facts is often therefore a means to contest the power arrangements that they justify, and asserting them is common in calling for social and political reform deemed necessary for treating persons justly. Signatories to the US

Declaration of Independence did not claim that "all men are created equal" in order to press a factual dispute about biology with the British crown, but as an emancipatory effort demanding the legal and political equality that colonists had been denied. Likewise with contemporary equality movements such as Black Lives Matter, so named in order to call attention to social practices that imply otherwise.

## Factual and moral equality

The relationship between factual and moral equality is somewhat tendentious. While claims to moral equality often take the form of assertions about factual equality, being factually equal is neither a necessary nor a sufficient condition for being treated as an equal. Similarly, claims or evidence about natural inequality – such as the Nazi phrenology experiments designed to validate Aryan supremacy beliefs by comparing the size of human skulls, uses of IQ testing data on African Americans to justify their educational marginalization, or other forms of **scientific racism** – cannot validly impugn ascriptions of moral equality or ground related claims to moral superiority or priority. Why do arguments about whether or not to ascribe moral equality, and thus to afford other kinds of equality that have a necessary relationship with it, so often get made through claims about factual equality, either on behalf of or against it? We shall return to this question later without fully answering it here. Suffice for now to note that there is often thought to be such a necessary relationship between factual and moral equality, but this requires an argument that is rarely made and is never valid. Instead, it is a common but contestable social construct that the two have some necessary relationship – and one that ought to be contested in some cases, including one that we shall examine below.

The appearance of this tendentious invocation of claims about factual equality on behalf of ascriptions of moral equality is easy to identify in major canonical works. Hobbes claimed in the *Leviathan* that humans were by nature roughly equal, in the respect that the weakest human was still powerful enough to kill the strongest. Acknowledging that persons differed naturally in their physical strength as well as intellectual capacities, and were therefore unequal in power, his somewhat equivocal factual claim was nonetheless sufficient to ground his ethical one. Since none could be powerful enough in the state of nature to be impervious to harm, none could prefer that state to life under civil government, making everyone at least roughly equal in their vulnerability, and equal in the way that matters to motivating the social contract. Since the status of persons in political society is a social construct determined by the social contract itself, and all are symmetrically placed in their motivation to join into that contract, none can insist upon elevated status under it.

We see a similar dynamic between claims about universal fragility versus unequal vulnerability in the discourse around climate impacts. International cooperation to combat climate change is more readily secured by declaring it to be a common concern of humankind, as the 1992 UN Framework Convention on Climate Change does, rather than noting that some parties are extremely vulnerable to climatic impacts while some are only moderately so, and a few may benefit in some ways by such changes. Solidarity in cooperation can result from the stipulation of a rough situational equality, so that all are working toward the same objective. As with the Hobbesian motivation to leave behind the state of nature, the belief by any state that it is less vulnerable to climate change may undermine its incentives to participate in cooperative efforts to mitigate that phenomenon.

Following Hobbes, this premise about factual equality and its invocation in justification of moral equality became the norm within the liberal tradition, although this neither insulated it from challenge nor was sufficient to motivate its recognition within those societies in which the tradition was formative. Having claimed moral equality in the Declaration of Independence did not deter the framers of the US Constitution from declaring slaves to count for three-fifths of a person for purposes of apportionment of House seats, and to exist as mere property otherwise. In the American case, as elsewhere, declarations of moral equality are often aspirational, but do not always represent universally shared aspirations. In order to realize the various forms of equality to which moral equality aspires – legal, political, social, as well as some kind of economic equality – much more needs to change, even where equality is nominally recognized as a social ideal.

## Equality between species

Leaving aside the questions about equality among humans, are humans equal to other species of animals, or even to plants? How do we even begin to ask such a question, and what follows from its answer? Some, typically informed by a teleological or progressive theory of history in which the moral community is expanding over time, ascribing moral equality to more humans who had previously been excluded from it, but eventually being challenged to incorporate nonhumans along with them, have posed the question with an affirmative answer in mind. Aldo Leopold begins the chapter on his land ethic in his *A Sand County Almanac* by presenting such a history, as does Peter Singer in his 1975 *Animal Liberation*. Both invoke this historical trend in partial justification of arguments for expansions of moral standing but not moral agency, to borrow a distinction made in chapter 7. Singer argues for it on behalf of sentient nonhuman animals, and Leopold for the various constituent members of what he calls the **biotic community**. Both claim a kind of equality between species in defense of their extensions of moral standing to nonhumans.

Singer argues that a kind of factual equality justifies the ascription of moral equality (in terms of the "equal consideration of interests" principle by which the equivalent interests of humans and nonhumans would be given equal weight in consequentialist evaluation): that humans share **sentience** with many nonhuman animals, so it would be arbitrary to grant this status to some creatures but not to other relevantly similar ones. Granting the biological differences between humans and nonhumans in a manner parallel to Hobbes granting natural power inequalities among humans, Singer claims that humans are equal to other sentient animals in the respect relevant to moral standing or **considerability**. According to Singer, echoing Jeremy Bentham's similar invocation of sentience as requisite for moral standing, "if a being suffers, there can be no moral justification for refusing to take that suffering into consideration."[1]

Singer does not, he clarifies, intend to suggest that humans and nonhumans are identical in their capacities to suffer – the recognition of moral equality does not require factual equality in that sense. A human might, he argues, experience more psychological distress at being killed than would a dog, for example, so we might have some basis for preferring the nonhuman death in a lifeboat case where only one can be saved. According to his equal consideration of interests principle, we must treat like interests alike, not prioritizing human interests when compared against equal or comparable nonhuman ones. To the extent that we form such a partiality toward humans – and certainly if we act upon it – we exhibit *speciesism*, which Singer compares to other irrational and self-serving prejudices like racism and sexism (and it is a form of anthropocentrism, as discussed in chapter 8). Achieving genuine moral equality, whether among humans or between humans and other animals, relies upon changes in attitudes and beliefs and not just laws or behavior, as it involves an attribution of status rather than turning upon any set of natural facts alone.

## Human exceptionalism

Other scholars in animal ethics, or its counterpart in environmental political theory, argue for some sort of moral equality or standing from particular kinds of factual equality. This often involves the rejection of commonly invoked criteria for justifying **human excep- tionalism**, such as the possession of reasoning powers, language use, or other capacities assumed to be unique to humans. Such criteria are either claimed to be irrelevant for the justificatory purposes to which they are commonly applied, or else factually mistaken. For example, language use might be proposed as a criterion for moral standing, but the negative argument would question its uniqueness to humans or its relevance to moral standing. Many nonhuman animals use language – with recent research suggesting that trees also communicate and exhibit mutualism through underground mycorrhizal networks, coined as the "wood wide web"[2] – and some humans do not. Similarly, if rationality is claimed as a justification for human exceptionalism, the "argument from marginal cases" would reply that infants and those lacking the capacity as the result of illness or injury are nonetheless accorded such standing. This line of argument is intended to cast doubt upon the justification for extending moral standing to all humans but no nonhumans, proposing a version of the equality ideal, as opposed to what it reveals to be an irrational prejudice against other species.

The premise of moral equality for animals in ethics would require what environmental philosophers call moral standing or considerability, which, if attributed to nonhuman animals, would mean that they can be wronged by human actions. Full *personhood* (which few propose extending beyond the human realm) would extend agency, so that nonhumans could also commit wrongful acts and be held morally responsible for them. Legal personhood would extend (some of) the same rights and liberties granted to other legal persons, and is often associated with justice (discussed further in chapter 10). Martha Nussbaum uses a positive version of the argument from factual to moral equality for extending justice principles to nonhuman animals, claiming that possession of any of the same capabilities for human flourishing that she defends as being the currency of distributive justice involves criteria for extending moral status to nonhumans. As she writes: "if a creature has either the capacity for pleasure and pain or the capacity for movement from place to place of the capacity for emotion and affiliation or the capacity for reasoning, and so forth (we might add play, tool use, and others), then that creature has moral standing."[3] While Nussbaum does not argue for the extension of the full set of rights granted to humans (political and economic rights would not be extended, for example), she does argue from a kind of factual equality (about nonhuman animal capacities) to a kind of moral equality, here on behalf of extending the "frontier" of justice beyond the human realm.

In this, we see both continuity with and departures from prior conceptions of the equality ideal in applications to animal ethics or normative research motivated by concerns about the environmental crisis. Ascriptions of moral equality are thought to have some relationship with claims about factual equality and are used to justify and advocate for other forms of equality to be realized through politics and in society. The importance of factual equality as a basis for moral equality, which begins to decline with Hobbes but remains a part of the standard trope, declines significantly with those arguing for some kind of moral equality between species. As with many arguments against ascriptions of moral inequality among humans, they acknowledge differences of various kinds but deny that these justify the marginalization or mistreatment of the Other. The premise linking factual equality to moral equality or standing remains in some form, but has been significantly transformed in order to fit this new application. Such approaches are thus called *extensionist* in that they maintain some continuity with existing ethical or political theories in their form and content but seek to extend these beyond the human realm, rather than inventing entirely new normative theories applicable to environmental issues. In this way, the equality ideal's wider application has sought to broaden the moral community and, in so doing, to criticize manifold human actions and practices that harm nonhuman others.

Political theorists have likewise turned their attention toward amending concepts and institutions that are currently based in human exceptionalism, remaking these in light of less anthropocentric and more inclusive value premises, as well as in calling for schemes whereby nonhuman interests could be more effectively represented in political processes. Insofar as politics is about collective decision making through which a kind of political standing is accorded to those whose interests ought to be taken into account, or to whom the collective is to be accountable, the ideal of equality has been mobilized on behalf of widening that community and making it more responsive to a broader array of parties. To the extent that schemes seek to represent a wider human community – for example, by representing future generations or those residing beyond national borders – they might invoke the all-affected principle, which is central to the democratic ideal. To the extent that they seek to represent nonhuman interests, they may seek to mobilize similar value theory arguments against human exceptionalism to those noted above.

## Rights and equality

Legal rights are important institutional mechanisms for promoting social and political equality, and are implicitly premised upon moral equality and grant equal legal standing to right-holders. Given tendencies within democracies to prioritize the interests of the majority at the expense of minorities, rights offer an institutional protection of those interests that would otherwise be imperiled. Possessing a legal right allows a party whose rights have been violated to access state power through the courts, which can order that those rights be recognized and protected. It allows those protected by rights to make claims, rather than appeal to the sympathies of others, on behalf of their legally protected interests. As Joel Feinberg notes, this activity of claiming "makes for self-respect and respect for others" and "gives a sense to the notion of personal dignity" for those exercising their rights.[4] Rights therefore give force to the ideal of equality and have become one of its primary expressions in liberal democracies.

Although rights function as checks on majority actions, as previously noted they should not for this reason be considered antidemocratic, as they function to protect and promote those forms of equality that are essential to democracy itself. From the distinction in chapter 4, they can protect substantively democratic values against erosion through democratic procedures, as voting rights protect political equality against numerical majorities that might seek to disenfranchise minorities within their polity. In an environmental context, rights to participate in environmental decision making can help to guarantee that decisions are responsive to those affected by them, which reflects a core democratic principle. Community rights to know allow those vulnerable to pollution and other environmental hazards to more effectively protect themselves, promoting the democratic value of transparency. The rights to a free press also advance this democratic interest in transparency, as journalists often uncover stories about environmental hazards and can help apply public pressure to force governments to mitigate them. Rights of free speech, assembly, and association are vital to effective organization and mobilization of environmental advocacy, without which movements on behalf of environmental protection would not have been able to play the opposition role that has been responsible for most environmental legislation in countries such as the United States.

In the US domestic context,[5] rights can be created by statute or in the national or state constitutions. Both require judicial interpretation in order to determine the full nature and extent of the right, which courts perform through their power of judicial review. Because amendments to the national and state constitutions require onerous supermajority approval, constitutional rights are more robust than statutory rights. Arguably, "new" constitutional rights can be created by judicial review rather than constitutional amendment, as with the identification in *Roe* v. *Wade* of a right to abortion from the "penumbra" of related privacy rights in legal precedent, but such rights are also insecure in that changing compositions of Supreme Court justices can revoke them through the same judicial review powers. They are still more robust than statutory rights in that federal and state Supreme Court justices serve longer terms than legislators, with the ideological balances of power in the judiciary changing less frequently than in the legislative branch, making its rights-affecting tendencies more stable. In addition, the **stare decisis doctrine** weighs against overturning established legal precedent in a way that has no parallel in the legislative branch.

Several important legal rights have featured in US environmental litigation, and thus warrant some attention here. As discussed in chapter 10, for example, the "equal protections" clause of the Fourteenth Amendment, which serves as the constitutional basis for most US antidiscrimination law, was used to litigate the first important environmental justice case, and later served to frame race-based environmental struggles as involving racial discrimination. In this case, the ideal of equality was invoked in a manner consistent with its use in opposition to segregation and other civil rights litigation, but used in a new way, to resist the siting of a toxic waste facility near an African-American neighborhood. Here, we see continuity with the way that the equality ideal was invoked in earlier civil rights struggles – as a demand for social equality by way of redressing a source of inequality – along with transformation of that ideal, here in the discursive framing of anti-toxics campaigns in terms of environmental racism and environmental justice, which was novel.

Other existing legal rights have been invoked on behalf of environmental protection objectives, in addition to the participation and transparency rights noted above. Antipollution statutes such as the Clean Air Act create a statutory right not to suffer harmful air pollution, with the Environmental Protection Agency legally required to identify and regulate harmful pollutants, maintaining levels sufficient to protect public health. Affected plaintiffs can legally challenge the agency's failure to do so, and have done so successfully on several occasions, including the 2007 case *Massachusetts v. EPA*, where the US Supreme Court held that the Clean Air Act required EPA to regulate dangerous airborne pollutants, and that the agency's internal science was sufficient for carbon dioxide to be covered by this mandate. (That EPA still hasn't complied with this directive is illustrative of the limits of such legal powers.)

## Environmental rights

Some propose creating new and specifically environmental rights to supplement this use of existing rights to protect against environmental threats. A common proposal for such a new right would be one to a safe environment, an example of which can be found in the 1972 Stockholm Declaration, which declares the right to "adequate conditions of life, in an environment of a quality that permits a life of dignity and well-being" (delegates rejected the proposed stronger wording calling for a human right to a safe or wholesome environment). A similar formulation is found in the Brundtland Report, which claims "the fundamental right to an environment adequate for their health and well-being" for all humans. At the domestic level, such a right could be declared by statute or through constitutional amendment, with the latter offering more robust protections for reasons noted above. As Tim Hayward notes, "a constitutional environmental right would both signal a commitment to better balance between economic and environmental interests, and provide the basis for some means of achieving this in practice."[6]

Because rights apply equally to all right-holders, guaranteeing the rights to an adequate or safe environment would rest environmental protection imperatives upon the equality ideal. As Hayward notes, the "most obvious application" for such a right would be "with respect to pollution, waste disposal, and other sorts of toxic contamination, since the most immediate threats to health and well-being concern contamination of air, water, and food."[7] If such a right was legally recognized, it would provide more robust protections for politically marginalized minorities against the imposition of unequal risk discussed as *environmental injustice* in chapter 10, offering those whose rights are now threatened access to the judiciary rather than merely the majoritarian branches of government. If it was constitutionally protected, as Hayward advocates, it would insulate the right against retrenchment through routine revision – to which it would be susceptible if established by statute or judicial decree – as well as manifesting a kind of equality under law.

Rights beyond the nation-state, such as those created through international humanitarian law in such conventions as the Universal Declaration of Human Rights (UDHR), likewise rest upon a foundational equality claim and can be used in pursuit of environmental objectives. Like the natural rights of early modern political theorists, human rights are seen to be universally held, rather than being contingent upon approval or protection by existing states, extending a conception of legal equality to all persons, regardless of their nations of origin or residence. Such rights might comprise key resources in struggles to protect the global environment. As Simon Caney argues, such basic human rights as those to life, health, and subsistence could be made to apply to climate change, furnishing a powerful justification for nation-states to act in order to mitigate the phenomenon's worst impacts.[8] A 2005 petition brought to the Inter-American Commission on Human Rights by the Inuit people alleged that the United States violated their human rights to culture – which, as Dinah Shelton notes, "is inseparable from the condition of the lands they have traditionally occupied" – as well as their rights to their territory, which was being dramatically transformed by climate change.[9] Delegates to the 1972 Stockholm Convention considered, but ultimately rejected, declaring the human right to a safe environment, in part because they believed it implicit in the right to an adequate standard of living in Article 25 of the UDHR.[10]

Unlike global justice, for which there exists no legal basis and minimal political support among the world's most powerful countries, human rights law is well instantiated in international law and enjoys at least the putative support of the powerful countries that have contributed to its development. As with international law generally, however, its limits lie in its dependence upon the support of the international community for its validity, making it unlikely that it could be used against the strong opposition of the same states that it requires for support. Nonetheless, the proliferation of human rights represents an important development for the equality ideal over the course of the past half-century, with a wider public brought under their protection and vested with the ability to make the claims that Feinberg celebrates. In challenging the notion that legal equality is to be circumscribed within nation-states only, human rights challenge more traditional scope limitations on rights as institutional instantiations of the ideal, with environmental human rights pushing the conceptual envelope further by seeking to provide basic threshold levels of environmental quality for everyone, regardless of nationality or territorial residence.

## Equality as equivalence: the issue of carbon offsets

The ideal of equality operates within conceptions of justice in various ways, one of which involves the notion of *equivalence*: that two or more different things ought to be treated in the same way on the assumption of their relevant similarity. We see this operating in a number of contexts in environmental politics and theory, and through different conceptions of justice. From the imperative to treat like cases alike, which is a classic formulation of impartiality norms, the importance of equivalence arises. Within legal justice, the observation that accused murderers are more likely to receive the death penalty when their victims are white than with non-white victims suggests the role that equivalence plays in defining justice. Racial differences among victims *shouldn't* matter, we think, because all human lives have equivalent value regardless of any such differences. What matters is the seriousness of the crime, and the equivalent crime warrants equivalent punishment. Here, we must decide which equalities to merely stipulate (like the value of human lives) and which to rest upon empirical facts, and with the latter decide which facts should matter and which should not. Even then, we must make contestable assumptions about equivalence, whereby, if we err, a decision that would otherwise be just becomes unjust.

Issues regarding equivalence arise in numerous contexts, but we shall consider two in the area of environmental politics. The first is simply an environmental application of the above objection to weighing the value of human lives differently, from the intersection of international inequality and the trade in pollution and toxic waste. While Chief Economist at the World Bank in 1991, Larry Summers authored what was intended to be an internal memo but which was leaked and later used to illustrate the economic logic behind environmental injustice. In it, he recommends that the Bank encourage migration of "the dirty industries" to poor countries, on the basis of what he describes as "impeccable" economic logic. Among his cited reasons are that "measurements of the costs of health impairing pollution depend on the forgone earnings from increased morbidity and mortality." In other words, it is cheaper to compensate people whose illness or death is caused by industrial pollution when their employment prospects are poor or their wages low, making the business case for moving pollution to where people's lives are worth less. Of course, wrongful death civil lawsuits in countries like the United States rely upon a similar calculation about lost wages in their compensatory judgments (a consideration that would not be reflected in any associated punitive judgment, where all lives are still assumed to be of equivalent value), but objections to this logic turn on the normative importance of equivalence. Human lives, we might think, should not be worth more or less based on someone's income, so all should be entitled (from the equality ideal) to have their lives treated as of equivalent value in such contexts.

## Carbon equivalence

The second application of equality as equivalence arises through the rules and regulations developed for the commodification of carbon as a climate change mitigation measure. In carbon offsets, some quantity (say, a metric ton) of carbon emitted through the combustion of fossil fuels is taken to be the equivalent of that same amount sequestered in a sink. When I plant a tree to offset my carbon from an airplane journey (or pay someone else to do this for me), I reason that the negative environmental impact of my carbon emissions will be negated by the positive effects of the sink, making my journey carbon neutral. When a company acquires the carbon credits needed to sell voluntary offsets like the ones I just described by planting an entire forest, there needs to be some kind of certification of equivalence between the carbon that is stored in their forest and the quantity of offsets that they are allowed to sell. Since a carbon credit of this kind is invisible, its value as a commodity depends entirely upon the credibility of the processes for certifying its value. As a credence good, its value cannot be observed by the consumer.

Research suggests that the rules and regulations governing the voluntary offset market are not very robust.[11] Despite the promulgation of several international private governance standards, including the so-called Gold Standard and Voluntary Carbon Standard, the procedures required for certifying offsets from reforestation projects in the voluntary offset market are not viewed as adequate to ensure the necessary equivalence. I may have no way of knowing whether or not my purchased offset really restores my carbon neutrality after my flight. Regulations for certifying compliance offsets – those used by nation-states to offset national emissions as part of their mitigation commitments in international efforts like those under the Paris Agreement – are more robust than those governing the voluntary offset market. With nearly a quarter of global greenhouse gas emissions arising from deforestation and forest degradation, incentives for forest protection and restoration comprise an important component of global mitigation efforts. The UNFCCC has, since 2005, been developing certification rules under its REDD+ (for 'reducing emissions from deforestation and forest degradation') program to try and ensure this equivalence, which is vital to the program's credibility and effectiveness.

Even if these technical and regulatory obstacles could be overcome and all carbon offsets represented equivalent removal of carbon dioxide from the atmosphere, several key normative issues would remain. For a carbon credit acquired by sink enhancement to be fully equivalent to the emissions it is designed to offset, it must have transitivity (or full quantitative equivalence in its climate effects, such that an emission and its offset would leave no remainder relative to not initially emitting). Such is the logic behind carbon offsetting and trading: since a ton of carbon added to the atmosphere has the same climatic effects regardless of its geographic point of origin or how it is released, a ton of carbon removed from the atmosphere should negate those effects regardless of where it is stored. In addition to the physical transitivity described above, we might require also that offsets be morally transitive: that we have no ethical reason to prefer a reduction in emissions to an offset of the same amount. Equality as a normative ideal may depend upon this physical equivalence but is not reducible to it. Combining the physical and moral, emitting 10 tons of carbon and then offsetting 9 of them through reforestation offsets should therefore be morally equivalent to emitting only a single ton.

## Offsets and equity in international carbon trading

If offsets were transitive in this way, there would be no reason to require rich countries to reduce their domestic emissions, rather than buying offsets or making their own through financed reforestation under REDD+. But this would be tendentious, as it would allow rich countries to meet their mitigation commitments through offsets alone, without actually doing anything to reduce their domestic emissions. If acquiring the offset is cheaper than reducing domestic emissions, as is typically the case, then national mitigation burdens (which are a function of abatement costs, rather than quantitative abatement impact) would not be equivalent across these different activities even if their effects were equivalent, and states would likely prefer to offset rather than reducing their domestic emissions. The result would be widening international disparities in per capita carbon access, as rich countries paid poor countries to reduce their emissions rather than reducing those domestically. Critics of proposed carbon trading and offsetting mechanisms based on this putative equivalence objected to them in the Marrakesh Declaration in 2001, which limited the proportion of credits toward emissions reductions called for under the 1997 Kyoto Protocol that could come from offsetting activities within developing countries, insisting that the majority of mitigation burdens come from reduction in domestic emissions.

One explanation for this objection might be false equivalence – that an offset ton is not equivalent to an emitted ton, and so allows increased warming – but this was not the critics' claim. Although they did not put it in this way, they objected to framing equivalence only in terms of climatic effects, rather than in terms of the respective burdens that different countries undertook in mitigation efforts. As is discussed further in chapter 10, burden-sharing equity in international climate change mitigation efforts can be conceived in different ways, with some viewing equity as requiring equal effort (measured in terms of expenditures) while others view it in terms of equitable emissions reductions. One problem with allowing compliance offsets in national mitigation commitments, then, is that the kind of equivalence that it involves does not match the conception of equity understood as operating in the climate convention. An element of this controversy remains even if offsets had the same economic costs as domestic emissions reductions, as critics also challenge the equivalence of reducing one's own carbon pollution and paying others to reduce theirs. While unsuccessful in setting a quantitative limit on how much of any state's mitigation commitments could come from offsets or carbon trading (called *supplementarity*), the 2001 Bonn Agreement does require that domestic actions comprise a "significant element" of developed country mitigation efforts, challenging the moral equivalence of offsets.

Controversy around the moral equivalence of carbon offsets arises also in climate ethics in relation to individual voluntary offsets. For example, John Broome argues that all persons are ethically obligated to become carbon neutral, which they can accomplish through an unlimited amount of carbon offsetting. They can, he claims, "cancel" any of their individual culpability in climate-related harm by purchasing voluntary offsets, since "emitting a tonne of carbon dioxide and offsetting it is exactly as good as not emitting it in the first place, providing the offset is genuine."[12] Critics have challenged the moral transitivity of this claimed equivalence, which would find no moral difference between a big polluter that emitted 10 tons of $CO_2$ but offset 9 of these, and a small one that only emitted a single ton. Jeffrey Skopec, for example, argues that allowing offsets to negate culpability "obscures the idea that the environmental ethic against wastefulness is not just about outcomes, but about an ethos – a type of character."[13]

A further objection to Broome's carbon neutrality imperative, which turns upon the moral equivalence of emitting and offsetting, concerns how regressive it is. To borrow a distinction from chapter 10, it assigns the **remedial liability** of mitigation according to a strict contributor-pays principle: all persons would be required to offset all, and only, the full amount of their personal carbon emissions. Variations in ability-to-pay are not viewed as relevant, with the rich and poor alike required to offset their emissions regardless of their financial ability to do so. It sets aside the fault-based distinction between the unavoidable first ton of emitted carbon that all need as a matter of maintaining human life at a bare subsistence level (let's say) and the tenth ton that is easily avoidable since it results from gratuitous affluence, treating survival and luxury emissions the same. Here again, Broome's focus upon equivalence of mitigation effects raises objections about other kinds of equivalence that might also affect our evaluation of these cases and emitters. As elegant as it may be to translate the equality ideal into the rule of treating like cases alike, the contested nature and role of equivalence in many cases complicate its easy application.

A related concern arises from an effect of allowing unlimited offsetting to countenance unlimited emissions, as Broome does. As Jonathan Aldred notes, "carbon trading extends the domain of distribution of goods based on willingness to pay (and ability to pay) in the market,"[14] allowing the affluent greater access to goods and activities with embedded carbon. Given existing economic inequality among persons, market trading allows the "extreme inequality of access" that currently characterizes market-distributed goods to be "spread to more goods," including travel and energy use. Since $CO_2$ "is a prerequisite for the fulfillment of basic needs," Aldred argues, its distribution by market principles can be "akin to regressive taxation" in that "the burden of a higher carbon price falls more heavily on the poor, because they spend a higher proportion of their income on goods whose production requires carbon emissions."[15] Again, the objection arises insofar as the ideal of equality allows for a carbon trading system whereby these regressive impacts manifest, as alternate conceptions (for example, that all are entitled to basic carbon access, beyond which further emissions incur liability) of equality avoid it.

## Equality and sufficiency: competing standards

How should the ideal of equality be applied to questions about natural resource access or distribution? Are all persons entitled to an equal share of earth's natural resources, as resource egalitarians claim, meaning that those using more than their share must compensate those deprived of theirs as a result? Or is there some other principle by which resource entitlements ought to be allocated (e.g. distribution in accordance with political or economic power)? Should principles of distributive justice apply to whole bundles of goods, including social goods and political powers as well as environmental goods and services, as is claimed by **global justice integrationists**,[16] or do different principles apply to particular goods? Can we insist upon equal rights and liberties but allow massive disparities in individual access to carbon emissions, water, or outdoor meat-based protein? Contrarily, if persons are entitled to unequal shares of the world's natural resources, or if nation-states are entitled to unequal access to resources on a per capita basis, what justifies this unequal entitlement?

Many of these questions strike at the heart of the ideal of justice, and several of them are discussed further in chapter 10. Here, our interest lies in the equality ideal, so we shall focus on the question of whether equality (and if so, in what form) or some other distributive principle ought to serve as the basis for allocating access to global environmental goods and services. Based on Michael Walzer's account of *complex equality*, we might observe that different distributive principles can apply to different goods (and perhaps also to the allocation of hazards or vulnerability, but we'll return to this matter later). As he explains, "complex equality means that no citizen's standing in one sphere or with regard to one social good can be undercut by his standing in some other sphere, with regard to some other good."[17] By this account, some goods may be allocated on the basis of need (health care, for example), while others might justly be allocated on the basis of ability to pay (e.g. luxury goods such as yachts), and still others equally (e.g. votes in an election). Distributive injustice quintessentially arises for Walzer with the emergence of a dominant good that is unequally distributed but can be used to access a wide range of other social goods. In a society marked by large economic inequalities, like the contemporary US, distributive injustice would arise if income and wealth (as a dominant good) allowed the rich disproportionate access to many other social goods, but Walzer also means to identify a range of goods for which a market allocation might not be unjust, so long as other goods are not allocated in the same way.

## Alternatives to equality

Let us consider several goods for which distributive principles other than equality might be more suitable. While food is a commodity rather than a natural resource, it requires resources like arable land and water for its production, so we might be thought to consume or claim these resources when we claim food (as implied in the concept of **virtual water**). Different human bodies have different caloric needs, with need appearing as the more appropriate distributive principle as a quantitative measure, and with nutritious and culturally appropriate (qualities that the UN Food and Agriculture Organization includes alongside sufficient caloric content in defining **food security**) as qualitative measures that structure what kind of food persons ought to have access to. Deprivation and excess in food both cause serious public health concerns in various parts of the world, as does the inability to access the right kind of food. A just distribution of food would be one in which all have access to adequate quantities and appropriate quality of food in accordance with their needs. Having access to less than is needed involves unjust deprivation, and having more food than is needed involves waste and avoidable environmental impacts from agriculture.

Water needs can vary significantly, as does preference-based demand for water beyond what is required for meeting basic needs. Meeting basic needs ought to take priority in water allocation decisions, and strict equality would probably be too insensitive to variable water needs to serve as the best distributive principle. How water ought to be allocated after basic water needs have been met is a matter of contention. Water for irrigation of lawns or gardens, as "virtual water" embedded in unnecessary meat-based diets, or in wasteful household or industrial use falls into a non-basic category that would enjoy lower priority than water access necessary for basic needs, and all such luxury uses become contentious when drought conditions compel municipal water authorities to ask customers to conserve in these areas. Some call for market allocation of non-basic water access based on ability to pay, while others would allocate on the basis of **prior appropriation** or proximity to its source. Equality – where all are entitled to equal shares of water resources, requiring some users to compensate others for using more than their share – is also a plausible candidate principle for water allocation, but is not the only one. One can imagine other bases for claims on water resources, including culture (e.g. with fishing rights for indigenous tribes), national residence (e.g. with those in water-scarce countries receiving less and those in water-rich countries more), and efficient use (with those using their resources more efficiently – for example in irrigation – being granted more resources than those wasting water used for the same purpose).

## Sufficiency and sufficientarianism

Some dispense with much of this nuance by asserting a relatively modest distributive principle that is grounded in humanitarian concerns for meeting basic needs rather than global egalitarian resource justice claims about common ownership. Sufficiency, they suggest, ought to determine the allocation of some environmental goods and services, since what matters is that all are able to get enough of critical resources such as water or energy to live decent lives, not whether access to resources is equal beyond this level. As Thomas Princen describes its logic:

> Sufficiency as a principle aimed at ecological overshoot compels decision makers to ask when too much resource use or too little regeneration jeopardizes important values such as ecological integrity and social cohesion; when material gains now preclude material gains in the future; when consumer gratification or investor reward threatens economic security; when benefits internalized depend on costs externalized.[18]

Utilizing a sufficiency principle for allocating resource entitlements (or *sufficientarianism*, as opposed to egalitarianism) has obvious appeal, not least because it simplifies the question that we have been trying to answer here. As noted in chapter 10, a sufficiency principle would also be compatible with existing human rights doctrine, which guarantees persons access to those resources and powers necessary for meeting human needs and serving important human interests. It also involves a different conception of the equality ideal, in that it ensures equal rights through equal basic access to critical resources in sufficient quantities, rather than calling for the equal resource entitlements advocated by resource egalitarians.

Reliance upon sufficiency as a distributive principle rather than equality does not avoid all difficult questions, however. One must still determine what counts as a sufficient share for each, which may be a function of geographical as well as cultural difference. Those residing in colder climates may need more energy to heat their homes or workplaces, for example, so a sufficient share of energy resources may vary by climate. Accounting for cultural difference may also require similar variation if social norms are taken into account. In his *Inquiry into the Nature and Causes of the Wealth of*

*Nations*, Adam Smith noted that while a "linen shirt" was not a basic necessity, in that many people historically had lived without one and many continued to do so during Smith's lifetime, it had become the case "through the greater part of Europe" that such a garment had shifted from luxury to necessity. In some places, but not others, he writes, "a creditable day-labourer would be ashamed to appear in public without a linen shirt, the want of which would be supposed to denote that disgraceful degree of poverty which, it is presumed, nobody could fall into without extreme bad conduct."[19] A similar case could arguably be made for the importance of automobile-based transport in areas not well served by public transport, requiring a larger personal energy budget in order to meet the sufficiency threshold.

Leaving aside the contestable premises in reaching such a conclusion, Smith's remark raises important questions that are relevant to evaluating claims upon environmental goods and services. Are persons entitled to more carbon emissions because they live in affluent countries where high per capita emissions are the norm? Should persons receive more water for irrigation because they reside in neighborhoods where others maintain large and water-thirsty gardens? More generally, as consumption expectations increase, do commodities or services such as mobile phones or air travel go from being luxuries to which none are entitled to needs that have to be accommodated under a sufficiency principle, but made relative to norms in the society or social subgroup to which particular persons belong? And if so, how does a society in which the majority subscribe to consumption norms that result in huge ecological footprints set itself on a path toward sustainable transition? As Mill observed in "On Liberty," one manifestation of the equality ideal is pressure toward conformity through social norms, but this kind of equality is ill equipped to address problems like unsustainable consumption where this is compatible with norms.

Note that reliance upon distributive principles other than equality does not mean that the premise of moral equality among persons has been abandoned. Indeed, that premise remains in place when allocating variable quantities of food or water on the basis of need, which assumes that all recipients are of equal moral standing but takes some differentiating facts about those persons to be relevant to how much of the good is needed to treat them equally. This norm of equal treatment – or what Singer calls the equal consideration of interests – undergirds reliance upon these other principles, which seek to establish or maintain some kind of equality. Limited inequality in access to some goods may be compatible with moral equality insofar as it reflects some morally relevant qualities among persons, like merit or differential effort in working. However, against the background of wide and increasing socioeconomic inequalities, it would be difficult to rationalize the wide environmental inequalities experienced by persons of putatively equal moral status. To such inequalities we therefore now turn.

## Inequality and the environment

International patterns of natural resource use are highly unequal, viewed on a per capita basis, and have been so since the start of what historians call the Great Acceleration.[20] Home to 5 percent of the planet's human population, North America emits 18 percent of its carbon dioxide. By contrast, Africa emits only 4 percent of its $CO_2$, despite being home to 16 percent of the population. According to an Oxfam study, the world's richest 10 percent are responsible for 49 percent of global lifestyle emissions, which is more than 60 times the carbon footprint of the poorest 10 percent, and the top 1 percent emit 30 times more than the bottom half on a per capita basis.[21] Similar inequalities can be seen across the range of ecological goods and services. For example, the US per capita water footprint is twice the global average, at 2,480 cubic meters per year, and more than three times China's per capita footprint.[22] As noted in chapter 2, the per capita ecological footprints of rich countries are nearly five times those of poor countries. An environmental version of the Pareto principle (or 80/20 rule) often approximates global inequalities in environmental access, with 20 percent of the population responsible for 80 percent of the resource exploitation that simultaneously drives economic inequality and creates negative impacts for the planet.

In short, the "great divergence" between development paths of global North and global South countries is, as Kenneth Pomeranz notes,[23] largely the result of differential capacities to exploit the planet's natural resources, which in turn runs parallel to the other "great divergence" of income inequality that Timothy Noah observes.[24] Rich countries became rich, he argues, by appropriating more of the world's valuable resources for their own. In an ecologically limited world, imperatives of sustainability are now unavoidably intertwined with those of equity. As Tom Athanasiou casts the "global New Deal" by which the planet must be equitably shared:

> [it] must compel the rich, the major consumers of the planet's resources, to profoundly reform their societies and make room

for others. And it must provide the poor with the means to raise their living standards without embarking on a futile effort to copy the Northern model of affluence and development. Above all, it must make "sustainable development" into something more than a cruel slogan.[25]

While Athanasiou does not go so far as natural resource egalitarians in interpreting the equality ideal as requiring equal entitlements to the planet's natural resources, he condemns the wide disparities in historical and current resource exploitation patterns (as well as calling for equal per capita carbon emissions entitlements, which is discussed further in chapter 10).[26]

## Conclusions: environmental imperatives and the equality ideal

One way that a revised conception of equality could help address such environmental inequalities would be through a modification to Locke's proviso on property acquisition, which we examined in chapter 3. Recall that Locke acknowledged that allowing for property acquisition through labor would result in significant inequality, but was not troubled by this implication, since he believed that God gave the world to all but intended it to benefit "the industrious and the rational." Clark Wolf reinterprets the proviso as a kind of harm principle that prohibits excess appropriation.[27] Applied across generations – as Wolf argues it should be if members of each generation are to have equal moral status – it would confer only limited usufructuary rights, through which current owners have a right to use but not "degrade, consume, or destroy resources in which future persons have an important stake."[28] So viewed, the right to acquire property would only make its owners a temporary steward of the resources they owned, deriving this stewardship ethics from a conception of intergenerational equality.

More radically, resource egalitarians like Hillel Steiner engage Locke in defense of an equal right of all persons to planetary resources. Steiner follows Locke's assumption about the earth originally being commonly owned to claim that "each person's original right to an equal portion of initially unowned things amounts to a right to an equal share of their total value." Even if they never get to use those resources themselves, he argues, they deserve compensation for their losses when others appropriate more than their shares, since "any person's possession of a just title to any such thing encumbers him with a duty to pay every person an equal share of its value."[29] From Steiner's point of view, if 20 percent of the world's population used 80 percent of its resources, that 20 percent would owe the remainder of the population significant compensation (or "ecological debt") for their overuse.

The concept of "climate debt," which is key to contemporary climate justice discourse, turns on this same resource egalitarianism, and also makes use of a version of the Lockean proviso: limiting each person's emissions to what is compatible with others having "enough, and as good" of carbon access within the boundaries of sustainability, and incurring debt above this (equitable) amount. Whether grounded in Locke, some other canonical text, or in ideals of justice (as examined in chapter 10), conceptions of equality are instrumental in critiques of existing environmental inequalities, and may therefore play some role in rectifying them.

Likewise with the other engagements between conceptions of equality and our relations to the more-than-human world, environmental rights, and the use of carbon offsets to mitigate climate change, where our efforts at sustainable transition may disrupt settled conceptions and require their transformation, or else bring these conceptions into new and productive use in environmental politics. Unlike several of the other social ideals explored in the book, equality does not so much create an obstacle to the sustainable transition as offer a fruitful basis through which to theorize elements of that transition. Its understanding as such is thus essential to our constructive and critical thinking about contemporary environmental challenges.

# 7 Agency and Responsibility

Agency and responsibility do not so much function as social ideals in themselves as operate as key components of ideals in ethical action, social and political accountability, environmental stewardship, and remedial justice. Persons, states, and non-state actors should all act responsibly, or be held responsible for their contributions to problems such as climate change. Their relationship to each other, as well as to these social and political ideals, will be the focus of the first part of this chapter. Its second part will examine how conventional constructions of agency and responsibility have been challenged by sustainability imperatives, and how in a symbiotic fashion they have been transformed in order to become more serviceable to those imperatives. Together, the chapter will explore how issues in environmental politics have constrained and directed how we think about and formulate agency, in an effort to better protect against environmental degradation or promote responsibility in sustainable management of the environment.

## Key concepts in agency and responsibility

To begin with a few definitions, *agency* generally refers to an entity's capacity to engage in voluntary or self-directed action. Social science debates about the relative impact of agency and structure on a phenomenon are thus questions about the extent to which behavior or actions of persons are freely chosen or are heavily influenced by constraints such as economic incentive structures, social class, or culture. *Moral agency* refers to this capacity in an ethical sense, whereby voluntary or self-directed action is informed by an understanding of right and wrong, and for which the agent can be held morally responsible. Only moral agents can act wrongly or be held morally responsible for their actions. Both senses are thus related to freedom or free will, which is the subject of chapter 3, as well as to the Kantian concept of *autonomy* (often understood as a kind of freedom), which is defined as action in accordance with categorical imperatives of ethics rather than the hypothetical ones of mere prudence. Agency in a more colloquial sense involves the power to act, and can be undermined by the scale of global environmental problems that seem too big for anyone to meaningfully address.

*Moral responsibility* refers to the status of agents as warranting praise or blame, reward or punishment, or being assigned some kind of remedial liability, usually by virtue of some kind of previous act or omission, and often in conjunction with or contingent upon some kind of mental state at the time. A murderer can be responsible for her victim's death, or a rescuer can be responsible for saving a child from drowning. Non-moral forms of responsibility also deserve mention here, as these can refer to designated roles in which some agent acts on behalf, or in the interests, of another agent, or some thing or objective. A physician can be responsible for prescribing the correct dose of a medication, or the EPA can be responsible for protecting the US public from harmful pollution. To complicate matters further, a purely causal notion of responsibility can be distinguished from both of these normative concepts, as we can and often do distinguish what an agent can be held morally responsible for from what they merely have some role in causing. We even speak of non-agents having this kind of responsibility, as when we speculate that an asteroid collision was responsible for prehistoric extinctions.

Finally, assignments of moral responsibility typically involve a third-party assessment, whereby some impartial observer assesses X's actions with respect to Y, determines whether X is morally responsible for those actions or their outcomes, and assigns that responsibility in one of its several forms. Juries do this in tort cases, deciding whether involved parties are responsible, and then whether to assign compensatory liability. There is an associated first-person standpoint, by which we hold ourselves responsible for actions or outcomes as an impartial observer might, or are motivated by a sense of responsibility for others or for objectives such as environmental protection. We blame ourselves for acting (or failing to act) in circumstances where we (often after the fact) determine that we could have made a difference, sometimes punishing ourselves accordingly. This sense can be either moral or non-moral, so it is possible for us to believe that we have failed in some responsibility of ours but done nothing wrong, as when someone under our care is hurt despite our having exercised proper vigilance. This latter kind of responsibility – in which persons assign themselves, or are assigned by others, a contributory or caretaking duty for something – can also be inculcated in others, as with animal welfare concerns or stewardship ethics that are encouraged by a kind of environmental education. Environmental awareness campaigns urge this kind of responsibility, trying to make everyone feel responsible for doing their part to save the planet.

Agency and responsibility also function as components of the democratic ideal. When we participate in collective decision making around public issues, and especially where we are able to deliberate about normative principles and their application to specific issues, we can exercise what John Dryzek calls "formative agency," which allows participants to "give shape to the normative principles of justice that should be adopted in a particular situation."[1] This conception operates as an ideal insofar as the practice of citizenship involves the exercise of such agency, and democratic institutions should embody or foster it. Mechanisms of accountability designed to ensure that states and other institutions are responsive to those affected by them involve another kind of agency and responsibility, which is alternately conceived as "responsible government" or the act of holding other agents responsible. The US Congress is electorally accountable to the voting public, which means not only that legislators are responsible to their constituents in the formal sense of having their power delegated to them by those constituents, but also that elections allow those constituents to end this principal–agent relationship at the next elections. A parallel sense applies the same accountability function to private actors, as in corporate social responsibility movements, which seek to make corporate boards accountable to their shareholders. Finally, we can identify a version of the responsibility ideal that is concerned with environmental protection or stewardship, as when (to be discussed further below) Wendell Berry commends his readers to "eat responsibly" or otherwise adopt responsible environmental behaviors.

## Agents and agency

Within the Western philosophical tradition, *moral agency* is paradigmatically exercised by individual persons. Some contend that agents can *only* be individual persons, denying that the kind of normative assessment made of individual actions can apply to collectives unless in some sort of metaphorical or reductive way. From this point of view, blaming an angry mob for an atrocity like a lynching is a kind of shorthand for placing that blame on each member of the mob, whether in an equal or differentiated manner in which some are held to be more blameworthy than others, given their roles in the act. Others endorse a kind of collective agency by which the actions or decisions of groups can be evaluated apart from any comparable evaluation of the actions of individuals that comprise it. This kind of collective agency is often thought to be constitutive of democracy, which is the subject of chapter 4, but is also on display in climate ethics, as when we assign liability to an entire polity for climate change remedies, despite our being unable to hold some members individually responsible for climate change. We shall thus be interested in this chapter in how this notion of collective responsibility has developed, and how it has interacted with key challenges of the environmental crisis.

The status of agent or capacity of agency is limited to persons within that tradition. Some persons cannot be agents by virtue of their lacking the requisite cognitive capacities to determine right from wrong, as with some forms of mental illness or disability. Those unable to be found criminally culpable are non-agents, and are presumed to lack this moral power. Ignorance of the harmful impacts of action is sometimes taken to excuse agents from responsibility for it, as when nation-states claim ignorance related to greenhouse gas emissions prior to 1990, when the first Intergovernmental Panel on Climate Change assessment report was published. Claims of absent or impaired agency are sometimes contested, as with the so-called "affluenza defense" that was unsuccessfully invoked on behalf of the Texas teenager charged with recklessly killing others, but defended by the claim that he had been morally impaired by his social and economic privilege. Most persons become agents at some point, which under law is assigned at a specified age (often the eighteenth birthday) rather than on the basis of any assessment of the relevant capacities involved, especially as, like puberty, these occur at different ages for different people, or, like moving out of a parent's house, are sometimes delayed well past legal adulthood. Some lose their agency near the end of life, which is why advanced directives concerning end-of-life health care are often the only means to ensure that one's preferences during this period will be respected.

The Western philosophical tradition has conventionally denied agency to nonhumans of all sorts: individual nonhuman animals are not considered to be agents in the sense that allows us to ethically assess their actions or to hold them responsible for those.

The lion is not culpable for killing the gazelle, and, even though we kill animals for having attacked humans or pets, we cannot justify this through moral responsibility or on punitive grounds. Likewise, nonhuman collectives cannot be agents in the moral sense, whether as an entire species of nonhuman animal or the "biotic community" within an ecosystem, including plants and animals alike. This is not to say that individual, or collectivities of, nonhumans cannot have morally relevant interests, or that they cannot be the beneficiaries of moral obligations or even the holders of rights, as agency is distinct from these other kinds of status. Environmental philosophers use the term "moral patient" to refer to those recipients of moral obligations that cannot reciprocate those obligations.

## Moral and legal standing

The concepts of moral and legal *standing* are related to these issues. Moral standing is the status associated with being a moral patient, or of having interests that must be taken into account by moral agents with a capacity to affect those interests. Debates within animal ethics, for example, often concern the moral standing of nonhuman animals and what this requires of human agents who can affect them. As Mary Ann Warren notes, for an entity to have moral standing, we must regard it as having a kind of intrinsic value whereby it is recognized as having a good of its own, and "its needs have moral importance in their own right."[2] Those with such standing can make claims (or have claims made on their behalf) for their needs to be taken into account or protected, even if such claims can be overridden by competing interests. Whether pets, trees, or landscapes can have this sort of intrinsic value is an important question, since we would treat damage to them differently if viewed as a wrong against them rather than an injury to some owner suffering a loss to their property.

Legal standing parallels its moral counterpart in some respects, in that it concerns interests that can be taken into account but is more specifically defined in terms of who or what can be party to a lawsuit by virtue of having suffered some kind of harm. Along with *mootness* and *ripeness*, it is one of three requirements of justiciability under US law. Parties that lack legal standing cannot have their claims legally considered on their merits, as standing functions as a precondition for courts hearing legal complaints. Humans can be contingently denied standing – for example, if they cannot demonstrate that they have been materially injured by someone else's actions or the court would be unable to provide an appropriate remedy – but some kinds of things are categorically denied any legally protected interests. Curiously, some nonhuman entities (e.g. ships and corporations) have been granted legal standing, connoting that they have an important good of their own that is not reducible to human owners, but most other nonhuman entities have been extended no comparable status by US courts. As a result, no one can be held to be legally responsible for harming them – the law can only recognize their loss as an injury to humans.

Christopher Stone's advocacy of extending legal standing to trees was thus concerned with meeting the court's procedural requirement that plaintiffs (represented in the case for which Stone developed his analysis as an *amicus curiae* brief by the Sierra Club) demonstrate a legally justiciable injury in their effort to halt the construction of a ski resort within a national forest.[3] While unsuccessful in its objective of broadening the standing doctrine to include nonhuman nature, Stone's analysis was influential in Justice Douglas' dissent to *Sierra Club v. Morton*, in which he calls for legal protection "in the name of the inanimate object about to be despoiled, defaced, or invaded by roads and bulldozers and where injury is the subject of public outrage." Had it been successful, environmental groups could have challenged environmentally damaging development by showing that forests would suffer from it, rather than having to demonstrate injuries to group members, allowing such groups to serve as legal agents in advocating on behalf of nature itself, rather than human users of it.

## Ethical individualism and the environment

Who or what is responsible for global environmental threats like climate change, and what follows from this responsibility? Are we responsible as individual persons, even if our individual acts cannot make a difference to the global climate? Do the consequences of group actions impugn the individuals that comprise such groups equally, so that all Americans are equally responsible for what the nation does as a collective agent (if it is one)? On the other hand, is it possible for us to absolve ourselves of responsibility for climate change – for example, by becoming carbon neutral – even if we belong to a group like the US that is collectively responsible for climate change? These questions, which have been central to climate ethics for over two decades, raise a number of issues for environmental political theory, as well. They are important, in part, because our answers to them determine what remedies may be available for problems like climate change; in part because they specify who or what must undertake such remedies; and partly because they instruct us how to think about and evaluate the contributions to large and diffuse problems like this. In order to more effectively address these questions about responsibility for climate change, we must first examine the relationship between individual and collective agents and agency, and the challenges associated with collective responsibility.

*Ethical individualism* assumes that individuals, rather than collectivities such as nation-states or humanity as a whole, ought to be of primary importance for ethical evaluation, in two respects. First, individuals and their welfare or freedom are taken by this view to be primary, with any evaluative characteristics associated with collectivities reducible to the individuals that comprise them. From an ethical individualist perspective, a group cannot flourish without members of the group also flourishing, with that experience being felt by individual persons rather than the group as a whole. The same is true for harm, which from this perspective cannot be suffered by any collective without its individual members also suffering. While persons might be more likely to experience some kind of harm as a result of their membership in some group – members of a racial minority experiencing discrimination in a way that persons who are not members of the group cannot, for example – they would, from this perspective, suffer the effects *qua* individuals (if also in solidarity with other members of the group). To say that a group suffers would, according to this view, be a kind of shorthand for saying that the individual members of the group suffer.

Second, ethical individualism assumes that only individual persons can exercise agency, which is the key condition for the ethical evaluation of actions. To hold someone responsible in a moral sense (along with related attributes such as culpable, complicit, or blameworthy) is to assess their role as involving agency, or willful involvement in, or connection to, an action or outcome. While responsibility in a merely causal sense can be attributed to things or forces that lack agency (that "the wind is responsible for knocking over the trash can"), moral agency is needed for ethical assessments to be made. According to ethical individualism, no collective can be responsible for committing some harmful act unless individual persons in the group are also responsible, and without remainder. Here, saying that "the United States is disproportionately responsible for climate-related harm" is again understood as a kind of shorthand for saying that the nation's responsibility is merely the sum of a set of constituent individual responsibilities.

## Challenges to ethical individualism

Environmental threats are not unique in challenging this ethical individualism, but they have underscored the need to retool our normative imaginations to accommodate ideas about collective harming, collective goods, and collective culpability. A prime example of how harm to a collective can exceed the sum of individual harm is the existential threatening of an entire people through genocide. Over and above the harm done to individuals killed because of their group membership during genocide, an additional harm is thought to be done that is irreducibly collective. It is not only the bodies of victims to which violence is done, but the identity of the group, which undergoes a process of erasure with genocide that Claudia Card describes as a "social death," to distinguish it from other mass-murders.[4] Whereas the memory of a person and the physical manifestations of their existence might persist after their death, whether carried on through their progeny or the persistence of their group's cultural practices, harm to groups of this sort aims to erase these residual manifestations. Since the collective harm involved in genocide exceeds the individual harm suffered by each group member, ethical individualism cannot fully capture its wrongness in the way that Card does with her more capacious ethical conception.

Like genocide, biodiversity loss involves a similar kind of irreducibly collective form of value that is not fully captured under an individualistic analysis. When an entire species goes extinct, the nature of that loss is not fully captured by accounting for the losses of individual members of the species. To view species extinction as a unique form of loss or harm, we must be able to conceive of it as being suffered by a collective in a way that exceeds the harm suffered by its constituent members. In this sense, the threat of biodiversity loss resembles the threat of genocide in that it involves a unique kind of collective harm beyond what can be accounted for in individualistic terms alone. To express this kind of loss, we need a conception of collective harm or value. While the irreversibility of extinction partly captures this loss, since it denies the possibility of existence for any future members of the species as well as involving losses to its current members, the collective has a value independent of and not reducible to those of its individual members. This collective value can perhaps be best appreciated by comparing the loss of a breeding pair from a healthy species to that of the last breeding pair of an endangered species, where the additional loss in the latter case can only be accounted for collectively.

Somewhat more controversially, collectives may flourish in a way that does not reduce to the flourishing of their individual members. Predation of prey animals in nature can be viewed as good for the collective despite the obvious harm visited upon those group members whose lives are sacrificed for the sake of the larger whole. When the wolf kills the elk, it is obviously harmful to that particular elk whose life is ended, but this predation can strengthen the herd of elk by eliminating its weaker members. In wildlife ecology, we can also speak of the health of a species in reference to its population being kept in check by predation, with benefits for natural selection arising through survival traits that allow some members to increase their chances of avoiding predators. As Aldo Leopold shows in *A Sand County Almanac*, we can even talk about the health of entire ecosystems in a way that doesn't reduce to the health of any particular species groupings within those systems, as when the biotic pyramid grows as the result of increasing complexity or greater **trophic diversity**. Here, we're asserting a kind of collective value that doesn't reduce without remainder to value experienced by individual group members.

Unlike collective harm, however, this kind of collective value characteristic of **ethical holism** can take on a more insidious form when applied to human communities. Sacrificing any one person for the sake of a social community is ordinarily regarded as morally repugnant, with individual rights asserting the priority of individuals to collectives in human contexts. Perhaps our attitudes about the distinctions between humans and nonhumans may change someday, but at present we generally refuse to regard the deaths of more vulnerable persons as good for either local human communities or humanity as a whole, whereas we often make the opposite judgment about nonhuman predation. Respectable environmental philosophers can defend therapeutic hunting as beneficial for a population of ungulates when its natural predators decline in number, but only a fascist would recommend sacrificing individuals for the sake of the group in any but the most extreme circumstances.[5] Our ingrained normative commitments to individualism preclude our recognizing (much less advancing) a good for human groups that comes only at the expense of its innocent and vulnerable members.

## Collectivities, value and moral standing

Our thinking about collective goods is nonetheless an important part of environmental value, and thus a product of environmental theorizing. The Gaia hypothesis, first advanced by the physicist James Lovelock almost half a century ago, posits the earth as a kind of living system, with the exchange of carbon dioxide for oxygen through respiration and photosynthesis forming a kind of planetary respiratory system, and its cycle of precipitation and movement of surface waters a kind of circulatory system. This expresses one form of such a collective entity that might be regarded as having a good of its own.[6] Lovelock was joined in support of the idea by microbiologist Lynn Margulis, who defined Gaia as "the series of interacting ecosystems that compose a single huge ecosystem at the Earth's surface," which, although not itself an organism, is "best regarded as alive."[7] Now regarded as the Gaia theory, the idea received substantial support in the Declaration of Amsterdam from a 2001 meeting of the European Geophysical Union, claiming that "the Earth System behaves as a single, self-regulating system with physical, chemical, biological, and human components."

A collective ontology such as that of the Gaia theory would recognize collectivities like ecosystems or the earth system as being a kind of entity that functions as a system, but it would take a separate argument to claim that ecosystems had moral standing, much less agency. Aldo Leopold claimed this standing in his land ethic, in which he treats "the land" as a recipient of moral obligations but not an agent in its own right. His idea of a "biotic community" reflects a collective ontology inherent to all the organisms within an ecosystem, but regarded as a whole system rather than as its constituent parts, and is discussed further in chapter 8. By claiming that an entire biotic community can flourish or decline, he offers an account of ethical holism. Here, our interest lies in its claim to the possibility of collective harm, which challenges ethical individualism. If collectives can be harmed in a way that is not fully captured by harm to their constituent members, this may pave the way for conceptualizing collective forms of agency and responsibility, which in turn might help us make sense of the kind of responsibility that is endemic in climate change.

Such collective agency and responsibility defy the individualism that remains dominant in contemporary ethical theorizing. Our foundational concepts of agency and responsibility were developed for a world of simpler interactions between persons, requiring no complex collective analysis. One person might harm another, whether from malicious intent, negligence, or by accident, and our assessment of their culpability is formed on the basis of our assessment of their agency in the matter and responsibility for the outcome. Whatever responsibility we attribute is assigned to one individual rather than divided among several, with causation for harm relatively direct rather than dispersed or aggregative. Homicide involves one person killing another with full agency, while manslaughter involves diminished agency and correspondingly reduced responsibility, and accidental killing involves neither agency nor responsibility. When two or more agents are involved in killing a victim, we might parse their agency depending upon their level of involvement – perhaps holding the participant inflicting the wound to be more responsible than the lookout, the getaway driver, or the participant holding a weapon but not landing a blow – but there is no group culpability that cannot be attributed to particular group members. A purely individualistic conception of agency and responsibility can suffice.

## Individualism, collective responsibility and climate change

But large-scale environmental threats have dramatically raised the stakes for collective responsibility, requiring more extensive and detailed normative evaluation of group liability and how this relates to the actions of, or responsibilities assigned to, individual, members. Climate change offers an illustrative case. No single person's greenhouse gas (GHG) emissions would be sufficient to raise atmospheric concentrations of those gases and, because of this, any climate-related harm, but the collective emissions of large groups do change the climate and harm others as a result. From an individualistic account of agency, it is not possible for a collective to be held responsible for harm without at least some of its constituent members also being responsible for that harm in some way, yet this appears to be the case. States are assumed to be collectively responsible for climate change, affirming this in the UNFCCC's identification of "common but differentiated responsibilities" of nation-states, with states understood as the level of analysis for the remedial responsibility associated with climate change. Without an adequate account of how this responsibility functions or can be justified, the treatment of climate change at this level of analysis would not be coherent, as it would be forced to choose whether to assign remedies to individual parties that may not be responsible for climate-related harm, or to collective ones that could not exercise agency and so could not be held responsible for outcomes of their actions.

Some attribute forms of individualism as causes of the environmental crisis, claiming that the possessive individualism characteristic of Western modernity encourages an excessively materialistic focus upon private acquisition and consumption over more social virtues, leading to ecological degradation through the demands that industrial capitalism places on the environment to support such vapid and self-oriented, but ecologically demanding, preferences. Others blame atomistic individualism for its denial of the webs of interdependence that connect us to each other and our environment, for its ontological insistence upon our self-reliance and independence from others and denial of our vulnerabilities and embeddedness. In some ways, these criticisms overlap with and reinforce those against anthropocentrism, which is discussed more thoroughly in chapter 8. As we shall explore in the following section, some of these shortcomings of ethical individualism could be remedied through the development of a kind of collective agency through which groups could be held responsible for actions of the individuals that comprise them, without the objectionable assignments of vicarious responsibility that critics of the concept worry about.

## Climate change, agency, and responsibility

While individual persons causally contribute to the various harms associated with climate change through their greenhouse gas emissions, for several reasons it remains difficult to hold them morally responsible for those harms. Part of the problem is that no person by themselves causes any climate-related harm, doing so instead when the effects of their actions join effects of several actions by several billion other persons. The moral wrongness of a person individually contributing toward climate change is in some question, for two primary reasons: that agency and causality at work in climate-related harm appear to defy conventional standards for moral fault and liability; and that the requisite knowledge and intentions for establishing such fault may often be missing in cases of individual greenhouse gas emissions. These two sets of problems defy conventional ethical analysis, leading to what Stephen Gardiner calls the "perfect moral storm" of difficulties in holding persons responsible for contributing to climate change,[8] but may rest on what Derek Parfit terms "mistakes in moral mathematics."[9]

Anthropogenic climate change is caused by pollution from billions of point sources that each make minute contributions toward increased atmospheric concentrations of such gases, with most of these emissions too small to be classified as other than benign. Each time we exhale, for example, we emit carbon dioxide, and the provision of such basic needs as food and shelter likewise contribute toward climate change. It is also true of each of these individual sources of greenhouse pollution that no unique harm results from it entirely. The harm associated with climate change instead results from aggregate levels of greenhouse pollution, and then only from those emissions beyond a sustainable threshold within which planetary sinks can safely absorb them rather than allowing them to accumulate in the atmosphere. Given this threshold effect, whereby emissions below the sustainable threshold are benign but those above begin to cause harm, it is impossible to specify that any particular emission causes harm, since it would itself be benign if not for the many like emissions released by others. Harm appears to be collectively caused, but in a way that cannot easily be disaggregated to individual emissions.

## Threshold effects, harm and responsibility

Standard approaches to addressing threshold effects would seem to be most effective in countering this problem. Rather than only looking at the threshold-exceeding act as harmful – as when the world's sinks have absorbed all the pollutants that they can and the next emissions (and perhaps those to follow within a given period) are faulted for causing climate-related harm – we might differentiate permitted from excessive pollution regardless of when it occurs within a period or with respect to reaching the threshold. Insofar as harm arises when humanity as a whole emits beyond the limit of what planetary sinks can sequester, we can identify excessive global emissions as those beyond this threshold, then assign fault to those contributing excessive emissions at scales below the global level. The emissions for which parties would be held responsible would not be those occurring after a threshold was reached – for example, faulting all greenhouse gas emissions after July 1 when the planet's annual sequestration capacity is exceeded after six months – but those occurring at any point during the year when judged as excessive.

One way of identifying excessive individual emissions would simply divide a sustainable global carbon budget by the planet's human population and then assign to each an equal share of that sustainable planetary budget, faulting persons for any annual emissions that exceed their per capita sustainable threshold. Another would draw on the distinction (central to moral responsibility in ethical theory) between emissions that persons cannot avoid because they are associated with meeting biological needs only (or *survival emissions*), and emissions beyond this level, presumed to be avoidable and resulting from affluence or the satisfying of wants rather than needs (or *luxury emissions*). Both seek to define faulty emissions in terms of excess, with the former relying upon an equitable rationing system and the latter defined instead in terms of the functions or activities with which emissions are associated. While the latter more closely follows distinctions relevant to the assessment of moral responsibility in other contexts, as necessity is typically an excusing condition for fault, it lacks the correspondence with global sink capacity that allows us to be confident that excusable emissions are not also harmful.

This imperfect correspondence between emissions that are faulted as involving moral responsibility for harm, and those which exceed biophysical limits and so begin to cause harm, challenges a conventional assumption in consequentialist ethics that actions are right or wrong, depending on the good or bad that results from them, along with an assumption also common to non-consequentialist ethical theories that rightness or wrongness attach to particular actions in a categorical rather than contingent manner (hence Kant's term for such an ethical prohibition in his deontological ethics as a "categorical imperative"). For an act-utilitarian (perhaps the most common form of consequentialism), actions are right if they result in good consequences, and wrong if they cause bad outcomes to obtain. Faulting an action that may not cause harm – as in the distinction between survival and luxury emissions, where some luxury emissions are possible within a sustainable global threshold – could not be justified from act-utilitarian premises.

For a deontologist deriving moral rules from principles like the categorical imperative, certain kinds of actions are always wrong, regardless of their consequences (lying is an oft-cited example in Kantian ethics, since he claims that it is wrong even where it results in good consequences). But either distinction (i.e. based on the equitably allocated sustainable sink threshold or that between survival and luxury emissions) would sometimes allow particular actions (e.g. driving a car) as morally permissible, but other times condemn them as morally faulty. A person exceeding their sustainable threshold of annual emissions in October would do so by committing the same kind of actions that they engaged in during February and August, so the difference lies not in the action itself but in another threshold effect. Fault thus attaches to individual persons through their patterns of behavior, not their individual actions, and to entire communities through their aggregate emissions rather than discrete actions.

## Fragmented agency and responsibility

While standard accounts of culpability rely upon some agent making a decision that results directly in another person being harmed, the way that individual persons cause the harms associated with climate change features a fragmented agency that is shared among many persons, groups, and institutions, and an indirect causal chain in which it would be impossible to trace any one person's polluting acts to any discernible harm suffered by another person. According to Feinberg's model of contributory fault, which requires a direct causal connection between some faulty action and a related harm, persons could not be held liable for the harmful consequences to which they contribute through their individual greenhouse gas emissions. Since this is true of everyone, and since it is also true that at least a substantial portion of existing greenhouse gas emissions are unnecessary, this model precludes finding anyone culpable for the enormous set of avoidable harm that anthropogenic climate change is expected to cause. Some address this apparent paradox of massive and avoidable but faultless anthropogenic harm by turning to collective accounts of culpability, eschewing individual responsibility for climate-related harm altogether.

A further complicating consideration in assessing moral fault for individual contributions toward climate change concerns the agent's knowledge and intentions surrounding the polluting acts in question. At least insofar as judgments of moral fault depend on finding that someone ought to have acted otherwise, and could reasonably have been expected to do so, the mental states of an offending agent enter the picture. By this analysis, it is not enough merely to have caused some harm as the result of one's action, in order to become culpable for that harm. One must also be at fault for that causal contribution, and fault requires, at minimum, that the agent in question must have been able to anticipate and avoid the harmful consequence of her action, whether or not she does either in fact.

## Uncertainty and responsibility

The problem with individual contributions to climate change is that they are shrouded in various forms of uncertainty. Some may erroneously believe that the scientific evidence demonstrating the existence of climate change or its anthropogenic causes is uncertain, and claim that this uncertainty renders all causally contributory individual actions blameless. Unless we can know for certain that we are causing the predicted harms of climate change, this approach suggests, we cannot be blamed for those problems if they obtain and we played some role in bringing them about. But this objection is easily addressed through the precautionary principle: so long as we have sufficient evidence that some categories of actions cause serious problems, even if some uncertainties regarding those causal connections remain, we cannot justifiably delay remedial actions designed to minimize those contributions to harm. The mere existence of some scientific uncertainty, particularly in the context of such a well-supported hypothesis, cannot cancel the culpability of agents that continue to act in ways that are widely predicted by the weight of peer-reviewed scientific evidence to be harmful.

Other kinds of uncertainty likewise plague judgments of culpability for individual contributions to climate change. Many people are simply ignorant of the findings of genuine climate science, either having been persuaded by climate skeptics that there is no scientific consensus on anthropogenic climate change, or else believing the conspiracy theories that acknowledge such a consensus but attribute this to dishonest researchers using scare tactics to extract research grants from frightened governments. Others may simply be uninformed, having ignored both the scientific information on behalf of anthropogenic climate change and the contrarian case against it. In both cases, faulting them for their contributory actions requires the judgment that they should have known that their actions were causing harm, whether or not they did in fact do so. In other words, persons contributing toward climate change from ignorance could be blamed in the same way as those doing so out of sheer indifference to the suffering of others, since in both cases the agents in question should have known better and acted accordingly. Such cases fault ignorant persons in part for their ignorance, and more particularly for the actions that they commit as the result of a culpable failure to assimilate widely disseminated information on basic climate science.

But this judgment can appear to be objectionably harsh in cases where climate skepticism is disseminated by trusted public officials, as it was in the United States under the presidency of George W. Bush. Faulting persons for believing their government, which propagated climate skepticism and suppressed scientific evidence linking human activities to climate change, sets a very high bar for what ordinary citizens are expected to discover on their own, in some cases against the information sources that many rely upon and trust. Nonetheless, some kind of culpable ignorance comes into play when people commit harmful acts in cases where a reasonable person could have foreseen and avoided that harm, and this analysis would seem to apply to individual contributions toward climate change. At minimum, liability to economically compensate those harmed by climate change can be attributed to those who cause climate change through their individual actions, as in strict liability, even if (as some argue) moral blame is inappropriate.

## Agents and levels of analysis: who should act?

Related to, but distinct from, the question of which agents *can* be held responsible for climate change is the question of which *should* be. The UNFCCC system has generally held states to be remedially liable for climate change, whether in terms of mitigation commitments or of obligations related to adaptation or compensation for loss and damage. Under the 2016 Paris Agreement, states pledged to reduce their greenhouse gas emissions (through nationally determined contributions, or NDCs) and were urged to finance institutions such as the Green Climate Fund, which assists in international mitigation and adaptation projects. Representatives of states serve as negotiators in the Conferences of the Parties under the UNFCCC, which, as an international agreement, is supported by state parties to the convention.

The UNFCCC's normative analysis also relies upon states as primary agents, calling upon them to act "in accordance with equity and their common but differentiated responsibilities and respective capabilities" (or the CBDR principle, which is discussed further in chapter 10). Groups of states are also recognized as agents under the convention – for example, developed country parties – and function as negotiating blocks at Conferences of the Parties (COPs) based on their shared interests, as with the Alliance of Small Island States (AOSIS). From the distinction between developed and developing country parties under the Framework Convention, as with its imperative that the former "take the lead" in responding to climate change, the 1997 Kyoto Protocol assigned all Annex 1 developed country parties some kind of binding mitigation targets, but required no such commitments for non-Annex 1 developing countries, creating a division between groups of states, based on levels of development, that those exempted from mitigation commitments under Kyoto have sought to maintain.

This "firewall," whereby "differentiated responsibilities" was taken to mean that only developed countries would be required to take on binding mitigation commitments, became controversial upon the expiration of the Kyoto Protocol's commitment period in 2012, and in the context of debates about the shape of a successor treaty framework, as rapidly developing states such as China were the fastest-growing sources of emissions and China overtook the US as the world's largest emitter, prompting critics either to claim that China (and perhaps other states in the non-Annex 1 group in 1992) had "graduated" into Annex 1 status, or else to reject divisions of states into such groups altogether. With the Paris Agreement's rejection of binding mitigation commitments in favor of NDCs, this division is now largely superfluous, but states continue to negotiate in blocs, and states remain the primary agents under the terms of the UNFCCC.

As a result of the focus within the UNFCCC process upon state agents, to which equity principles are applied and which were to be held responsible for their contributions to climate change under the convention, climate justice tends to be applied at the same level of analysis. Disparities in national emissions, especially when viewed alongside inequitable vulnerabilities by which countries least responsible for causing climate change are expected to bear the bulk of its impacts, suggest an international frame for climate justice. Remedial liability – responsibility for solutions to climate change, whether in the form of mitigation, adaptation, or compensation for loss and damage – has likewise been focused on states in the UNFCCC process, and theorized for states in much of the climate justice literature. Justice principles might apply at other levels of analysis, however, and agents other than states could be assigned remedial liability.

How, for example, should a state's mitigation burdens be allocated internally, as part of its effort to comply with its NDC under the Paris Agreement? Similar equity and responsibility principles might apply within a domestic burden-sharing context. Given the imperative to reduce national emissions overall, one might assign the greatest mitigation burdens to those persons with the highest current emissions, or those whose personal income or wealth give them greater capacity to reduce their personal emissions. Within this second burden-sharing stage, once GHG reduction burdens have been justly assigned among nation-states, we must also attend to issues related to the just allocation of burdens within those states, lest climate justice demands only be partly met. Questions about agency and responsibility arise anew in this stage, given the kinds of agents that might potentially be assigned remedial liability within particular states.

## Non-state agents and responsibility for climate change

In addition to persons, other agents might be held responsible for climate change, being assigned some kind of remedial liability for their role. Several non-state institutions might be good candidates. Multinational corporations are an obvious choice, as these are responsible for a large share of global emissions but are not captured within assessments of national responsibility, given their multinational status and consequent ability to offshore significant aspects of national carbon footprints. A 2017 study by the Carbon

Disclosure Project estimated that just 100 fossil fuel producers were responsible for 52 percent of all global emission since the industrial revolution (1751), with over half of global emissions since the first international convention on climate change in 1988 attributable to just 25 fossil fuel producers.[10] An oil and gas company releasing methane from an arctic drilling operation contributes to climate change, but since its emissions take place outside of the national territory that controls or profits from that activity it would not be counted toward that nation's carbon budget using standard production-based accounting. The only ways to assign responsibility for those emissions would be through either treating the company as an agent and counting them where they are produced, or treating persons as agents and counting the emissions where consumed.

Corporations as well as other kinds of institutions claim responsibility for abatement of their emissions, as with carbon neutrality or reduction commitments that they take on and often publicize in order to enhance their reputations as good environmental stewards. Indeed, much of the decarbonization activity taking place in countries lacking regulatory limits on greenhouse gas emissions can be attributed to private actors, since those actors have been the primary source of such emissions and therefore have maintained control over them. Termed "private governance" by Michael Vandenbergh, these efforts by private-sector organizations have partly filled the void left by the US federal government, which, as Vandenbergh notes, has not passed a major new environmental statute for nearly three decades, leaving carbon governance imperatives to other levels of government as well as nongovernmental organizations.[11] But credit-claiming for efforts to reduce companies' emissions is only one side of agency and responsibility. Those firms must be held responsible for their failures to act, not just benefit by such voluntary actions.

## Individual agents and remedies

Individual agents may also play a role in remedial responsibility for climate change, whether in terms of actions outside of the mandates of state climate policies or through equity principles or mechanisms that apply specifically to persons. In thinking about responsibility at this level, individual persons may *take* responsibility for their environmental impacts, or they may be *held* responsible for those impacts by a collective such as the government. Thus far, our interest has been in responsibilities that are assigned by others, but what would it mean for someone to voluntarily take responsibility for their role in collectively caused environmental impacts? We might distinguish a cognitive dimension of responsibility-taking from an action dimension.

For me to take responsibility for my role in contributing to climate change, I must first acknowledge a causal link between my actions and the larger problem. As previously noted, this link can be tendentious, given the vanishingly small share of greenhouse gases that I emit on my own and the equally tiny likelihood that my actions make any difference. These problems aside, we can acknowledge a causal role in climate change without viewing ourselves as necessary or sufficient causes of any climate impacts, and many persons do in fact acknowledge this kind of personal responsibility. This acknowledgment establishes an affinity connection with those affected by the problem, whereby we view ourselves or our actions as contributing toward some potential harm that the remedial sense of responsibility therefore asks us to rectify. Because we're responsible for causing a problem, we understand, we have some responsibility for its remedy.

Here we might distinguish between causing through our actions and causing through our failures to act, in order to capture an important driver of personal responsibility-taking. Where we could help to alleviate someone else's suffering, even if we had no previous role in causing that suffering, our failure to act could be regarded as causing the harm by omission. While we may think of this as a less serious form of responsibility, which yields less demanding remedial duties than if we had also played a causal role, sometimes the mere capacity to assist is all that is needed for persons to take responsibility for some harm. In this sense, it parallels the capacity and responsibility principles for collective liability discussed above. Such Samaritan duties arise because we are in a position to prevent a serious harm, and while we do not directly cause the harm, we might think of ourselves as potentially responsible insofar as we could remedy it.

## Holding persons responsible for climate change

Persons can be held responsible for their role in climate change without them acknowledging any role in causing the problem, as when they are made to pay a carbon tax on their fossil fuel consumption. But they cannot hold *themselves* responsible without such an acknowledgement. Those denying any causal role and disavowing any affinity connection with sufferers – whether because persuaded by science denialism, from sheer ignorance, or due to skepticism about any direct causation linking their actions to a global environmental problem that they believe to be anthropogenic and serious – cannot take personal responsibility in the relevant sense. Even if they consent to being held responsible for their actions – for example, by accepting a share of the national mitigation or adaptation burdens – they are here not assigning remedial liability to themselves so much as allowing others to assign it to them. Responsibility-taking requires this state of mind in which persons accept a link between what they have done and what they now must do.

Our response comprises the action dimension of responsibility-taking. Less effective responses include feeling guilty and developing anxiety but not changing one's behavior in any constructive way. Many people feel personally guilty about their roles in factory farming, plastic pollution, and climate change, but fail to take any constructive remedial action in response. They may not know what else to do, or doubt that they personally can make any difference, despite believing that they should do something to help. Perhaps those accepting some responsibility for climate change also suffer from *eco-anxiety*, which psychologists have identified as a maladaptive worry about the present or future environment that often leads to exhaustion and immobilization, preventing constructive responses such as responsibility-taking.[12] Others may decline to take responsibility out of a recognition of the collective action dilemma inherent in problems like climate change, being willing to cooperate if others also do their part, but knowing that others, by free riding, will undermine any positive effects produced by contributors.[13] More effective responses, and the kind that interest us in this section, involve behavioral change or other measures undertaken to reduce one's ongoing contributions, or offers of assistance to or compensation for those adversely affected. With climate change, these amount to individual mitigation, adaptation assistance and compensation. When we connect such personal measures with a sense that we ought to do something to help, we take responsibility for that problem.

How do persons now take responsibility for their role in climate change, and how could others be encouraged to join them? Before we begin to answer, some may take issue with the question itself, which implies what has been called the "individualization of responsibility." Michael Maniates, for example, argues that assigning environmental protection responsibilities to individual persons (as, for example, through **green consumerism**) leaves "little room to ponder institutions, the nature and exercise of political power, or ways of collectively changing the distribution of power and influence in society."[14] For Maniates and other critics of individualized responses to environmental threats, the focus upon individual rather than collective agency fails to take advantage of the potentially most effective solutions, which involve governance. But the inculcation of a sense of responsibility as described above need not be individualizing in this way, as it encourages taking action in response, including collective and political action.

## Transparency and responsibility-taking

Given the cognitive aspect of responsibility-taking – whereby persons must acknowledge their role as contributors to problems such as climate change before they assign to themselves some kind of role in its remedy – information and transparency about such links and impacts can play important roles. While disclosure and transparency requirements for polluters can be effective in encouraging their improved environmental performance and can allow members of the public to better protect themselves against the threats they cause, it is from the awareness in individuals of their personal carbon footprints that the cognitive aspect of responsibility-taking might arise. If I know what my carbon footprint is, which among my current activities contributes most to it, and how it compares to others, and what would be sustainable, this would be potentially empowering information that I could effectively use to reduce my footprint if I was to take responsibility for it. Insofar as that information can both raise my awareness about my role in climate change and assist me in more effectively reducing my contributions, it assists in responsibility-taking.

Critics may again object that such "informational governance" approaches, by relying on voluntary individual actions rather than institutions and regulations, fail to take advantage of the potentially most effective remedies, which rely upon collective agents like states, rather than individual ones like consumers. To the extent that disclosure and transparency are considered as alternatives to institutional or regulatory approaches, the critique is stronger. Individual persons have limited capacity to effect social or economic change on their own, and face significant collective action problems in doing so. Many lack the motivation needed to seriously reduce their carbon footprints, and many others lack the economic means to take advantage of some sources of individual carbon abatement. On its own, transparency is limited in its capacity for change. But the action component of responsibility-taking is not limited to individualized and private action only, as it relies upon the cognitive aspect to generate a commitment to respond in some way to the problem. There is no reason to suppose that it rules out effective responses, and indeed it may be a key component for mobilizing collective and political action.

## Collective responsibility

A conception of collective responsibility may help to alleviate some of the objections that have been made against the way that climate change holds individual persons responsible, but collective responsibility is also conceptually fraught. Perhaps most importantly, collectives are comprised of individual members, and collective responsibility can hold some of those members responsible *qua* members of a collective when they could not be held so *qua* individuals, which some find objectionable. Yet forms of collective responsibility through which we dissociate our evaluation of collectives from that of the individuals that comprise them are common in politics, as polities are one such example of a collective that exhibits a kind of agency and responsibility.

As Michael Walzer suggests, democracy can be regarded as "a way of distributing responsibility," and insofar as citizens have some control over their collective decisions, they must also be held responsible for them.[15] Those with more control – whether by virtue of their office or influence in democratic societies, or their being in a better position to resist collective decisions outside of standard political processes – may be assigned greater responsibility for collectively produced harm than those with less control, even if all citizens are to some degree responsible for what they do together. Collective responsibility in wartime and its aftermath therefore sometimes extends even to those citizens who opposed the war at the ballot box or public forum, insofar as they did not do all they could reasonably have done to stop it. Here, citizens are the principals that collectively bear responsibility for the decisions of the state, which acts as their agent.

Collective responsibility can in this way serve a valuable social role in expressing and strengthening the solidarity of groups that share mutual interests or bonds of affection, strengthening norms and encouraging cooperation. But it also raises objections from the principle of responsibility, since the group's fault does not readily reduce to the faults of all individual members held liable for group actions and decisions. The same is true of collectivized responsibility for climate change, as fault that is widely disparate among fellow citizens is obscured by blanket assignments of group liability.

David Miller, whose account of collective national responsibility has been influential in political theory, defines the nation as "a community of people who share an identity and a public culture, who recognize special obligations to one another and value their continued association, and who aspire to be politically self-determining."[16] His aim here is in part to distinguish nations from states (nations often act *through* states but are distinct from them), but he seeks also to emphasize the importance of common culture, solidarity, and self-determination in attributing collective responsibility for national decisions. Solidarity is a key ingredient for collective responsibility, as can be seen in the vicarious pride and shame felt by some group members for the actions of others, but it is self-determination that plays the larger role for Miller. Only policies adopted by democratic states can be assumed to be authentic expressions of a national culture, he argues, even if some citizens disagree with them.

Democratic self-determination confers prerogatives of governance upon citizens, but with these come responsibilities, including the responsibility to abide by and own up to bad policies adopted by the collective, regardless of any individual citizen's private preference or public political choices. As societies become more democratic, the extent to which all individual citizens must be seen as responsible for group decisions likewise increases, to the point where the perfectly democratic society represents a fully empowered agent of the state acting on behalf of the informed consent of its principals within the citizenry. At this point, no citizen is held vicariously liable for the state's bad actions, for each endorses them through participation in the processes by which collective decisions are made, regardless of individual preferences or votes. Hence, he claims, it is only in democracies that "the policies pursued by the state can reasonably be seen as policies for whose effects the citizen body as a whole is collectively responsible, given that they have authorized the government to act on their behalf in a free election."[17]

Climate change may be caused by individual actions, but significant contributing causes of those actions are state policies and social norms, and in the contemporary United States neither of these prohibits individual emissions at levels well above those which are globally sustainable. Despite its several democratic deficits, the US government remains answerable to its citizens during periodic elections and through inter-election pressure groups, so the American citizenry must shoulder some share of responsibility for the failure of its government to make adequate domestic climate change mitigation policy, and perhaps also for its continued obstruction of global climate policy efforts, given its widespread passive support for its government's active opposition to global efforts to reduce emissions.

But the US government's failure to adequately address global climate change is not merely an institutional shortcoming, since social norms are too permissive of pollution to generate genuinely democratic support for taking the necessary policy steps to avoid dangerously high greenhouse gas concentrations accumulating, much less to achieve that aim in the absence of coercive policies. Part of the problem is a public culture constructed around the personal automobile, large living spaces, high resource consumption, and little regard for the consequences of these upon the world's less fortunate. Democratic decisions ultimately reflect this culture, and the shared values and common identity it fosters create the necessary conditions for attributing collective responsibility, as well as generating the preferences for which such attributions are necessary. Prior to those political decisions lies a culture that is inimical to meaningful action to reduce emissions, and that culture can only be the product of society taken as a collectivity, and irreducible to individuals.

## Conclusions: agency and responsibility and the environmental crisis

It may be trite to remark that environmental problems would not occur if all agents simply took responsibility for their actions, insofar as this means that they would prevent the effects of those actions from having deleterious consequences for others. But most persons are not responsible in this way, so we might like, as a second-best alternative, for institutions to hold persons and other agents responsible for their actions, in the sense of preventing impacts from one agent adversely affecting another. As we have explored above, this kind of responsibility involves assignments of liability for remedies and can be clouded by debates over whether or how different agents can be held responsible for their contributions to environmental problems. Individual responsibility is difficult to extricate from actions and choices of groups, as when a person's carbon footprint depends upon their community's energy and transportation systems, and the fragmented agency and diffused responsibility inherent to global environmental problems such as climate change can complicate assessment of whether anyone is responsible for remedies, let alone how much remedial liability ought to be assigned to them.

Nonetheless, we can and do invoke responsibility as an ideal at various levels and for a wide variety of purposes, whether we're seeking responsible political parties or governments or trying to persuade business leaders to direct their enterprises in a responsible manner. As we've seen in this chapter, the responsibility ideal can be influential in shaping particular remedies, especially in its normative meaning, by which it is associated with a conception of justice that seeks to ensure that persons are held responsible in some cases and prevented from bearing responsibility in others. Understanding its theoretical dimensions can thus assist in projects like developing and applying remedial justice principles to climate change, where the model of "common but differentiated responsibilities" from the UNFCCC text suggests that responsibility plays a crucial role. However we construe it, identifying the right agents to hold responsible, and determining what responsibility entails in assessment and remedy, are challenges that reveal some key fault lines in competing approaches to environmental theory.

# 8 Community

Community has become something of a tendentious social and political ideal. To even assert its status as such requires an explanation, given recent reactions against it. On the one hand, it has a long historical provenance as a vital aspect of the good society, dating back at least to ancient Athens – from the praise of its democratic aspirations in the funeral oration of Pericles in Thucydides' *History of the Peloponnesian War*, to Plato's call for development of a "community of pleasures and pains" two decades later in his decidedly anti-democratic *Republic*. Cast as *fraternity*, it served as a motto for democratic revolution in France, and continues to serve as part of the nation's tripartite motto, along with ideals of liberty and equality. It has also served a role in ethnic nationalist movements from Nazi Germany to contemporary white supremacism in the United States, revealing the concept's xenophobic associations and, in so doing, accounting for the widespread antipathy toward its current status as an object of social aspiration. As a social ideal, it has always been plagued by this two-sided character, as it intensifies affections for and loyalties toward fellow members of the community, calling for solidarity and even self-sacrifice, but can simultaneously motivate hostilities toward outsiders, whose differences from group members are often exaggerated in order to differentiate and marginalize them.

Antipathy toward the ideal of community has thus come from a variety of ideological orientations. Former British Prime Minister Margaret Thatcher was rejecting the welfare state as a service provider for the disadvantaged when she claimed that "there is no such thing as society. There are individual men and women and there are families." Society, or social community, for Thatcher would raise the possibility of a common good or collective political action through the welfare state, and with these some constraint upon the atomistic individualism of her economic conservatism. Ethical cosmopolitans mean something quite different when they reject special obligations toward fellow nationals,[1] as will be discussed further below, asserting community to be an arbitrary basis for differentiated treatment of persons. Their opponent is a provincial sort of partiality that rationalizes global economic privileges that Thatcherism would defend. In debates in political theory during the 1980s, "communitarians" claimed, against liberals, that persons were constituted by their social identities, rejecting the abstract proceduralism of John Rawls' method of deriving justice principles from hypothetical contracts between deracinated maximizers,[2] or, to come full circle from Thatcher, rejecting individualism more generally.

In examining its conflicts and compatibilities with the environmental movement and its imperatives, and as an ideal that has been appropriated, resisted, and in both cases transformed within environmental politics and political theory, we should keep this dual aspect in mind. The ideal offers a rich source for developing progressive ecological ontologies capable of motivating social transformation of the kind demanded by the environmental crisis, but its "blood and soil" variant risks joining strong environmental values with hostile and anti-social political associations that oppose such imperatives. Claims to community, especially when attached to evaluative or action-oriented commands, are by their nature social constructs, and must be assessed as such. They are, as Benedict Anderson claims of their manifestation as nation-states, always *imagined*, rather than corresponding with or revealing realities, even when based on real differences.[3] The focus of this chapter will thus be upon how and why they are constructed, and what values they serve or obstruct, in creating a politics appropriate to the environmental challenges we face.

To what community or communities do we belong, then, and what is entailed by our claimed membership in them? To the extent that belonging creates thicker ties with some of our fellow members but also highlights the absence of such ties with those deemed outside of its boundaries, does the notion of community exacerbate privilege or otherwise lead to unwanted hierarchy or bias? Have some communities exhibited hostility toward others, whether through settler colonialism or through other forms of oppression, and if so, how does this affect the community ideal, or future relations among and between such communities? If community membership involves a common good or set of interests that are distinct from those of any of its constituent members, what is this good or these interests, and how do we resolve conflicts between the community and its members when they arise? Insofar as our community or communities involve virtues of citizenship, what are these and how are they cultivated? These are just a few of the questions that arise when considering the ideal of community and its potential application within contemporary environmental politics.

## The ancient ideal of community

We might begin by observing the use of community as an organizing and motivational principle in ancient political thought. While Plato's invocation of it in the *Republic* is aptly identified as exhibiting a form of what would later be called *nationalism*, or an inward-looking orientation that seeks to construct thicker bonds between members of the polity at the cost of a greater suspicion of outsiders, he had good reason for both. Athens had recently been sacked by Sparta, with blame for the city-state's vulnerability variously cast, but with some faulting the city's democratic commitments. Among other motivations, Plato wanted to differentiate his own utopian city from both Athens and Sparta, even if he looked fondly to both for inspiration. On the basis of the strong social bonds that he aimed to instill, he claimed of his imagined city that it would be capable of repelling attacks of the kind that Athens had suffered, with its guardians able to reliably distinguish between friends and enemies – a boast that would have commended this quality of his design to his contemporaries, and perhaps to ours. Still, his proposed insular and suspicious community stands in contrast to the open and outward-facing Athens celebrated in Pericles' funeral oration and associated with the ancient democratic ideal.

On the positive side, Plato sought to establish a community that was unified in common purpose – even if divided into three differentiated social classes – and to overcome the pernicious partialities associated with kinship. By promulgating the myth that all its citizens were born of the earth into a single family, rather than allowing for the formation of rival kin-based groupings, he aimed to establish something like the sense of fraternity associated with more contemporary uses of the *brotherhood* metaphor. His aim was to widen the natural affection associated with family ties to encompass the entire community, reducing one kind of internal differentiation by magnifying distinctions between insiders and outsiders. Classical ideals of political community often derive from this text and its formulation of the ideal, or else from Aristotle's insistence in the *Politics* that a political community be no larger than a person can walk in a day, in order to preserve the face-to-face interactions that he saw as essential to its maintenance. Community here entails familiarity and similarity, seeks to create and maintain common purpose and shared values, and appeals to feelings more than to reason or advantage.

## Community in modern political thought

Modern political thought is typically defined, in part, by its rejection of this ancient ideal, with moderns like Hobbes describing the kind of society without a sovereign as undermining everyone's personal security by allowing unmitigated conflict. Embracing an early modern form of individualism, Hobbes did not seek to unite persons into a civil order on the basis of fellow-feeling or common purpose, but sought a political authority that could keep them all in awe and maintain order. That different persons have different values and want different things in life was for Hobbes a natural fact, and, when combined with natural selfishness, a key contributor to natural conflict, so getting people out of this natural state and into an artificial one, based on contract and fear and not the bonds of community, was his primary imperative. But the artificial community of Hobbesian society is merely transactional, created for the instrumental purpose of providing security and order, with members bound together by contract, rather than affective ties or common identity.

For Locke, too, the modern individualistic ontology of his classic liberalism displaced the ancient communitarianism of Plato and Aristotle, with individuals relating to others only for purposes of mutual advantage in society. By the time that Locke wrote the *Second Treatise*, community had receded significantly as an ideal, displaced by a focus on and concern for the individual, whose rights against others in the community had priority over any natural duties that anyone might have to other members of it. Given the turmoil of the English Civil War and the religious animosities that drove it, Locke's work reflects a well-founded skepticism about developing a singular vision of the common good in a social community that had been deeply divided along religious and political lines for half a century. As he implies in his "A Letter Concerning Toleration," religious communities may be unified around a shared view of the common good but political communities (at least those comprised of multiple and competing religious sects) cannot. His use of the term "commonwealth" (or common *weal*, or good) was not based on this ancient community ideal of a society organized around common values or conceptions of the good, but rather followed its usage under the Cromwellian regime to refer to the state itself.

As noted above, enthusiasm for community ebbs and flows throughout the history of Western political thought. That ancient notion of the ideal as a source of common bonds or identity would return in various guises, whether through the socially constructed commonality of Rousseau's general will, or through the nation-building projects of the nineteenth and twentieth centuries that Anderson describes as the construction of a "deep, horizontal comradeship," through which "in the minds of each lives the image of their communion."[4] Sometimes it appears in a transformed condition, as in contemporary identity politics, where community encompasses social subgroups rather than society as a whole – or in postcolonial theory, where an imposed and damaging social identity is cast off so that an older community can be recovered. When joined with national claims to territorial resources, as discussed in chapter 9, it appears as selfish and insular. In its manifestation in the global human community claimed through the UDHR, it takes on a diametrically opposed aspect. Over time, this conception of a single human community has generated some of humanity's noblest aspirations, but it now stands also accused of contributing to an ecologically insensitive form of human exceptionalism and a narrow-minded and ultimately destructive anthropocentrism. It is to these transformations, or at least their assessment by environmental theorists, that we must now turn.

## On anthropocentrism

*Anthropocentrism* (or human-centeredness) takes on several forms, all of which involve dimensions of the community ideal, including its dual aspect. As before, its positive dimension warrants first mention, as the focus upon common humanity has historically opposed various kinds of arbitrary status inequality and mistreatment. Humanitarian duties, human rights, and human development all derive from this notion of belonging to a single human community, without distinction based on race, gender, ethnicity, national identity, or any of the other sources of division that have contributed to conflict and injustice in recent centuries, and continue to do so today. However, its negative aspect looms large in environmental theory, as its distinction between the species *Homo sapiens* and all other species on the planet, complete with a status hierarchy that has been used to justify brutal exploitation – and even extermination, at times – has attracted the force of a powerful environmental critique. This critique, along with the desire to overcome at least the insidious force of anthropocentrism, has in several key ways helped to identify and orient environmentalism as a social movement, and environmental political theory as a scholarly research area, serving as the focus of one of the field's first important texts in Robyn Eckersley's *Environmentalism and Political Theory*.[5]

Ontologically, anthropocentrism orients humans to each other by virtue of a putative commonality and corresponding difference from nonhumans, encouraging us to view ourselves and our identities as constituted in part by this group membership. Humanity is something that we share and that defines us, potentially encouraging us to think about our common interests and common fate, from which a planetary species-wide solidarity might emerge. Consequently, it downplays or diminishes distinctions frequently made among humans that detract from forging a common identity based on species membership. Since those distinctions are often emphasized by those stoking conflict or advocating war, this ontological anthropocentrism can oppose or dispel forms of ethnocentrism averse to humanitarian and ecological objectives. Of course, ethnocentric and anthropocentric attitudes and beliefs can and do coexist in the same persons, but insofar as anthropocentrism reinforces that boundary by emphasizing commonality within the species, it aims to diminish the perceived differences among those within those boundaries.

Ethically, it prioritizes the interests of humans over those of nonhumans. In some forms, this priority merely attaches greater weight to human interests than to otherwise comparable nonhuman interests, while in others it allows for absolute priority of all human interests over even the most basic of nonhuman interests, but without denying that nonhumans have morally relevant interests at all. For example, one might believe that animals in agriculture can permissibly be eaten even though adequate nutrition can be had from plant-based diets – claiming that the human interest in satisfying particular dietary preferences outweighs the most basic interests of animals raised for food – but still think it wrong to be gratuitously cruel to such animals in the process of converting them into food and fiber. In its strongest and most objectionable form, which has been prevalent throughout most of modern history in the West, ethical anthropocentrism denies that nonhumans have any morally relevant interests or can be recipients of any moral obligations, treating them instead as mere objects to exploit.

## Anthropocentrism and the environmental crisis

It is for such reasons that some critics of either ontological or ethical anthropocentrism accuse it of complicity in the environmental crisis,[6] or call for the development of new and non-anthropocentric ontologies or normative theories, rather than relying upon existing ethical and political theories designed to govern human relationships or oriented around human interests only. Like patriarchy, ethnocentrism is accused of justifying dominion by a dominant group over a subordinate one and encouraging the latter's exploitation by the former. Insofar as ethical anthropocentrism denies that we have any direct duties to nonhumans, leaving only indirect duties that reduce to concerns about the impact of our actions on other humans, it undermines the normative basis for much environmental protection, as well as our ability to conceive of nonhumans as having a good of their own, independent of our experiences or welfare.

At its worst, anthropocentrism parallels forms of belligerent nationalism in encouraging us to regard those outside of our species community as a threat, and to imagine that we are at war with them. Farmers who view insects as hostile opponents to be exterminated, or ranchers who view livestock predators such as wolves in the same way, exhibit this kind of anthropocentrism. In condemnation of it, Rachel Carson describes this hostile attitude in *Silent Spring*, where "man proceeds toward his announced goal of the conquest of nature," which involves "slaughter of the buffalo," a "massacre of the shorebirds" and a "crusade against insects."[7] This imagined war, as Carson suggests, often manifests as very real mass killing of our imagined enemies. Describing humans as being at "unintentional war with Gaia," James Lovelock uses a similar metaphor. He urges humans to "make a just peace with Gaia while we are strong enough to negotiate and not a defeated, broken rabble on the way to extinction."[8] Whether Lovelock's just peace involves the end of anthropocentrism, or merely a cessation of hostilities between opponents for the purpose of prolonging human survival, is a question that may determine the efficacy of his war metaphor.

Not all environmental theorists regard anthropocentrism as inherently antithetical to a strong normative basis for environmental protection, however. Bryan Norton, for example, distinguishes between a consequentialist ethic that seeks the satisfaction of felt preferences only (which he calls *strong anthropocentrism* and identifies with the critiques of anthropocentric ethics noted above) and a *weak anthropocentrism* that seeks instead to advance only considered human preferences.[9] Like the distinction between higher and lower pleasures that John Stuart Mill introduces in order to defend utilitarianism against charges of countenancing a shallow hedonism, Norton argues for a weakly anthropocentric environmental ethic that he believes can justify humans living in harmony with nature, based on values of experience with natural objects or undisturbed places, thus overcoming the tendency toward domination and exploitation of nature noted above. According to Norton, the problem is not merely that human preferences are prioritized over those of nonhumans, but that extractive and exploitative human preferences are allowed to take precedence over those associated with good environmental stewardship.

Understanding ethical anthropocentrism in terms of its prioritization of human values over those of nonhumans, Norton's distinction suggests that another cleavage may be relevant to the assessment of normative environmental concepts. Rather than viewing all anthropocentric values as inherently averse to environmental protection, we may distinguish between those that seek to justify protection of the nonhuman community against human impacts on it from those that justify those impacts. The ideal of justice (as will be discussed further in chapter 10) is in its conventional conception an anthropocentric value, in that justice obligations are owed only to other humans, but it has likewise been developed on behalf of justifying strong environmental protection. In doing so, it defines the justice community as involving only humans (including future generations of them), treating environmental degradation such as climate change as a kind of injustice to other members, but it need not devalue non-members in the process.

## From biotic to planetary community

Insofar as anthropocentrism is complicit in the environmental crisis, perhaps some alternative conception of community can help to transition to more sustainable relationships between humans and nonhuman nature. What would a non-anthropocentric conception of community look like, and would it be more disposed toward advancing sustainability imperatives? Aldo Leopold develops such a conception in his land ethic, or moral imperative for humans in their relationship with the biotic community (which includes animals and plants as well as waters and soils).[10] Belonging to such a community entails a recognition of our mutual dependence upon it, along with an egalitarian ethic whereby we do not prioritize our own interests over those of the community – and, for Leopold, prompts our treatment of it with "love and respect." Rather than maintaining a "land-relation" that entails "privileges but not obligations," as he believed was common to human relationships to the environment, Leopold calls for the development of a sense of community with the land, from which such obligations might arise. Developing such a sense, he writes, is an "evolutionary possibility and an ecological necessity."

Inculcating an ethical sense of our connections with this wider community involves what Leopold calls an "ecological conscience" and grounds in a non-anthropocentric ontology that he locates in the science of ecology and the recognition it suggests for our inter-dependence with the land. The failure to develop such a conscience, which he claimed can disabuse us of our anthropocentric tendencies, owes for many to social and economic relationships of production, and the geographic and cognitive distance from the land that many such relationships can impose on our thinking:

> Your true modern is separated from the land by many middlemen, and by innumerable physical gadgets. He has no vital relation to it; to him it is the space between cities on which crops grow. Turn him loose for a day on the land, and if the spot does not happen to be a golf links or a "scenic" area, he is bored stiff. If crops could be raised by hydroponics instead of farming, it would suit him very well. Synthetic substitutes for wood, leather, wool, and other natural land products suit him better than the originals. In short, land is something he has "outgrown."[11]

The separation that Leopold laments – physical, economic, epistemic, psychological – results from social and economic arrangements whereby the "true modern" person not only fails to properly appreciate the links between ecosystem health and the continued satisfaction of their material preferences and lacks any feedback mechanism for identifying changes in ecosystem health, but falsely comes to believe humanity to have "outgrown" or transcended nature itself. We falsely believe, that is, that we do not belong to this community and thus are not affected by changes to its health, which in turn undermines our stewardship of it.

The view of humans as separate from and conquerors of nature, or as seeking mastery over it, runs through much of the Western canon. From Aristotle's natural teleology – through which he posited a hierarchical natural order in which all other beings served human interests – to the desire for mastery of nature expressed by political theorists as ideologically opposed as Locke and Marx, the canon largely reads like a history of anthropocentrism itself. Treating nonhuman nature as largely inert and without value, the dominant ontology of humans in the natural world – but not of it

– not only is anthropocentric but barely even acknowledges instrumental value within nature, as with Locke's claim that nature was bereft of value until humans "improved" it with agriculture. As a community, humanity has been characterized by insularity and shortsightedness, not unlike the many bounded social communities that comprise it.

## Human exceptionalism

*Human exceptionalism* refers to the claim that humans are categorically different from the rest of nature and exempt from laws that apply elsewhere in the natural world. It is thus related to anthropocentrism, linking its ontology of humans as outside of and superior to the rest of nature with an attitude that encourages human domination, control, and transformation of nature. Whether in the form of what Peter Singer calls "speciesism," defined as the irrational prejudice against nonhumans,[12] or in what Val Plumwood calls the desire for mastery of nature,[13] which seeks to dominate and control nature as an inferior but threatening Other, exceptionalism is another target of critics that see its conception of community as both factually mistaken and ethically repugnant – but nonetheless influential in orienting humans against nature. By thinking of ourselves as exempt from laws that apply to other species, we fail to appreciate the extent to which we share a common fate with other residents on the planet, and, by viewing ourselves as authorized to dominate those other species, we are more likely to harm our shared planet.

As Lynn White has persuasively argued, the historical roots of this human exceptionalism date to early Christian rejection of Franciscan *animism* – the belief that places, objects, and creatures in nature possess a spiritual essence of their own that is worthy of reverence – at which point the ontology of humans as outside of and superior to the natural world was developed, as well as to the nineteenth-century separation of science from technology, with the latter oriented around the human transcendence of natural limits. Both reinforced human exceptionalism and promulgated a conception of community in which humans saw themselves as outside of nature but entitled to manipulate it for their own benefit. White suggests that modern Christianity (which he calls "the most anthropocentric religion the world has seen") should seek to recover a community conception that he associates with St Francis of Assisi, whom he calls "the greatest spiritual revolutionary in Western History" and "a patron saint for ecologists," and to whom he attributes "the idea of the equality of all species."[14] While numerous indigenous religions also maintain similar animistic views, and would therefore reject this pernicious form of human exceptionalism, White claims that, "since the roots of our troubles are so profoundly religious" (and specifically Christian), so also must the remedy focus on internal reform of the same religious traditions (a view that is shared by contemporary "Creation Care" and similar movements within Christianity).[15]

Environmental philosophers have engaged in critical work to recover a sense of human embeddedness within nature, with the identification of character traits such as humility as among the environmental virtues that might signal a retreat from an ontology of what Leopold cast as viewing humans as "conquerors," to viewing them as "plain citizens" of the biotic community.[16] Others have sought to recover a similar ontology from indigenous religion and environmental philosophy, casting this effort to recover a more sustainable ethic of human–nature relations from centuries of Western domination as an act of "decolonizing the Anthropocene" of effects of colonization on how we think of ourselves in the world.[17]

Scholars of political ecology have likewise sought to under-stand how colonialism and coloniality have contributed toward pernicious ontological divisions between humans and nature,[18] as have ecofeminists[19] and scholars of postcolonial theory.[20] All view a dominant conception of community as complicit in human domination of the environment, as well as of some humans by others, and seek to recover alternative conceptions from older tradi-tions or marginalized peoples.

## Cultivating planetary community

How do we overcome this human exceptionalism and the sense of planetary entitlement that it confers, and restore or inculcate the kind of ecological conscience that Leopold recommends? The spatial and consequent cognitive distancing that Leopold mentions suggests one strategy for trying to more closely connect persons with their shared environment. If the "true modern" has "outgrown" the land in thinking herself no longer dependent upon its health or connected to its systems, restoration of that cognitive connection could initiate the process of inculcating a sense of affinity, or developing an ecological conscience. This is, at least, a premise of environmental education, which seeks to develop such a conscience by exposing students to the sources of their food (for example, though field trips to farms) or the location and impacts of the wastes (with field trips to landfills) that they produce. The larger goal is to get students to view themselves as living within a food or materials *system*, rather than regarding themselves as isolated nodes whose actions have no further repercussions, with the direct experiences with other aspects of that system eliminating that distance noted by Leopold. This kind of systems view, illustrated by the metaphor of "Spaceship Earth," serves as the basis for ecological economics and its concept of the steady-state.[21]

Wendell Berry's food activism illustrates this strategy. Berry begins his essay on "The Pleasures of Eating" by recommending that his reader "eat responsibly."[22] In order to do this, he argues, they must overcome that social and cognitive distance that Leopold notes. For the typical consumer, he suggests, "food is pretty much an abstract idea – something they do not know or imagine – until it appears on the grocery shelf or the table." While the "passive" or "industrial eater" fails to acknowledge the existence of a food system, or any connection between eating and the land, the empowered or responsible eater exercises greater control over her own health as well as the welfare of the planet as a whole. Berry commends the sort of experiences that environmental educators often use, whereby consumers can learn through observation and experience about food systems, food production, and sustainable food practices. Only through these, and with the ecological conscience that they inculcate, can one experience genuine pleasure from eating, which depends on "one's accurate consciousness of the lives and world from which food comes." One thus rejoins the biotic community as a plain citizen, to paraphrase Leopold, and in so doing inculcates a sense of interdependence, coproduction, and shared fate.

Cultivating a sense of planetary community might, therefore, rely upon similar cognitive connections. While the earth system is even more abstract than the ecosystems that Leopold and Berry seek to deepen human connections to, one might seek to inculcate that sense of community by the same kind of education and experience of it. For example, the iconic "Blue Marble" photograph of the Earth taken by the *Apollo 17* crew on its way to the moon in 1972 is viewed by many as capturing the unity and fragility of the planet, providing visual stimulation for forging such connections. Education in climate science and in the human and environmental impacts of climate change can yield insights into this earth systems perspective, but direct experience of climate change is elusive, given its scope and scale. Visual representations of glacial retreat, such as those produced through the Extreme Ice Survey,[23] might serve as a proxy for such experiences by capturing dynamics that would otherwise be unavailable to human perception, showing how earth systems or the planetary community is being affected by human activities. Systems are communities of interdependent parts, with cognitive recognition of this interdependence prompted by some of these images. From this recognition might come a sense of solidarity, shared fate, and common concern, mobilizing the constructive potential of the community ideal while minimizing its more destructive tendencies (at least until it is mobilized in the service of fomenting interplanetary conflict).

## National identity and environmental protection

Nationalism has become something of a pariah in contemporary political theory despite its continued popularity within contemporary politics. While it is viewed as influential in shaping identity and can clearly be powerful in mobilizing power, many view its contributions as primarily negative: in promoting conflict and war, in justifying privilege and exclusion, or in obscuring common humanity and our shared planetary boundaries. At a time in which nationalism invokes right-wing populism and its associations with ethnic nationalism or white supremacism, resurgent authoritarianism, and reaction against multilateral cooperation, nationalism and national identity seem like poor conceptions of community to invoke for environmental purposes.

Invocations of an insular form of nationalism have a long and sordid history within the US environmental movement. As detailed in chapter 3, critics of US participation in famine relief efforts such as Garrett Hardin appealed to an insular form of nationalism in which rich countries like the US are like a "well-equipped lifeboat," relatively well supplied with resource wealth and thus able to assist famine victims and economic migrants from the poor countries, which Hardin compared to "under-equipped lifeboats" with too few resources to support their populations – able, he argues, but they should resist doing so. His xenophobic environmental nationalism would later be echoed by others – as, for example, when Edward Abbey suggested closing the US–Mexican border in order to block immigration by the "morally-culturally-genetically" inferior peoples of Latin America,[24] prompting Murray Bookchin to denounce deep ecologists like Abbey as "barely disguised racists, survivalists, macho Daniel Boones, and outright social reactionaries" guilty of "a crude eco-brutalism."[25]

The manifestation of the community ideal as a conception of anti-immigrant nationalism has embroiled environmental advocates in the past and threatens to do so again. Following the passage of California's controversial Proposition 187 in 1994, which sought to deny education and other services to illegal immigrants, the Sierra Club found itself divided over whether or not to associate itself with the sentiments behind that law. The group had declared its support in a 1989 policy statement for a US population policy, aimed at curbing domestic population growth, that focused on numbers rather than national origins, noting that "it is the fact of increasing numbers that affects population growth and ultimately, the quality of the environment."[26] In February of 1996, seeking to avoid the backlash from immigrant and minority communities, the Club's Board of Directors reversed course, adopting the following resolution: "The Sierra Club, its entities, and those speaking in its name will take no position on immigration levels or on policies governing immigration into the United States. The Club remains committed to environmental rights and protections for all within our borders, without discrimination based on immigration status."[27] Dissidents within the group objected to what amounted to a reversal of longstanding Club policy, bringing the issue to a membership vote in 1998. While 40 percent of the membership voted to restore the official policy position calling for limits on US immigration, the initiative lost. The group's official position became instead: "The Sierra Club can more effectively address the root causes of global population problems through its existing comprehensive approach."[28] These approach includes sustainable development, anti-poverty efforts, and pressing for rights for and empowerment of women, especially in developing nations. According to then-Director Carl Pope, the opposing nationalist view held that "the United States' ecosystems can be saved, even if the rest of the world's environment is being damaged by overpopulation, by reducing birthrates and immigration here."[29] Especially during a time of resurgent ethnic nationalism driven by a pernicious anti-immigrant populism, this experience provides a cautionary tale on the perils of seeking to harness nationalism in the service of stronger environmental protection.

## Nations and peoples as allies of environmental protection

National community membership may nonetheless be mobilized in protection of territorial environments, but not without some caveats and risks. Claims to territorial natural resources have been justified by the attachment that develops over time between a people and the forests, waterways, and landscapes that its territory contains. Avery Kolers, for example, claims that attachments form as "the character of the people for instance, their dwellings, cuisine, and eventually social relations and kinship patterns develop over time due to features of their environment such as climate, soil, and so on."[30] Sentimental associations between a people and some territorial resources may motivate their stewardship, insofar as threats to or degradation of those resources is seen as threatening national identity itself. Drawing on patriotism rather than nationalism, Robyn Eckersley defends as "a *nonexclusive* attachment to, and responsibility for, the national environment" on the basis of this potential.[31] Harnessing US national identity on behalf of protection of national parks, for example, might provide such a motive.

Linking patriotism or nationalism with environmental protection or stewardship assumes several important risks, however. The mere association between territory and identity involved in "blood and soil" Nazism ought to give pause to anyone seeking to link the two rhetorically. Attachment to territorial resources, like sentiments associated with national membership more generally, may develop enhanced connections with territorial resources at the cost of diminished connections with non-territorial resources, undermining a planetary stewardship ethics. At best, the attachment is to particular resources, and often for the benefit of particular people, with such claims used to exclude non-citizens from their benefits. In the context of attachment theories of territorial rights, such as Kolers develops, the entitlement claims they justify are often used against cosmopolitan common ownership claims that seek to conserve global resources for the benefit of humanity, rather than losing them to national extraction or degradation. Granting entitlements to territorial resources on this basis may also undermine prospects for egalitarian resource justice, maintaining existing and highly inequitable allocations of national resource wealth.

On the other hand, when threats to territorial environments (as opposed to their resources, which implies instrumental and possibly extractive usage) can be viewed as threats to a people or its culture, the ideal of community may be more effectively used to promote the protection of both. In the context of climate change, for example, rapidly changing landscapes are viewed as threatening the human rights to territory and to culture of the Inuit people. Melting permafrost, disappearing sea ice, and rising sea levels all threaten indigenous peoples like the Inuit or Sámi. As noted in chapter 6, the invocation of human rights to protect their territories, culture, and ways of life may offer a means (thus far unsuccessful) to protect their landscapes. Here, the value of such threatened cultures may find expression through a conception of community that views its preservation as sufficiently important to protect it through collective rights. Unlike nationalism or patriotism, which are invoked from within a community and for the purpose of motivating its members, this conception of the community ideal relies upon an appeal to outsiders, and rests upon imperatives to protect traditional and vulnerable communities.

Where communities that are vulnerable to climate change face significant or even total territorial loss, as with residents of small island states like Tuvalu or the Maldives, this threat to the ongoing identity of their people can be very serious. Many face the prospect of dislocation, with resettlement options elsewhere being tenuous and very likely quite damaging to the group. Raising the specter of a choice between what is euphemistically called a "managed retreat" as "we lose parts of the habitable earth," and a "hasty and violent" chaotic retreat, Bill McKibben notes that sea level rise and desertification from climate change mean that "the earth, for humans, has begun to shrink, under our feet and in our minds."[32] While, on the one hand, our psychological and cultural attachments to territory may motivate stronger protections against the ecological forces now threatening them, on the other, as McKibben notes, our future may require a post-territorial mindset as the habitable world shrinks and humans must accommodate displaced others into the remaining spaces, where environmental nationalism could potentially backfire.

## Nationality, territory, and environment

As Avner de-Shalit suggests, environmental displacement "involves a loss of home and therefore a loss of a sense of place," which can be especially damaging for people with lengthy attachments to places lost as the result of environmental change. Since these attachments to place help to form and maintain a people's culture and identity, the loss is not merely to property, or ability to be self-governing within a territory, but often includes loss of cultural identity, as well.[33] For this reason, de-Shalit argues that climate displacement involves a "strong and special case of environmental injustice" that cannot be rectified through adaptation measures, or compensated as loss and damage. The harm suffered by the climate migrant, for whom the protections under international law governing the treatment of refugees are not available, is both individual and collective. While lost property can be compensated, the losses to the community that result from its lost territory cannot. Concerns for the future welfare of those people most threatened by climate change have consequently become a focal point for efforts to increase the ambition of global mitigation programs, with a conception of the community ideal as concerned with territorial identity and place-based cultural attachment motivating those concerns.

So close is this link between nationality and territory that the *nation* (or people, a distinct political community with some claim to self-determination) is often conflated with the *state* (or political apparatus of government for a political community). Nation-states are those nations that have their own state, or ability to satisfy that claim to self-determination. This typically requires that they have their own territory, since, as we will see in chapter 9, political sovereignty is among the set of territorial rights, and sovereignty is necessary for self-determination. Numerous examples of national minorities residing within the territories of other states, such as indigenous peoples residing within settler colonial states like the US or Australia, suggest the difficulties inherent in maintaining those political communities over time. Language laws, economic marginalization, and other assimilationist pressures imperil their continued existence as distinct communities, even where they have some territorial claims, as with the reservation system in the United States.

Sometimes, national communities claim the prerogative to degrade their territorial environments under the guise of territorial rights and self-determination, as with Brazil's refusal in August 2019 of $50 million in international aid committed to fighting Amazonian fires. Here, we might recall our analysis of democracy in chapter 4, where we observed that procedurally democratic decisions could undermine democratic substantive commitments. In such cases, we saw democracy as in need of some limits or constraints as required to maintain that democracy over time. With democratic decisions that intensify natural resource scarcity beyond that which is compatible with the continued maintenance of democratic culture and institutions, we must limit democracy where needed to maintain its necessary material and environmental conditions. A similar constraint might apply to the ideal of community, where we defer to a people the prerogative to collectively decide how to live within its territory, with the constraint that community-enhancing sovereignty or self-determination cannot be used to destroy its community-supporting territorial environment. In balancing these competing ideals and their associated claims, we must ensure that excessive adherence to one doesn't undermine the other.

What conception of community might allow for a better balance between stewardship of the global environment and respect for the autonomy of distinct national communities? To the extent that nation-centered conceptions of community strengthen some associations at the cost of others, we may applaud appeals to nationalism when these lead to better protection of territorial environments, but worry about them when they undermine a global stewardship ethic or lead to the export of environmental impacts from human activities, rather than their reduction. The ideal of community to which states or other actors appeal can be evaluated in terms of the ends for which it is being enlisted. To the extent that it is wielded for inclusive and humanitarian purposes, as nationalism can be, the conception might be a good one. To the extent that it is mobilized on behalf of xenophobic and exclusionary political programs, as with contemporary right-wing populism, we might find the ideal to be repugnant. We might be tempted to conclude that, since nationalism is most often invoked on behalf of insidious political projects such as war and the reinforcement of internal ethnic hierarchies, any conception of community that is built around the nation-state is more likely to cause harm than good, and simply avoid all such conceptions. But, given the scale of the challenge, we must enlist all potential sources of motivation to undertake significant change in the interest of sustainable transition, leaving some conception of community that includes recognition of nationality as significant to the ideal.

## Cosmopolitanism and the global community

The term "cosmopolitan" originates in ancient Greece with an alleged response by Diogenes of Sinope to the question of his home, with social identities during that period being closely identified with city-states of origin. He allegedly replied: "I am a citizen of the world (*kosmopolitês*)," simultaneously claiming to be a citizen of everywhere and nowhere. Several interpretations of this remark are available, some of which were developed by Stoics sympathetic to Diogenes, with others viewing it in a more contemporary context. All are instructive in understanding what cosmopolitan has meant in the past and what it connotes today, and together these suggest a role for a cosmopolitan conception of community in theorizing human relationships to the environment and each other.

One interpretation of Diogenes' remark is that humans can simultaneously dwell in their city of origin, where locality and cultural difference matter, and in a transcendent or universal world of abstract ideas, where they do not, and that Diogenes was merely asserting this latter kind of philosophical disposition. Like Plato's stargazing ship's captain in the *Republic*, he may have been claiming to be in the world but not of it. Another interpretation, also from Stoic conceptions of cosmopolitanism, involves simultaneous membership in communities that extend outward in concentric circles, marked by different connections and with diminishing levels of affinity as these extend outward from the self, expanding through communities of kin groups, neighbors, compatriots, and finally all of humanity. Thicker obligations to others may arise from membership in closer communities, but Diogenes could have been asserting his recognition of or membership in this final community that binds all persons by common humanity. Neither would be inconsistent with recognizing special obligations to co-nationals. Finally, to interpret his remarks as calling for ethical cosmopolitanism, Diogenes could have been linking obligations to community membership but denying his membership in any community smaller than that of all of humanity, treating national borders and membership as irrelevant to ethical considerations.

Regardless of the intentions of Diogenes or whether he actually uttered that remark, these possibilities suggest the role that community membership plays in ethics, and several competing views about which communities exist and are most important. Many take offense at Peter Singer's claim that it would be wrong to spend money on birthday presents for our own child if more good could be done (as it nearly always can) if spent on a distant stranger,[34] implying a belief in the legitimacy of partiality toward family members. Others bristle at the suggestion that their charitable donations be used to combat poverty among distant strangers rather than the poor within their own communities or countries, indicating two other circles of partiality. One could formulate these objections in terms of an account of concentric circles of community: without denying that we have any obligations to distinct strangers, we have more and thicker ones toward those closer to us (literally and/or metaphorically), and fewer and thinner ones to those further away. Here, our ethical obligations are a function of our community memberships, recognizing humanity as one of the multiple communities to which we belong (perhaps including planetary membership beyond this). Having stronger ethical ties to those closer to us need not necessarily preclude having some significant ethical ties to distant strangers, so belonging to a more local and parochial community need not preclude our having some kind of cosmopolitan identities.

Contemporary ethical cosmopolitans reject this concentric circles conception, taking the third interpretation of Diogenes remark as their guiding claim and rejecting all forms of partiality based in shared community membership. While political philosophers disagree about whether justice extends beyond national borders – a point to which we will return in chapter 10 – the premise of moral equality is axiomatic among moral philosophers, with persons on both sides of any national border having the same status in terms of our ethical obligations toward each. While shared social membership may often make it easier for us to notice and respond to the suffering of those close to us, they argue, this cannot justify our prioritizing otherwise comparable suffering on grounds of our shared community membership. Membership in any particular political community may be constitutive of our identities and provide a cultural context through which our lives have meaning, but it would be morally arbitrary to differentiate between persons on the basis of their national identities when it comes to basic ethical obligations to avoid harming, as well as to assist in avoiding suffering. The wrongness of avoidably harming someone is not diminished by any geographical or social distance, even if our awareness of who and when we harm is often diminished by this same distance. Because national community membership can be perilous in prioritizing some persons over others on the basis of such distance, most moral philosophers are ethical cosmopolitans, recognizing that any such distinction would be morally arbitrary. Most non-philosophers, however, are not ethical cosmopolitans, identifying with smaller and local communities and believing distant strangers to have a different status than those residing nearby, even if they also accept some obligations as arising from their membership in a global – or even a planetary – community.

## Ethical obligations and distant strangers

Especially insofar as we regard ethics as primarily involving negative duties not to harm others, rather than the sort of positive duties of assistance that Singer defends, denying the relevance of shared national membership should be relatively uncontroversial. We might think the prohibition against harming distant strangers to be mostly superfluous, assuming that we rarely or never have the opportunity to do so, but this is different than denying its wrongness. As noted in chapter 7, this cognitive disconnect of our actions from their global impacts is partly the result of the fragmented agency and diffuse causality in global environmental problems such as climate change, whereby we often fail to see our actions as contributing toward harm because they only do so as small parts of large sets of like actions, where our unique contribution may be little more than notional. We assume, falsely, that the mere fact that problems like climate change would happen without us can excuse our role in it, since that role is relatively small. That is, we either deny that distant strangers are harmed by other humans through climate change, or we deny that we are among those others contributing to this harm, but most would not claim that it is okay to intentionally harm an innocent victim merely because they belong to a different political community.

While this assumption that we cannot harm distant others may once have been safe, it no longer is, now that we live in an increasingly ecologically interdependent world in which humans are changing the global climate, violating negative duties not to harm. Setting aside various challenges to our assumptions about individual moral responsibility for climate change (discussed in chapter 7), it can be challenging to come to terms with our potential to harm distant strangers in our increasingly interconnected world. Many persons would react with shock and revulsion if confronted with the working conditions of some laboring in supply chains for consumer products they purchase, or at living conditions for those faced with hazards resulting from US trade, military, or other foreign policies, but nevertheless remain blissfully ignorant of some of the impacts of their consumption and the collateral damage of their voting preferences. Faced with the cognitive dissonance between the moral decency that they value and try to maintain and such impacts of their own actions upon distant strangers, many likely embrace denial about either the impacts themselves or, at least, their personal complicity in them. Geographic and social distance between actions and impacts makes this easier, with harm that is out of sight easier to keep out of mind. Against this tendency of cognitive distancing to reinforce isolationist beliefs that we cannot be harming distant strangers, however, are the increasingly interlinked global environment and global economy, both of which make it increasingly possible for us to harm distant strangers.[35]

Even if most persons concur with virtually all moral philosophers that national borders are irrelevant to negative duties not to harm, positive duties to assist those in need are more controversial. Several considerations may account for this apparent equivocation on the question of whether all persons *qua* human warrant membership in a single moral community, or whether members of a political community can permissibly be treated differently than non-members. With regard to assisting those in need, we may view this as an act of charity that warrants praise when we perform it, but not as an ethical requirement that involves wrong or blame when we do not. They are, according to this view, morally optional, and if we cannot be faulted for failing to perform acts of charity at all, it would seem to follow that we cannot be blamed for acting charitably toward some but not others. In ethical theory, this involves the contrast between *duties of justice* (for which we can be faulted if we fail to perform them) and *duties of charity or beneficence* (for which we can only be praised if we perform them, but not blamed if we do not). From the perspective of those in need of assistance, duties of justice confer a kind of right or entitlement that duties of charity do not, legitimizing the view that those denied assistance required by the former have been wronged in a way that those denied the latter have not. Feeding the hungry offers an example of a positive duty that some cast as a duty of justice (as, for example, in the identification of a human right to subsistence), while others view it only as a duty of charity.

As the demandingness complaint against Singer's famine principle suggests, many find duties of assistance to distant strangers to be understood better in terms of charity than justice. This comports with the judgment that, while it might be morally commendable for someone to give most of their income toward global poverty relief, rather than spending that money on themselves or their loved ones, it would be inappropriate to criticize them for failing to do so. Others may distinguish between doing and allowing, viewing harm resulting from their actions as culpable but regarding harm that results from their omissions or failure to come to another's aid differently.[36] Finally, popular attitudes about differences between negative duties to refrain from harm and positive duties to assist may be complicated by the relative complexity and challenges associated with each. Complying with a negative duty to cease causing harm requires only that we stop the harmful action once we recognize our contributory role in harming. By contrast, assisting those in need requires that we initiate a new action – often incurring an additional expense or bearing a new cost – and that we ensure that it actually helps the person in need. Would-be Samaritans may shy away from assisting distant strangers because of the difficulty in ensuring that their contribution actually makes a difference, or even out of fear that their intervention may cause harm in other ways. (Contrary to popular belief, Good Samaritan laws do not require bystanders to come to the assistance of victims but seek to address this latter worry by insulating them from potential lawsuits if they provide reasonable assistance to those in peril.)

Notice that none of these considerations impugn ethical cosmopolitanism, which maintains only that national borders are irrelevant to ethical duties between individual persons. If causing harm is wrong but failing to rescue an imperiled victim is not, the intervention of a border between those two persons makes no difference. Likewise with prioritizing a loved one over a distant stranger in how we spend our time and money – if we think this to be morally permissible (and many do, against Singer), our judgment probably does not depend upon whether that distant stranger belongs to the same political community. Even the right-wing populists and ethnic nationalists who currently malign immigrants and others for political gain do not draw the border of the moral community at the boundary of the political community, often applying their ethnocentric rhetoric against some legal members of the political community that they consider to be outsiders, and declining to use it against some legal outsiders who share the ascriptive characteristics with insiders. If Diogenes was making a point about what he owes other persons as a matter of individual ethics, his claim to share a single moral community with all humans would probably resonate with much of the lay public, if in a somewhat smaller proportion than among professional moral philosophers.

Cosmopolitan justice, however, is another matter. Since distributive justice is concerned with the manner in which social institutions distribute goods within society, with egalitarian versions typically recommending significant redistribution of goods to the least advantaged, the stakes are higher in maintaining that social membership ought to be irrelevant, as extending most principles of distributive justice globally would require massive transfers of wealth from rich states to poor ones (with the large tax increases and steep declines in government services that are perhaps the most reliable impetus to an involuntary career change for elected politicians in any affluent democracy). But its actual or expected popularity is not a reason to reject it. As noted in chapter 10, many of those political theorists and philosophers who maintain egalitarian justice commitments at the level of the nation-state reject its application beyond those borders. They don't do so because of its general unpopularity or demandingness, of course. Rather, their claims focus on the nature of justice (as distinct from ethics), of community, and the relationship between the two, and so are of interest to us here. Our question concerns only what follows from a conception of community that includes (at least) all of humanity, and whether identifying as a member of such a community (even if persons also viewed themselves as members of national and subnational communities) could facilitate our sustainable transition.

## Theorizing cosmopolitan and planetary membership

What would it mean to claim membership in humanity as a whole, or to belong to a global community? National membership confers a set of powers and privileges as well as obligations. Formally, citizens typically have political rights, such as the right to vote, stand for office, or be represented in government. In exchange for these, they accept political obligations, such as jury duty, the potential for military conscription, as well as social obligations, among which are some stewardship duties for their shared local environments. Belonging to a community means taking responsibility for one's fair share in maintaining the community's public goods, including its environment. Some privileges apply to those without full membership status, including resident aliens – such as rights to work and to receive social benefits like access to public education, – while others are denied to those without membership status, such as tourists being denied free access to health care where it is freely available to full members. Obligations to obey the law apply to all residing within national territories on an undifferentiated basis, with the law protecting all on the same basis. But national membership is defined by whom it excludes and what they are denied, as much as who is included and what they receive.

In this sense, cosmopolitan membership appears to be markedly different from membership in bounded human communities, since everyone is a full member, so its privileges must be defined not in terms of who is excluded from them, but rather in terms of the common goods that are protected or created, and its obligations are defined in terms of what is necessary to create or maintain those goods. A habitable global environment is surely among these privileges, as many threats to it imperil all, regardless of national membership, and refraining from actions that degrade that environment must also be its corresponding obligation. While the absence of a government with executive power at the global level may mean that such obligations cannot be legally enforced, as smaller communities (such as nation-states) enforce some of their obligations of citizenship, it is nonetheless useful to consider how civic duty may appear in the context of our membership in communities without coercive power of their own. Within political theory, citizenship is not only a legal category that is reflected in one's passport, but also involves a range of activities and relationships that exist within communities, along with a set of civic virtues that are viewed as necessary for the community to flourish.

Since an important aspect of the community ideal is this notion of civic virtue (reflected in the idea of being a "good citizen"), identifying and seeking to inculcate character traits associated with the community's preservation and the advancements of its interests, cosmopolitan or planetary membership may involve an applicable set of civic virtues for its expansive polity. Ecological virtues offer one example of what it might mean to claim cosmopolitan or planetary membership. Such virtues are a subset of more general civic virtues in a sense, but depend upon the identification of the environment as at least a vital resource for the community, if not a constitutive element of it. They are oriented toward the welfare of the entire community, not distinct national communities or other subsets, and so might serve as counterweights to nationalism-based claims to degrade the global environment or destroy the environments of other peoples. As virtues, they link character traits with what tends toward the flourishing of the community as a whole, which in the case of a planetary conception would include the more-than-human world, in addition to the whole of humanity.

## Environmental citizenship and its associated virtues

*Environmental citizenship* names a kind of affiliation and set of affective ties to a larger community, and one associated with the inculcation, and dependent upon the exercise, of these virtues. Environmental virtues differ from civic ones and environmental citizenship differs from national citizenship, however, in that their orientations are toward protecting the integrity of the environment in which the polis is nested, not advancing any particular regime type, ideology, or creed, or favoring any specific political community. Membership is defined through ecological rather than social or political boundaries, with the relevant virtues oriented toward the advancement of the interests of this wider community. Within political theory, it refers to a kind of ethical sensibility, as well as a set of practices that the sensibility connotes, and those necessary for inculcating the relevant virtues within a polity. Emerging from the republic tradition rather than classic liberalism, environmental citizenship stresses the obligations of membership rather than its rights, and seeks to develop character traits that serve the interests of the polity (which, in the case of a cosmopolitan or planetary polity, would highlight environmental dependencies and shared vulnerabilities as the bases for such an account).

As originally developed by Environment Canada, a popular construction of the ideal of community expressed in environmental citizenship notes that: "Each of us has an effect on the environment every day; the key is to make this impact a positive one. We must all take responsibility for our own actions, whether as individuals, or as members of a community or an organization." Andrew Dobson has developed a conception of what he terms "ecological citizenship," whose community is "created by the material relations of cause and effect" rather than defined by territorial borders or cultural distinctiveness, but it "is a space in which political obligation operates." According to Dobson, our "embodiedness" in the world "gives rise to the ecological footprint," which aims to measure the extent of our personal impacts upon that world, which he understands as "a network of effects that prompts reflection on the nature of the impacts they comprise."[37] Fleshing out the Environment Canada conception, we take on a responsibility for others and our common environment by seeking to use no more than our equitable share of planetary resources, as conceived through the ecological footprint, according to Dobson.

Terence Ball proposes a similar model of what he calls "biocratic" citizenship (related to his idea of biocracy, discussed in chapter 4), through which states inculcate ecological virtues in their members through processes akin to those Leopold describes as necessary for developing an ecological conscience:

> Biocratic citizens will have an ecocentric outlook, viewing themselves and their species as a small but important part of a much larger and more inclusive biotic community; they will be motivated by a love of and respect for the natural world and its myriad creatures; their satisfactions and pleasures will not, in the main, be materialistic; their wants will be few and satisfiable in sustainable ways; they will whenever possible act non-violently; their time horizon will extend into the further future; and their moral and political community will consist of creatures and entities which are not human, not necessarily sentient and not (yet) present.[38]

All attest to the importance of cultivation of attitudes, beliefs, habits, and inclinations among the members of the polity as essential to a just and sustainable transition, rather than focusing only upon the development of effective governance institutions. To the extent that the community with which this kind of citizenship is associated transcends national boundaries and so requires a more expansive conception of global community membership, we must next consider the rise of ethical cosmopolitanism as an important instantiation of this conception.

## Global community and common heritage

An important manifestation of this ideal of cosmopolitan community can be seen in the notion of a *common heritage of mankind*. Drawing upon a cosmopolitan community ideal of a single human community, the reference to shared species experience and value seeks to leverage the partiality of nationalism without its limits, much as Plato sought in the *Republic* to extend the affinities associated with biological families by promulgating the myth that all citizens shared a common biological heritage. Belonging to a shared community means sharing some cultural heritage with fellow members, and the common heritage idea allows for the conception of global community to be used on behalf of protections for sites and artifacts that are declared to be of significant value for humanity as a whole, Since some of these are natural sites, the notion may also be compatible with a conception of planetary community, whereby humans share some of our common heritage with our fellow inhabitants of the planet.

Developed in the wake of World War II and its destruction of many cultural sites and artifacts, the idea was expressed through the 1954 Hague Convention for the Protection of Cultural Property in the Event of Armed Conflict, which declared that "damage to cultural property belonging to any people whatsoever means damage to the cultural heritage of all mankind, since each people makes its contribution to the culture of the world." This "Common Heritage of Mankind" idea was applied to the seabed and ocean floor under Article 136 of the UN Law of the Sea Treaty in 1982, extending its construction to include ecological resources as well as human cultural artifacts. By conceiving of space, the oceans, and Antarctica as a kind of global public good belonging to humanity as a whole, rather than having control over these contested by separate human communities, the common heritage idea replaces one potentially dangerous conception of community with another that is regarded as benign or even beneficial.

Applied to shared features of the global environment, it expresses the loss that all would suffer if these goods were degraded, as well as the loss that many would suffer if they were to be claimed for exclusive enjoyment by any state or group of states. Its meaning is somewhat different as applied through the Hague Convention to the intentional destruction of cultural property, as the loss is surely felt more deeply by the members of those cultures whose sites are targeted (as is the intention of those seeking to erase their adversaries' cultures) than it is by cultural outsiders. So, while particular sites and artifacts may belong to particular cultures, rather than humanity as a whole, in the sense of being more valuable to them, and perhaps validating claims to their possession (e.g. with plundered artifacts such as the Elgin Marbles), culture in general is part of the common heritage of mankind (a sentiment also reflected in Article 27 of the UDHR, which grants all "the right freely to participate in the cultural life of the community"). Threats to any particular culture could thus be viewed as threats to culture everywhere, as Martin Luther King Jr. wrote about injustice anywhere.[39]

The idea can also be seen in the United Nations Educational, Scientific, and Cultural Organization (UNESCO), which has since 1972 been charged with protecting the "natural heritage" of humankind along with its cultural heritage, which it does in part through its protection of World Heritage sites. Among the 1,007 designated sites are 197 natural sites, 19 of which are considered to be endangered. By appealing to a common human community, the idea of common heritage mobilizes this affinity on behalf of some environmental protection already in its limited applications within international law, but could more broadly serve as an antidote to the partiality associated with appeals to nationalism while drawing upon similar sentiments. Since it trades upon a conception of cosmopolitan or environmental citizenship, generating stewardship obligations from a sense of belonging to a community that includes all of humankind, it requires that persons be able to identify with and act on behalf of such a community, even while also belonging to and identifying with communities at other scales.

## Conclusions: environment and the community ideal

As we've seen, appeals to the ideal of community invite skepticism as feasible bases for environmental values when these communities are defined in terms of the nation-state, especially when these also contain elements of the sort of ethno-nationalism that is currently popular among right-wing populists. But, as we've also seen, other conceptions of community may be more tenable bases for environmental values. These include cosmopolitan conceptions that seek to transcend the nation-state and, in so doing, create a more inclusive and egalitarian social order, along with planetary conceptions of community that seek to overcome anthropocentrism and foster deeper affective ties between persons and the planet, or to inculcate environmental virtues as equivalents to the civic virtues for members of the polity.

At its core, the ideal of community involves the effort of constructing bonds between members in order to temper selfishness and foster cooperation, which is an objective that is well suited for many environmental problems. So long as it can avoid defining its commonality and fostering its common purpose against an excluded Other, as frequently occurs with invocation of this ideal, community can potentially serve as a motivating ideal as well as an aspiration that is capable of critiquing many of the forms of partiality that currently reinforce objectionable forms of hierarchy and domination.

# 9 Sovereignty

Ever since the 1648 Peace of Westphalia ending the Thirty Years' War established the legal basis for the modern nation-state, the legal norm of state sovereignty has assisted, but also frustrated, efforts at multilateral cooperation in pursuit of common objectives that transcend national borders Insofar as it provided a basis for international peace and the internal stability necessary for promoting the political and economic development of sovereign states, recognition of sovereignty was instrumental to securing the material bases for domestic prosperity and the development of peacetime institutions. By offering some measure of protection from external threats, sovereignty allowed states to engage their neighbors in mutually beneficial exchanges, such as those arising from cooperation, without threats to territory or political independence. Through the vessel of the nation-state, which would later serve interests of self-determination as early modern conceptions of sovereign authority gave way to democratic aspirations, sovereignty helped to usher in a democratic age. Later, it would serve emancipatory interests against imperial and colonial rule, asserting prerogatives of popular and independent rule against powers that opposed both. Historically, sovereignty has served as a progressive force in modern politics, and, as an ideal, has been as capable of challenging oppressive power relations as defending them.

Now, and for reasons to be explored in this chapter, the principle of sovereignty and system of sovereign states often finds itself aligned against progressive change and emancipatory politics, including protection against global environmental threats such as biodiversity loss and climate change. As a result, some critics have come to view sovereignty as an outmoded and ultimately regressive concept, pointing to its use by those with interests in maintaining an oppressive or unsustainable status quo against pressures and conditions that would call for its curtailment or substantial revision. Here, we shall examine these pressures and conditions to consider their relationship to the principle that they seek to challenge or modify, as well as whether sovereignty is inherently opposed to progressive change or whether an evolved construction of the principle might be able to accommodate such demands. As a principle that has evolved considerably over time, which we shall briefly examine, the question ought not to be whether its dominant existing conception is up to the task of regulation in an environmentally interdependent world, but whether a recognizably developed alternative can be adapted to the task.

Our questions, therefore, are several. To what extent does state sovereignty in the current international system help to advance sustainability imperatives such as biodiversity protection or the mitigation of climate change, and to what extent does it stand as an obstacle to such efforts? Where sovereignty in its conventional form stands as an obstacle to such imperatives, can we identify a reformed or evolved conception of the principle that would better suit such objectives, or do all conceptions of sovereignty obstruct such efforts? How do associated concepts and ideals like territoriality and self-determination fare under green alternatives to conventional sovereignty, or in a post-sovereign world? To these questions we shall soon turn, but first we must briefly examine the concept's meaning and history.

## Sovereignty as principle and in practice

As an international legal norm, sovereignty claims, for a people or nation, the collective *prima facie* right against coercive interference in its domestic affairs by foreign agents. The right can be overridden – for example, when a state commits large-scale abuses of its resident peoples, which is held under the "responsibility to protect" doctrine to justify **humanitarian intervention** to protect those vulnerable to such abuses.[1] Other occasions that might allow sovereignty norms to be overridden are discussed below. Sovereignty protects only against significantly coercive interference, including acts or threats of military force or interference in processes of selecting government officials. Whether it is threatened by less coercive means such as economic sanctions or trade embargos is a matter of some contention, but sovereignty is typically thought not to prohibit **soft power** interventions designed to persuade or shape preferences without coercion.[2] This distinction between coercive and non-coercive (or between hard and soft) power is likewise contested and will be further discussed below. Similarly, the range of activities that is protected as among the domestic affairs of a people offers another area of contestation, with implications for how a state may manage its territorial resources as well as its treatment of resident aliens. Sovereign states may have the prerogative to degrade their own environments, so long as they don't affect those of neighboring states or injure or violate the rights of their residents, but, as we shall see, even such imprudent decisions may be incompatible with some conceptions of sovereignty.

In practice, sovereignty is most frequently invoked to protect states, but, for reasons to be explored further below, is better construed as a collective right of *peoples*, or the principals for which states are agents, and is related to their right of self-determination. Where states reflect the will of their people, and the nation is coterminous with the state (in *nation-states*), sovereignty is exercised simultaneously through both states and peoples, and no conflict exists between sovereignty and self-determination. Insofar as states do not always represent the collective will of their people but can nonetheless be sovereign, the two principles are separable. Autocratic states can be sovereign while denying self-determination. Where multiple nations or peoples coexist within the territory of a single state, the ability of minority people may be threatened by the sovereignty and territorial integrity of the state, since sovereignty would imply the people's right to choose their own state with a distinct territory. This would require the minority people to secede from the state to which they currently belong, and there is no international legal process for secession. According to Allen Buchanan, sovereignty and territorial integrity ordinarily take precedence over self-determination where they conflict, but a remedial right to secede would be available for a people that had suffered serious injustices or human rights abuses, as a last resort.[3]

## Elements of sovereignty

Sovereignty is typically thought to contain three elements: **jurisdiction** within a territory, control over membership in the polity, and control over territorial resources. Jurisdiction applies to members as well as non-members within territorial borders, as both are subject to laws and other administrative functions. While the several exceptions are not thought to diminish the sovereignty of a state or its people – diplomatic immunity from most ordinary criminal charges, for example – threats to jurisdiction would include outside interference in national elections or undue influence upon government officials from foreign sources of power or authority. External sources of power or authority do not threaten sovereignty when they have been internally authorized, as with ratified treaties and sources of international law such as conventions and other legal agreements. Because states rather than governments authorize such external constraints upon domestic jurisdiction, later governments are no less sovereign for being bound by them, even if some (e.g. the Trump administration with the Paris Agreement) seek to justify their disregard for such authorized legal constraints by reference to their impacts upon sovereignty.

Control over membership is limited to authority over immigration, through which new members may be admitted to the political community and others may be granted permission to visit, reside or work within the territory, or be eligible for some state services. Seldom does this apply to new members born to existing ones, as birthright citizenship is a common (if currently contested) constraint on this dimension of sovereignty, and the border control that states exercise is asymmetrical, applying to entry but not to exit (rights to emigrate, except for those whose freedom of movement is restricted as part of criminal punishment, are absolute). As Sarah Song has argued, state sovereignty cannot be used to deny entry to some **necessitous migrants**, and the principle of *non-refoulement* prevents states from returning refugees to their countries of origin when this would threaten their lives or seriously jeopardize their wellbeing.[4] State sovereignty is, like individual autonomy or rights to property, a broad but not unlimited prerogative or power.

Control over territorial resources includes the right to develop and to profit from natural resources that reside within territorial borders (which, somewhat tendentiously, include oceanic or seabed resources that lie outside of formal territorial borders). This dimension of sovereignty was originally recognized in order to protect against the economic exploitation of resources by colonial powers, claiming these to belong to resident peoples and to serve development interests. As will be discussed below, however, when granted to undemocratic states rather than peoples, this aspect of sovereignty has been condemned (as the "resource privilege"[5]) as complicit in the so-called "resource curse," and has in other contexts been invoked against multilateral efforts at environmental protection. Given the relationships between justice, democracy, and sustainability discussed elsewhere in this book, developing a "green" conception of sovereignty requires confronting both of these points of conflict.

## Sovereignty as foe? The debate over the Convention on Biological Diversity

As an international legal norm, some conceptions of sovereignty can frustrate efforts to protect biodiversity, control pollution, and sustainably manage natural resources. In its strong form, the principle insists upon primacy over all internal matters for national governments (as putative agents of their people), rejecting pressures from other states to participate in cooperative environmental governance efforts. The United States, for example, occasionally adopts a very strong conception of sovereignty against participation in multilateral environmental governance efforts, along with other treaties such as those against landmines, protecting the rights of the child, and against the death penalty. Within international environmental governance, the US has invoked sovereignty interests against the ratification of the Convention on Biological Diversity (CBD) and the Law of the Sea, as well as the Kyoto Protocol and Paris Agreement on climate change. In citing national sovereignty as a motivating reason for rejecting a US role in these cooperative international schemes, critics of such efforts have implicitly associated particular kinds of policy objectives (usually those with humanitarian or environmental objectives) with threats to national sovereignty, in some cases despite explicit framing to avoid conflicts with the principle as conventionally understood.

Debates over ratification of the CBD illustrate the conception of sovereignty that opponents of multilateral environmental governance have sought to develop. According to this proposed reinterpretation of the principle, states may not enter into binding agreements with other states or delegate any administrative authority to international or multilateral bodies (a view that at present finds little support within international law). The Convention, which was negotiated alongside the UN Framework Convention on Climate Change at the 1992 Earth Summit in Brazil, aims to conserve biological diversity throughout the world, sustainably use its components, and equitably share the benefits of earth's genetic resources. Importantly, its main principle, articulated in Article 3, aims to protect state sovereignty:

> States have, in accordance with the Charter of the United Nations and the principles of international law, the sovereign right to exploit their own resources pursuant to their own environmental policies, and the responsibility to ensure that activities within their jurisdiction or control do not cause damage to the

environment of other States or of areas beyond the limits of
national jurisdiction.

Adhering to the conventional distinction between internal affairs
that are fully protected against interference by the terms of the
CBD, and those policies or practices that allow for transboundary
environmental impacts from activities carried out within the
boundaries of nation-states, Article 3 was intended to assuage the
worries of those seeking to prevent multilateral environmental
agreements from restricting the traditional prerogative of states
to willfully degrade their own environments and deplete their
natural resource stocks if they wished. The constraint noted in the
final clause against causing transboundary environmental damage
was not new under the CBD, reflecting conventional limits upon
sovereignty that prohibit externalized harm to other states, and is
reflected in other treaties.

Arguably, effective biodiversity protection would have required
a significantly retooled conception of the principle, in which
sovereign states or peoples have only a prerogative to injure
themselves, not other persons, peoples, or nonhuman life that
resides within national territories or is affected by actions undertaken under national policies. Here, sovereignty refers to a power
to command or control forces or events in the world insofar
as this control affects only the sovereign body, not all events,
forces, or entities within a territorial space. Such a conception
would follow J. S. Mill's distinction between self-regarding and
other-affecting actions, discussed in chapter 3, viewing state sovereignty's core imperative as a kind of collective harm principle
whereby a people's right of self-determination includes the prerogative to make imprudent decisions that risk environmental harm
to members of the polity, but not to non-members (or, possibly, to
future members[6]).

One can imagine objections to even such a constricted view of
sovereignty: collective decisions by a majority or powerful minority
within a society to transfer environmental risk onto a vulnerable
and disadvantaged group within its territory are aptly characterized as instances of environmental injustice and condemned for
their abuse of power, rather than viewed as protected if regrettable
byproducts of collective autonomy. But such a moderate conception
would allow more external interference and principled constraint
in a state's domestic environmental policies than does the CBD, and
would prohibit unsustainable resource management policies that
deplete natural capital to the detriment of nonhuman inhabitants of
threatened ecosystems or future generations of humans.

With the earth in the midst of a sixth mass extinction event, and the first anthropogenic catastrophe for the planet's biodiversity, a more critical examination of the principles ordering human–environment interactions may be needed, to avoid what Elizabeth Kolbert estimates may lead to a loss of between 20 and 50 percent "of all living species on earth" by the end of this century.[7] Any international order that allows sovereign states to exploit their natural resources and degrade their ecosystems, with no limit other than the CBD's prohibition of spillover effects onto neighboring territories, may be viewed as complicit in this pernicious anthropogenic threat to the diversity of life on the planet. In addition to migratory species that transcend national borders, and so are placed at risk if governments fail to protect their territorial habitats against impacts from resource extraction or other forms of development, many species of flora and fauna whose habitats lie entirely within the territories of single nation-states are placed at risk by a conception of sovereignty as strong as that accommodated by Article 3.

## Strong sovereignty and isolationist anti-environmentalism

However, an even stronger conception of sovereignty has been urged by anti-environmental populists such as Donald Trump and Jair Bolsonaro, both of whom cite the principle on behalf of their domestic deregulatory and anti-environmental agendas. Elected president of Brazil in 2018, Bolsonaro pledged during his campaign to lift protections against Amazonian deforestation, with one economic model predicting a 268 percent increase over 2017 levels of deforestation within Brazil as the likely result.[8] Since Brazil is home to 30 percent of the planet's tropical rainforests and 10 percent of all species of life on the planet, Bolsonaro's agenda is expected to intensify biodiversity threats. Importantly, Bolsonaro has suggested that he will invoke state sovereignty against international pressures to protect the Amazon, as he did during the campaign on behalf of his threatened withdrawal from the Paris Agreement.[9] Like Trump's fusion of right-wing populism and international isolationism in the US context, Bolsonaro's view of sovereignty has little to do with democratic self-rule, and is aimed primarily at undermining or circumventing external mechanisms of accountability and serving the resource exploitation interests of a tiny cadre of economic elites. Indeed, the assertion of state sovereignty against international efforts to protect the environment is among US ideological exports to countries such as Brazil.

The debate over ratification of the CBD within the US Senate illustrates this tension within the principle of sovereignty, as its interpretive flexibility and essentially contested nature open it to serving widely divergent political agendas. During the first ratification push in 1992, op-eds entered into the *Congressional Record* by Senator Don Nickles (R-OK) claimed that the treaty would "deny the USA and other industrial nations control of the dollars they donate to conservation," and that "money will be allocated to conservation projects through a financing mechanism controlled by the parties to the treaty, mostly the poor countries." Both are in reference to the CBD's reliance upon an international finance body, which is conventional for treaties of this kind and reflective of democratic principles. According to this view advanced by Nickles on behalf of his Senate Grand Old Party (GOP) colleagues, state sovereignty is threatened whenever the finance mechanisms of international organizations are not dominated by donor states or yield participation rights to developing countries. Such a strong conception of sovereignty would obviously be inimical to US participation in other multilateral environmental treaties.

When ratification was reconsidered two years later, GOP opposition was again expressed in terms of sovereignty, in the process widening the incompatibility between the conception of sovereignty wielded by Senators opposed to the treaty and any meaningful US participation in international environmental protection efforts. Senator Conrad Burns (R-MT) claimed that the CBD "could give a panel outside the United States the right to dictate what our environmental laws should say. That is wrong." Not to be outdone, Senator Larry Craig (R-ID) alleged that "environmentalists will stop at nothing in their zeal to extend the power of the [Endangered Species Act], regardless of the disruption and damage which results," and Senator Kay Baily Hutchinson (R-TX) added that ratifying any treaty would require implementation of its "essential nuts and bolts" at an international conference of the parties, which, if allowed, would mean that the Senate "will have given away one of its major constitutional authorities and will have betrayed the trust of the American people."

Beyond rejecting any international sharing of power over governance of the treaty's finance mechanism, the conception of US sovereignty advanced by the Senate GOP during this 1994 debate over the CBD rejected the establishment of any multilateral governance powers through the convention as an affront to sovereignty. If accepted, this construction of sovereignty would in practice nullify all international law and the authority of any multilateral institution, and with it any sort of US participation in cooperative international environmental protection efforts. This is despite the fact that sovereignty as conventionally understood allows for the empowerment of multilateral executive authority necessary for a treaty regime's implementation. Such powers form an essential component of international cooperation, without which treaties are impossible, and are fully legitimate when ratified by bodies such as the Senate under standard principles of international law. Indeed, their authorization through treaty ratification constitutes a key exercise of sovereignty, rather than an affront to it. Craig's comparison of the CBD to the Endangered Species Act – an authorized statute that embodies rather than threatens national sovereignty, but which Craig opposes for ideological reasons – betrays the motive and substance of this construction of strong sovereignty, in which Senators hoped to cloak an isolationist and deregulatory agenda under a disingenuous conception of the principle, and in so doing to claim greater power over foreign policy against a president of the opposing party.

## Assessing Senate GOP sovereignty claims

Indeed, as noted above, the CBD was carefully negotiated so as to avoid interfering in recognized and legitimate national sovereignty interests, and as such should not threaten the principle as conventionally understood. As William Snape III notes:

> Contrary to the rhetoric of some extreme ideologues who seemingly oppose involvement in any multilateral cooperative endeavor, the CBD creates a global structure that is implemented with wide latitude and discretion at the national level, specifically allows for negotiation (or rejection) of annexes or protocols, does not mandate binding dispute settlement and provides connection with other accepted international agreements.[10]

While opponents may have grounded their opposition in terms of sovereignty, their aims likely had little to do with enhancing popular self-determination over US internal affairs, and much to do with pressure from the biotechnology industry, which opposed the treaty's subordination of intellectual property rights to other rights recognized by the convention. According to then-EPA Administrator William Reilly, in a July 1992 memorandum, an operative from the Bush White House undermined his pro-conservation negotiating position at the Rio Earth Summit when "elements of that industry convinced the State Department, Vice President's office and White House that the Convention did threaten them."[11] Sovereignty, which in its standard construction enjoys wide support within international law and politics, merely provided a more acceptable pretext for treaty opponents than did their true aim of protecting corporate profits.

The view of sovereignty on display in the US Senate's rejection of the CBD combines two related claims about state power and authority. The first takes any formal limit upon state power – including any kind of power sharing with other states or the creation of any legislative, executive, or judicial power beyond the nation-state – as an inherent threat to sovereignty. US opponents of the United Nations, the Paris Agreement, and the International Criminal Court often cite sovereignty concerns in justification of their rejection of such institutions, irrespective of the substantive merits that they might provide. Strong sovereignty dogmatists reject all bilateral and multilateral agreements, all international organizations and institutions, and any other source of power or authority as infringements upon sovereignty. While not necessarily isolationist – advocates of this view are often hawks when it comes to the unilateral use of military force to advance national economic or strategic interests or against other perceived threats to national hegemony, and (perhaps hypocritically) tend to support institutions of neoliberal economic globalization – this view insists upon full control over the terms of engagement with other states.

The second claim concerns the basis or objective of such engagement, as this is closely associated with this strong conception of sovereignty, even if conceptually distinct from it. In rejecting the CBD, for example, Senators identified potentially forgone profits to US firms as among their objections to participation in the treaty, suggesting an additional constraint on international engagement. By this view, which is often associated with realism and contrasted with idealism in international relations, states may only use their power in international politics to promote their own economic or strategic interests. Ethical or altruistic objectives, such as the protection of human rights or the promotion of human development, would by this view threaten the strong sovereignty advocated by opponents of the CBD. Sovereign states are in this sense equivalent to individual ethical egoists, reducing all external actions to narrow self-interest, and participating in cooperative endeavors only insofar as these maximize national interests. Profits accruing to private industry like biotechnology, according to this conception of sovereignty, are treated as equivalent to or a source of national economic interests, while biodiversity protection or mitigation of anthropogenic environmental change are treated as illegitimate objectives.

Both claims are ideological and are largely peripheral to sovereignty as conventionally constructed. Rejecting idealism in international relations and rejecting multilateralism and the binding force of international law have been frequent, if inconsistent, strategies of ideological conservatives in the US, with the neoconservative embrace of post-war Iraqi nation-building a notable departure from both. The two claims are practically related in that establishing international institutions to which other states could voluntarily consent, or sharing power with other states in bilateral or multi-lateral treaties, often requires some concession to the interests of other participating states, rather than insistent pursuit of narrowly construed national economic and strategic interests only, but they remain conceptually distinct. Like the Platonic philosopher-king, a benevolent hegemon could altruistically serve the interests of all states without sharing any power with them, so the first kind of sovereignty claim is insufficient for the second to be realized; nor is it necessary, at least for non-hegemonic states, which must typically concede some power to other states or to multilateral institutions in order to realize the benefits of mutually advantageous cooperation.

## Dogmatic versus pragmatic sovereignty

One might contrast a dogmatic conception of sovereignty – in which national governments assert the primacy of their authority over all matters within their borders, while also holding to realist principles whereby they only enter into international agreements when they expect net benefits from doing so – with a more pragmatic view in which international cooperation is not seen as inherently threat-ening to state authority, and those realist principles are not always or necessarily applied. Under the former view, a state would only participate in a multilateral climate change mitigation treaty framework if it expected the domestic benefits of its participation to exceed its domestic mitigation costs of participation, whereas under cooperative sovereignty a different calculus could be used. For example, a cooperative state could participate if it viewed the objective as important, and the allocation of burdens under the treaty framework as fair, even if that state expected its domestic costs to exceed its domestic benefits; or could view its future partici-pation as required by considerations of historical justice, due to its responsibility for historical emissions, or of distributive justice, due to being relatively affluent while poorer states were more vulnerable to climate change.

Note that in the above distinction it is not sovereignty itself that makes states claiming strong sovereignty into such poor cooper-ators, but rather their realist bent, in which only the economic or security interests of the state or its citizens could justify ceding any power to an oversight body by which national compliance with the terms of bilateral or multilateral treaties could be enforced. One might thus retort that sovereignty is therefore not the relevant obstacle, but rather that the selfish orientation of the state's foreign policy prevents its being able to enter into cooperative efforts with other nation-states. This would be fair enough, except that sovereignty as a norm has come to be so closely associated with these realist premises (as realism is also so closely wedded to post-Westphalian sovereignty) that the two cannot easily be dissociated.

## Trump and the sovereignty principle

As seen in the episode surrounding ratification of the CBD and elsewhere, the US has routinely invoked its sovereignty on behalf of refusals to cooperate in international efforts to protect biodiversity, slow climate change, punish war crimes, and protect the rights of children, to name just a few occasions. In announcing the US withdrawal from the Paris Agreement and renunciation of its pledges to the Green Climate Fund, for example, President Donald Trump cited national sovereignty on behalf of his rationale for refusing to participate: "Foreign leaders in Europe, Asia, and across the world should not have more to say with respect to the U.S. economy than our own citizens and their elected representatives. Thus, our withdrawal from the agreement represents a reassertion of America's sovereignty."[12] Characterizing the Paris Agreement as "a massive redistribution of United States wealth to other countries," Trump suggests that sovereignty requires countries to refuse participation in treaty efforts that could potentially cost participating countries more than they receive in domestic benefits, asserting what Posner and Weisbach term **"international Paretianism"** as an element of sovereignty itself.[13] According to this view, sovereign states cannot participate in any cooperative international efforts that do not advance their (economic, political, or strategic) interests, even if such efforts are necessary to prevent injustice or protect human rights. As with the GOP Senators' rejection of the CBD, realist premises about what constitutes a legitimate objective in international relations are smuggled into a conception of sovereignty whereby issues of legitimate authority are conflated with ones about objectives.

## The Trump Doctrine

Trump's efforts to reshape the principle to embrace his economic nationalism and political isolationism can be seen elsewhere, as well. In a 2017 speech before the UN, he used the word "sovereignty" ten times, claiming it to occupy a central place in what might be termed the Trump Doctrine. Treating his address like a stump speech before his fawning base, he claimed: "In foreign affairs, we are renewing this founding principle of sovereignty. Our government's first duty is to its people, to our citizens – to serve their needs, to ensure their safety, to preserve their rights, and to defend their values." In a 2018 address before the General Assembly that provoked both gasps of shock and laughter, in which he used the term six times, he announced that the US "will never surrender America's sovereignty to an unelected, unaccountable, global bureaucracy."[14] Clarifying that his view of sovereignty rejected the authority of all international institutions, including convention-based international law and ratified treaties to which the US is legally bound, he claimed that "America is governed by Americans. We reject the ideology of globalism, and we embrace the doctrine of patriotism."

Since the Paris Agreement was negotiated under the 1992 UN Framework Convention on Climate Change, to which the US is a signatory, it had already been properly authorized and so involved no infringement upon sovereignty as conventionally construed. The US was legally a party to the Agreement – which contained no binding commitments or enforceable powers – and could not legally withdraw until 2018 under its terms. After months of internal debate within the US administration about whether to formally and prematurely withdraw or to remain within the Paris framework while ignoring its mitigation commitments, Trump followed the counsel of advisors seeking to do the greatest damage to international law and withdrew. His proposed revision to the concept of sovereignty in his rationale for doing so is thus best understood as an attack upon the rule of law, as one of the constraints on presidential power, for binding later presidential administrations to treaties ratified under previous ones. Not only would Trump's conception of the principle appear to reject the authority of all multilateral agreements and international law – it views sovereignty to be in conflict with the binding nature of the rule of law itself, in a domestic as well as international context. His willful ignoring of the Emoluments Clause, his preference for "acting" officials rather than properly approved ones, and other hostile rejections of US law limiting executive power or enabling institutional oversight all reflect his view of sovereignty.

In this sense, Trump's conception of sovereignty most closely resembles the view espoused by early modern political theorist Jean Bodin, for whom sovereignty requires that absolute power be vested in the person of a monarch (or *sovereign*). Bodin's conception, as with Trump's, treats any constraint upon executive power as a threat to sovereignty, as "sovereignty given to a prince subject to obligations and conditions is properly not sovereignty or absolute power."[15] As Joan Cocks notes, this early modern conception stands in sharp contrast to the view of sovereignty as a guarantor of freedom or popular self-determination characteristic of its later modern conception. "In a nutshell," she writes, capturing Trump's view of sovereignty as well as Bodin's, "the good of sovereign power for the Prince is such recognized superiority that he can impose his will on society without encountering inside that society the legitimate or effective opposition of another human will."[16] The conception of sovereignty on display in the Trump Doctrine, that is to say, calls for a return to a premodern worldview from a time (1576) in which kings rule by divine right rather than through popular sovereignty (which replaced divine right theories of political authority in the seventeenth century), and where law and other institutional constraints on executive power are anathema to sovereignty itself, rather than embodiments of it.

## Sovereignty and sustainability

Leaving aside the "globalist" conspiracy theories and longing for premodern absolute monarchy inherent in the Trump Doctrine's conception of sovereignty, mainstream conceptions of the principle likewise collide with imperatives of sustainability. For example, the *permanent sovereignty* principle – which was first articulated with UN General Assembly Resolution 1803 in 1962, and reaffirmed in Common Article 1 of the International Covenant on Civil and Political Rights (ICCPR) and International Covenant on Economic, Social and Cultural Rights (ICESCR) four years later – assigns natural resource rights to peoples within the territory in which those resources are located, rather than allowing wealth from their extraction and exploitation to be transferred by states to foreign interests, with no benefits from their extraction and sale accruing to the people. Resolution 1803 notes that such resource rights are to be "exercised in the interest of their national development and the well-being of the people of the state concerned," which – as Article 47 of the ICCPR and Article 25 of the ICESCR state – entails the right to "utilize fully and freely their natural wealth and resources."

Developed in response to patterns of resource exploitation by which residents of resource-rich developing countries saw little or no benefit from the extraction and export of natural resources by foreign states and multinational corporations, permanent sovereignty seeks to ensure some public benefit from private resource extraction and depletion, granting management authority over territorial resources to states, with the explicit charge that these be exercised in a manner that benefits the people. Under this principle, states could transfer ownership or use rights over some territorial resources so long as this provided some benefit for local people, understood in terms of advancing economic and political self-determination.[17] In practice, this "resource privilege" has been exercised by states rather than peoples themselves, with what Thomas Pogge describes as "disastrous effects in those many poor countries where the resource sector constitutes a large segment of the national economy."[18]

Of primary interest here is the permission that it grants, under the umbrella of sovereignty, to virtually unlimited resource extraction, including – and especially – of the fossil fuel resources that cause climate change and drive local air and water pollution. This element of conventional state sovereignty was reaffirmed in the CBD at the request of states concerned about the impact of international conservation efforts upon their domestic resource industries, and is on display in Article 3 as excerpted above. While gesturing toward a constraint against causing cross-border environmental externalities (states have the "responsibility to ensure that activities within their jurisdiction or control do not cause damage to the environment of other States or of areas beyond the limits of national jurisdiction"), the CBD expressly affirms a conception of sovereignty whereby development of territorial fossil fuels is a matter for national governments only, not one for global (climate change or biodiversity) governance. Consistent with the conventional interpretation of sovereignty as granting unlimited command and control within a defined territory to the people or its legitimate governmental agent, the CBD sought to assure reluctant state parties that international conservation and biodiversity efforts would not interfere in their prerogatives to deplete their mineral resources and degrade their domestic environments.

One might, of course, point to this clause in Article 3 as recommending constraints upon resource development when these contribute to global environmental change – constraints that would be consistent with the interpretation of sovereignty as collective freedom, in accord with something like Mill's harm principle – in which case the territorial limits of sovereignty might be thought to prohibit resource exploitation that caused transboundary environmental harm, as fossil fuels inherently do. But Article 3 is widely recognized *not* to carry this implication: fossil fuel development contributing to climate change is permitted as an aspect of permanent sovereignty. Instead, a December 2017 report of the CBD's Subsidiary Body on Scientific, Technical, and Technological Advice recommends the "mainstreaming of biodiversity into the energy and mining sectors" through the dissemination of best practices and technical assistance, rather than prohibitions or regulations upon extractive industries or practices. Despite noting that "the burning of fossil fuels is widely known to be a major cause of climate change, presenting a significant impact on biodiversity globally" and that energy resource extraction can also "have large direct impacts on biodiversity and ecosystem services," these impacts are not considered to warrant the kinds of international restrictions that a strong reading of Article 3 might suggest.[19]

Such tensions between the conventional conception of sovereignty and international biodiversity efforts ought to give pause to the supposition that the two can coexist. The CBD allows for the destruction of critical habitats through domestic natural resource extraction practices in deference to the sovereignty concerns of participating states (or nonparticipating ones, since the US is not a party), undermining its core purpose. It allows for the unlimited extraction and export of fossil fuels, which are the primary culprits behind the planet's fifth mass extinction, again prioritizing sovereignty over biodiversity or ecological sustainability. Insofar as this deference to sovereignty is likely to comprise the CBD's most serious limitation, we may wonder whether biodiversity protection is compatible with a world of sovereign states at all. Insofar as greenhouse gases transcend national borders but international laws seeking to reduce their emission cannot, sovereignty as conventionally understood may threaten our ability to maintain the environmental conditions for democratic self-determination to flourish, rather than allowing that quintessentially modern expression of popular sovereignty.

Clearly, the conception of sovereignty implicit in the ideological opposition to the CBD and Paris Agreement is incompatible with sustainability imperatives, as well as those of justice and human rights. But even conventional state sovereignty – insofar as it allows unlimited fossil fuel development and habitat destruction, as it appears, for reasons noted above, to do – may likewise be incompatible with such imperatives. The development of a "green" conception of sovereignty may therefore be among the preconditions for a sustainable transition. This would allow for the kinds of multilateral cooperation that are essential to successfully addressing global threats such as biodiversity loss and climate change while prohibiting the transboundary imposition of environmental harm, along with its imposition upon future generations and other marginalized groups by dominant political interests under the guise of sovereignty. In the next section, we shall consider what a green conception of sovereignty might look like.

## Greening sovereignty

One might wonder whether *any* conception of sovereignty could accommodate interests in preventing massive biodiversity loss or catastrophic climate change, given the international cooperation and constraints upon sovereign authority that are required to effectively address each. Perhaps, that is, a sustainable future must also be a post-sovereign one, where the decentralized authority of nation-states gives way to an ecologically minded global government. Similarly, as Bill McKibben has suggested, perhaps the planetary future will be a post-territorial one, since climate change entails, among other things, that "a period of contraction is setting in as we lose parts of the habitable earth."[20] Sovereignty is bound to be transformed as peoples increasingly lose significant parts, or even all, of their territories to sea level rise and desertification, with waves of necessitous environmental migrants overwhelming the current division of the planet into separate and autonomous territories. Even if humans manage to avert the catastrophic environmental change that McKibben describes, and without a Hobbesian transfer of national authority to a global environmental sovereign, the sustainable transition would seem to require the development of a conception of sovereignty that can accommodate objectives such as those of the CBD and Paris Agreement (both of which are modest and incremental reforms designed to maintain the existing international order). Given the threat posed by climate change and on display in the current mass extinction event, anything less must be abandoned as untenable, as well as inconsistent with the original objectives of the system of sovereign states.

But how might sovereignty evolve in order to accommodate environmental imperatives like those of global climate change mitigation and biodiversity protection? What problems has the principle confronted in the past, how was it able to accommodate those interests (which, as sustainability currently does, may have once conflicted with the conventional conception), and what guidance for the principle's further evolution can be gleaned from studying its history? In this section, I shall briefly sketch a history of the principle as it evolved in order to accommodate another objective with which it was once thought incompatible, drawing from this history a few observations about how sovereignty might evolve to accommodate sustainability imperatives. This *greening* of sovereignty describes the development of a conception that seeks to protect the collective interests of peoples as they are typically organized into nation-states, while also protecting against the kinds of anthropogenic global environmental threats that conventional sovereignty has struggled to accommodate and implausibly strong conceptions of sovereignty (such as those described above) have in recent years been invoked against.

As Karen Litfin notes, the "greening of sovereignty" requires that the principle evolve to meet the challenges of the present and future and not remain shaped only by the problems of the past. Insofar as "sovereignty is about divisibility" in that it divides power and authority into a set of territorially limited nation-states, then "ecological indivisibility" (or the kind of cosmopolitan and ecological ontology discussed in chapter 8, recognizing our mutual interdependence on the planet) "necessarily calls into question traditional notions of independent decision making, territorial control, and exclusive authority."[21] Sovereignty, Litfin suggests, must evolve to better account for the global and "indivisible" nature of threats such as biodiversity loss and climate change, or it risks undermining the material bases from which its original objectives can be advanced. Because of the collective action problems associated with decentralized authority under anarchic conditions (the international version of Hardin's "tragedy of the commons"), an ecologically sustainable world of sovereign states must allow for some power to coordinate among these separate states or it will incentivize degradation and resource depletion, eventually threatening to topple democratic governments through the exacerbated scarcity that it enables.

In order to better understand how sovereignty might be transformed by future challenges and threats, we might look at how it has been transformed by past ones. In response to atrocities committed during World War II, at the same time as institutionalizing sovereignty norms, the world's nation-states also developed a body of international humanitarian law designed to prevent future atrocities and better protect important human interests against pernicious threats. Finding its first articulation in the Nuremburg Trials, which spawned the notions of war crimes, crimes against peace, and crimes against humanity (categories of punishable offenses by which Axis leaders could be held accountable for wartime atrocities), but given a fuller and more robust expression through the 1949 Universal Declaration of Human Rights, the notion of universal and inviolable human rights grew over the latter half of the twentieth century to include less basic right protections – through, for example, the 1966 ICCPR and the ICESCR from that same year. Under the body of human rights law that these conventions have promulgated, states may have considerable autonomy to direct their internal affairs but they do not have the prerogative to violate human rights, which therefore serve as limits upon their sovereignty. In practice, these limits depend upon the will of the international community to enforce norms that it has constructed through international law, which in recent decades has left many victims of human rights abuses vulnerable, but the development of international humanitarian law has nonetheless shaped the sovereignty principle inasmuch as claims to a sovereign right to commit internal atrocities are formally rejected under law and viewed as an illegitimate invocation of the principle.

## Progressive sovereignty

This conception of sovereignty as constrained by humanitarian objectives, and as aiming for the reconciling of popular sovereignty and democratic self-determination with its application to nation-states, can be termed "progressive" in that it seeks the principle's evolution away from its early modern usage of justifying sovereign power as domination and toward modern interests such as securing effective freedom. Such a progressive redefinition of sovereignty and its related concepts can be seen in Allen Buchanan's work on secession, where he argues that territorial integrity (as part and parcel of sovereignty) serves "the most basic morally legitimate interests" of its residents "in the preservation of their rights, the security of their persons, and the stability of their expectations."[22] As among the set of territorial rights that accrue to states legitimately inhabiting a defined territory, alongside sovereignty, territorial integrity guarantees an effective jurisdiction within a bounded territory that persists over time, within which a people may exercise political authority. As Buchanan notes, it creates the conditions for effective sovereignty to be possible, which in turn makes possible the kind of legal order upon which the rights and other interests of persons depend. By insisting upon a progressive version of the principle, he grounds it in these humanitarian objectives, which justify sovereignty but also limit its application.

Sovereignty and territorial integrity must be bounded by imperatives of justice and human rights, Buchanan maintains, while also being instrumental to them. While they may be necessary conditions for rights-protecting state institutions, they are not sufficient for them, so Buchanan's "progressive interpretation" of territorial integrity limits the power to legitimate states only, allowing peoples whose human rights are being abused by illegitimate states the remedial right to secede, which would otherwise violate the territorial integrity of the offending state. This move, which reflects the emergence of human rights law in the wake of post-war sovereignty norms, combines two conceptions of sovereignty, while aligning both with humanitarian objectives. States would be protected against outside interference (or have *negative sovereignty*) if and only if they respected the human rights of their subjects and worked toward their democratic inclusion within collective governance arrangements (*positive sovereignty*).

Such a progressive interpretation reflects the normative commitments to humanitarian objectives found in the UN Charter, which also formalized contemporary sovereignty norms. According to Section 3 of its first Article, the system of sovereign states aims to "achieve international co-operation in solving international problems of an economic, social, cultural, or humanitarian character, and in promoting and encouraging respect for human rights and for fundamental freedoms for all." The UDHR gives expression to these objectives through its enumerated human rights, which limit what sovereign states may legitimately do within, as well as beyond, their borders. Against some contemporary invocations of the principle, sovereignty was originally intended to promote "international co-operation" in solving problems of an international nature, not to allow states to shirk their responsibilities to contribute toward such cooperative global efforts. Progressive sovereignty protects and advances human rights – especially the collective rights to territory and self-determination, which are threatened by interferences in the democratic governance of nation-states – and thus entails a mechanism of accountability whereby states that fail to do so can be checked by the international community.

## Humanitarian intervention and the evolution of sovereignty

While the doctrine of human rights did not immediately threaten state sovereignty, it did introduce a counterweight to it. Human rights are asserted as valid normative and aspirational legal claims for all persons and peoples, regardless of their countries of origin or the legal recognition of those rights by their home governments. Insofar as the UN Charter sought simultaneously to instantiate and strengthen state sovereignty interests by affirming territorial integrity and establishing an international quasi-legislative body composed by member states, and to increase protections embodied within human rights, it set up a tension that would eventually be resolved through the weakening of sovereignty norms through the doctrine of humanitarian intervention. Given the context of atrocities committed by and within sovereign states during World War II, the UN Charter affirmed the importance of sovereignty for warding off hostile foreign threats to territorial integrity, and in collective security, but also identified important human interests that could be threatened by the abuse of sovereign power and which therefore serve as its limiting conditions.

Half a century after adoption of the UN Charter and UDHR, in response to the growing concern about humanitarian crises occurring within the borders of sovereign states, the International Commission on Intervention and State Sovereignty (ICISS) released its *Responsibility to Protect* (R2P) report in 2001, promoting the sort of progressive reinterpretation of sovereignty principles described above. The report expresses two core principles. First, it asserts that sovereignty should not be construed only as a negative right against outside interference, but also in terms of positive obligations, claiming that "the primary responsibility for the protection of its people lies with the state itself." The identification of states as having primary responsibility for protecting human rights within their borders sets up the second principle, which identifies the international community, through humanitarian intervention, as having secondary responsibility to protect, limiting the sovereignty expressed in the first principle to rights-protecting states only: "Where a population is suffering serious harm, as a result of internal war, insurgency, repression or state failure, and the state in question is unwilling or unable to halt or avert it, the principle of non-intervention yields to the international responsibility to protect."[23] The report, upon acknowledging the instrumental value of sovereign states in maintaining a just international order, emphasizes that a changing international environment required a recognition of sovereignty's "dual responsibility: externally – to respect the sovereignty of other states, and internally, to respect the dignity and basic rights of all the people within the state" (1.35).

Rejecting strong formulations that would allow sovereignty to override human rights imperatives (noting that "the defense of state sovereignty, by even its strongest supporters, does not include any claim of the unlimited power of a state to do what it wants to its own people"), the R2P report frames its recommendations as a shift in emphasis, rather than a fundamental revision to the principle. Nevertheless, its declaration that states waive their territorial integrity if they fail to adequately protect human rights offers a key revision to the principle as formulated in the UN Charter, which allows the use of force only in self-defense. The doctrine's assertion of a right to intervene in the internal affairs of states in cases other than self-defense remains controversial, as evidenced by its informal status, with opponents typically claiming undue infringements upon national sovereignty on behalf of their opposition or against its invocation.

Its subtle redefinition of the sovereignty principle as also having this internal aspect aims to bound it within a human rights framework. Given that human rights include the collective right of people to self-determination, this evolution of the principle elevates the interests of the people relative to the state, emphasizing the democratic core of popular sovereignty and seeking to marginalize nondemocratic states that use their power against, rather than through and on behalf of, their citizens. In this sense, it shifts power away from states as agents to the people who are their principal, prioritizing the interests of the latter. As Cocks writes, "attaining freedom from monarchical power, which in real life proved more oppressive than Bodin and Hobbes theorized, has seemed to people in many centuries and many regions to be synonymous with wresting the prerogatives of sovereign power for themselves."[24] The modern evolution of sovereignty has consisted in a gradual shift away from merely authorizing the state and toward empowering its people, and as a progressive force in this evolution the R2P doctrine sides with the rights and interests of the people when the two conflict.

## Sovereignty and sustainability

What lessons can be drawn from the evolution of state sovereignty to accommodate human rights? When it comes to the potential incompatibilities between state sovereignty and sustainability imperatives, the greening of sovereignty could involve similar critical evaluation and reconstruction of sovereignty principles to those found in its progressive interpretation. That is, one might stipulate that global environmental degradation calls with similar urgency for states to effectively cooperate in pursuit of common objectives, ensuring that sovereignty conceptions facilitate and do not obstruct effective international cooperation in governing earth systems. To the extent that sovereignty is invoked to evade or obstruct such cooperation, it should be regarded in a manner similar to its use by states to avoid accountability for human rights abuses.

One could, for example, amend the second R2P principle to add severe resource scarcity or environmental degradation to the list of drivers of "serious harm," which would limit a state's sovereignty over contributing to such degradation and thereby triggering an international intervention. This amendment follows the expansion of security beyond its conventional association with conflict to include **human security** interests, in recognition of their growing importance as threats to human welfare. By adding environmental drivers to the existing conflict-based drivers of human insecurity, this revision could contribute toward the greening of sovereignty by explicitly identifying the full range of threats to the human rights on which the principle is based. While the threat of armed intervention in pursuit of more sustainable state environmental policies or behavior raises several objections to be discussed below, the formal recognition of ecological integrity as a limiting constraint on state sovereignty could potentially address a serious objection to the principle as currently defined under law, without affecting benign exercises of self-determination. One manifestation of this expansion would broaden the definition of refugees to include those threatened not only by violent conflict or persecution but also by environmental degradation, as with migrants forced to flee by threats to their lives and livelihoods by sea level rise, droughts, or other environmental changes.[25]

Robyn Eckersley proposes a similar conceptual expansion through the idea of "ecological intervention." Modeled upon the humanitarian intervention concept, an ecological intervention would involve the international community legitimately using force against a sovereign state if necessary to prevent grave environmental harm. In many ways, an ecological intervention would follow the legal and moral logic of R2P: assigning to states the primary responsibility for protecting the integrity of their territorial ecosystems, but reserving secondary responsibility for the international community to intervene in what would otherwise be sovereign authority, by force if necessary. The rationale would be similar: that sovereignty exists in order to facilitate effective international cooperation in addressing problems of an international nature and to promote humanitarian objectives, with the kinds of triggers for ecological intervention comprising either international environmental threats or else threatening human rights.

Most clearly compatible with existing legal norms, Eckersley suggests, would be actions necessary for preventing transboundary environmental harm originating within the territory of some sovereign state (e.g. "a Chernobyl-like nuclear explosion" in which "military intervention may be the only means of preventing an imminent transboundary ecological disaster"). Since sovereignty doesn't protect against threats that transcend state borders, no legal exception to it would be needed in such a case. Less clearly in line with existing norms, but compatible with R2P interpretations of them, would be what Eckersley terms "eco-humanitarian inter-vention," where intentional damage to the environment ("ecocide") is used against targeted peoples (e.g. "the decimation of the marsh region, the homeland of the Ma'dan, or Marsh Arabs, by Saddam Hussein's Baathist government"). Least compatible with existing legal norms would be intervention against ecocide (or "crimes against nature") that doesn't involve human victims, which, as Eckersley notes, is "the most challenging," as it "directly appeals to a moral referent beyond humanity." Nonetheless, such an extension of R2P principles to protect biodiversity "is no longer unthinkable," for many of the same reasons that the ICISS advocated the evolution of state sovereignty norms.

Similarly, Catriona McKinnon proposes the human rights crime of *postericide*, or "intentional or reckless conduct fit to bring about the near extinction of humanity."[26] As with the R2P doctrine, it identifies strong state sovereignty as in tension with human rights objectives and seeks to reconcile the two through a progressive redefinition of sovereignty. Like Eckersley, she argues that the further evolution of sovereignty that she proposes has only become thinkable as the result of large-scale anthropogenic environmental atrocities. McKinnon argues: "Human security only contingently requires a Westphalian world order. If well-ordered states are instrumental to human security then the arguments I make here also count as arguments for protecting the security of well-ordered states, which means protecting their sovereignty."[27] Asserting the critical role of ecological integrity in maintaining the material conditions needed for meaningful exercises of popular sovereignty and self-determination, and counterposing these to exercises of state sovereignty that erode such conditions, McKinnon seeks to progressively evolve the principle away from its premodern incarnation and toward a principle that is suitable for governing relationships between nation-states under contemporary contexts and conditions.

## Reconstructing sovereignty

A critical reconstruction of the sovereignty conception would seek to reorient its positive and negative dimensions so that they can accommodate ecological limits and other sustainability impera-tives. Its positive construction in terms of advancing democratic self-determination and popular sovereignty within and between states might follow the greening of democracy discussed in chapter 4. Insofar as the all-affected principle sometimes requires that decisions be made at scales higher than the nation-state, despite the centripetal force of conventional sovereignty in limiting the scope of collective decision making to the nation-state, a greener conception of sovereignty would endorse those multilateral or global environmental governance institutions that are necessary for protecting against transnational environmental threats. Nation-states that obstruct the development of international biodiversity protection or climate change mitigation efforts would thus be viewed as an affront to sovereignty, not enabled by it. When states engage in actions that degrade their territorial environment to the detriment of future generations, they would again be violating the sovereignty of an intergenerational community, rather than acting upon the sovereign prerogative of a single generation to soil its own nest.

Viewing sovereignty as a fundamentally democratic imperative and drawing upon the analysis in chapter 4, we might also view increased scarcity and pollution as threats to either the achievement or maintenance of popular sovereignty (through democratic self-governance), reconstructing sovereignty to ensure that it is not self-undermining. Conceived in this way, any action by an otherwise sovereign state that compromised either its future ability to maintain its popular sovereignty (e.g. by allowing increased scarcity to fuel conflict or authoritarian reaction) or the ability of neighboring states to do the same could not expect those actions to be protected by sovereignty. Like the denial of sovereignty to rights-abusing states, its restriction to those states that maintain the ecological integrity of their territorial environment and contribute their fair shares to cooperative international environmental governance efforts could be justified in terms of this positive and internal dimension noted by Buchanan and in the R2P report. Since an adequate environment is essential to the realization of other human rights – to use Henry Shue's distinction, it is among the *basic rights* – no less basic right (with popular sovereignty construed as a manifestation of the right of self-determination) can be allowed to undermine it.

A negative construction of sovereignty – as freedom from interference by other states in the territories of any nation-state – may also be invoked to advance sustainability imperatives. As Eckersley notes, the transboundary impacts of pollution and ecological degradation resulting from activities in one state "constitute a form of illegitimate intervention in the ecosystems of states," and so may be construed as violating their negative sovereignty. As she writes:

In the context of increasing global economic and ecological inter-dependence, such unwanted flows of pollution (e.g. acid rain), waste, or potentially harmful products might also be said to undermine the self-determination of nation-states, in this case, the freedom of national communities to determine their own levels of environmental quality and the ways in which they might wish to use sustainably or protect their natural resources and biological and cultural heritage.[28]

In order for sovereignty to protect against this kind of interference, it must be conceptualized as disallowing ecological degradation suffi-cient to imperil the global environment, rather than (as the Trump and Bolsonaro versions urge) enabling such degradation. Together, this kind of critical reconstruction of the sovereignty principle could help to transform the principle so that it is less useful to those seeking to shield unsustainable policies and practices against external scrutiny and popular accountability, thus facilitating rather than opposing a sustainable transition.

## Conclusions: sovereignty and the ecological crisis

At issue is *who* or *what* is sovereign, which mere reference to the term "state sovereignty" does not fully resolve. A state is an apparatus that can be alternately controlled by governments of different parties, so if sovereignty attaches to states, the elective decision by one government to participate in a multilateral environmental treaty would not threaten the sovereignty of a later government of the same state, as the persistence of the state itself connotes a lasting permission that cannot be later criticized as an infringement upon its sovereignty. States may be able to legally withdraw from such treaties (although it is not clear that prohibitions against this violate sovereignty when it is merely a particular government rather than the state itself that seeks to do so), but cannot justify such withdrawal through sovereignty itself. Insofar as sovereignty originates in the people and is only contingently entrusted to states, as agents through which the popular will and the rights and interests of the people remain paramount, and since govern-ments are only temporary agents within those states, a legitimately enacted sovereign commitment to a treaty framework can bind future governments without any limitations on sovereignty.

More generally, we must understand operative legal and political principles as subject to a process of evolution and adaptation to changing conditions, which include new social demands for inclusion or political independence, as well as changing environmental conditions. Given its origin in early modern resistance to democratic modernity, and its instantiation in a Westphalian order that was still under the sway of premodern notions of chivalry and divine right monarchy, we should be impressed by the concept's malleability and adaptability, rather than frustrated by those whose ahistorical and disingenuous invocation of sovereignty is meant to reinforce and ossify oppressive institutions, rather than empower emancipatory ones. It is a matter of great urgency whether or not the modern state system, with its legal and normative principles such as sovereignty, can adapt to changing political and environmental conditions. Some critics, of course, insist that it cannot, urging their preferred systems of social and political organization in its place, whether these are to operate at larger or smaller scales than that at which sovereignty now functions. Perhaps they are correct, and the state system is both complicit and beyond repair, in which case they too will need a conception of sovereignty that can be attached to the locus or power that replaces it. How the principle must evolve to meet contemporary challenges is thus independent of its limitations as currently used, demanding such critical reconception.

# 10 Justice

Of all the normative political concepts examined in this book, justice has been embraced for perhaps the longest, and yet has attracted the most attention from academic political theorists and philosophers over the past half-century. Plato, for example, held modern ideals such as freedom, equality, and democracy in little esteem, but devoted his *Republic* to articulating and defending a conception of justice. However, justice remained a secondary and derivative quality for most texts in the Western canon, with ideals such as liberty or equality occupying the central role in their accounts of political right. It was not until the publication of John Rawls' *A Theory of Justice* in 1971 that justice took its position as the most theorized social and political ideal in contemporary texts, as well as being perhaps its most contested.

Conceptions of justice have come to occupy a central place in contemporary social movements, from local campaigns against hazardous waste facility siting decisions to global efforts to mitigate the climate crisis. As will be explored further below, a wide range of contemporary environmental problems have come to be understood through the conceptual lens of justice, whether by understanding their threats as instances of injustice or by seeking to apply some conception or principle of justice to their remedy. The opponent in this chapter differs from several earlier ones in that it is not some older conception that has been identified as complicit in existing environmental problems, but rather the failure of prevailing or institutionalized conceptions or principles of justice to adequately capture the injustice inherent in those problems or to provide the kind of remedy that the ideal promises. In order to understand this development and mobilization of justice as a critical or constructive ideal for guiding environmental change, we shall first consider several variants of justice theory and then examine how related conceptions have been applied to environmental contexts.

## Rawlsian distributive justice

Declaring justice to be the "first virtue of social institutions" and reviving the modern social contract tradition on behalf of developing economic-focused principles of distributive justice, Rawls influenced a generation of political theorists and philosophers to either follow or challenge the scope or form of the "justice as fairness" conception that he defends. His is a liberal conception insofar as it remains indifferent to what he calls "conceptions of the good," which since Hobbes have been relegated to the private sphere, where they might guide their adherents in their personal lives but do not inform the design of public institutions. By focusing upon the distribution of what he calls the *social primary goods* – instrumental resources like rights and liberties as well as income and wealth, which are constructed, and to some extent allocated, by society – Rawls casts justice in terms of fair opportunities for persons to form and pursue life plans. Ancient foci like the social division of labor or personal virtues are not objects of Rawlsian justice.

As a theory of distributive justice, the two principles of Rawlsian justice specify how the social institutions that comprise society's basic structure may justly allocate those social primary goods that are its focus. Parties seeking their own advantage, but prevented by the "veil of ignorance" from knowing specific facts about their identities whereby they could effectively benefit themselves, would, Rawls claims, endorse principles that were fair to all, not knowing whether they themselves may be among society's least advantaged. From this hypothetical choice situation (a contemporary version of the social contract tradition known as *contractualism*), the two Rawlsian principles are generated and justified. Both concern the arrangement of social and economic inequalities. The *greatest equal liberty principle* calls for each person to "have an equal right to the most extensive total system of equal basic liberties compatible with a similar system of liberty for all," and takes "lexical priority" over the second principle when they conflict. The second principle has two parts: the *difference principle* (that social and economic inequalities may be allowed when, and arranged so that, they are "to the greatest benefit of the least advantaged"); and the *equal opportunity principle* (that they be "attached to offices and positions open to all under conditions of fair equality of opportunity").[1]

The Rawlsian difference principle has attracted the most attention from justice scholars, as it would allow some institutionalized social and economic inequality (raising the ire of strict egalitarians), but would call for significant redistribution of resources in highly unequal societies such as the contemporary United States. Rivals and critics within the distributive justice field have offered alternative principles (or rules for just distribution) or currencies (the objects to be distributed) of justice, as well as contesting the scope of justice (whether it applies within one society only, between states, or globally) and its form (whether it should be egalitarian, and then with respect to what, or whether it should be guided by a threshold of sufficiency rather than equality). Others accuse Rawls and his followers of focusing too narrowly upon economic distribution rather than on other sources or concepts of justice, of being excessively individualistic rather than attending to group-based injustice, or of ignoring the effects of structural injustice. While we shall explore some of these critiques later, for now it is worth contrasting distributive with other kinds of justice, since the former is not the only concept to have been further developed and applied in environmental political theory.

## Other conceptions of justice

*Retributive justice* originates in criminal justice, viewing offenses as upsetting a kind of equality within society when an offender wrongs a victim. Viewing the wrong from the point of view of the offender, it calls for retribution (usually some form of punishment, such as incarceration) against the offender in order to restore that previous equality. *Restitutive justice*, by contrast, views the offense and consequent imbalance from the victim's point of view, calling for monies or services to be paid to the victim in restitution and in order to restore equality. *Restorative justice* considers both perspectives at once, restoring the balance upset by some offense through actions by the offender (construed as rehabilitative, not punitive as in retribution) toward the victim, seeking to mend damaged relationships and restore harm to the community at large. All three are versions of corrective justice, which seeks to remedy past wrongs through present and future actions. As we shall see, versions of all three concepts are used in debates about climate change remedies, whether viewed from the perspective of the polluter or of the victim of that pollution.

In a post-conflict social milieu, *transitional justice* seeks to repair damage done to society as a whole by legacies of human rights abuse, and includes truth and reconciliation commissions, reparations to victims, criminal prosecutions, and other measures, both judicial and non-judicial. It is not to be confused with a *just transition*, which, according to the Climate Justice Alliance, is "a vision-led, unifying and place-based set of principles, processes, and practices that build economic and political power to shift from an extractive economy to a regenerative economy."[2] Support for the latter can be found in the Paris Agreement, which calls for "a just transition of the workforce and the creation of decent work and quality jobs in accordance with nationally defined development priorities," and in the proposed US Green New Deal. Since the objective of transitional justice is to repair a society that has been torn apart by violent conflict, its model may be less applicable to environmental politics, but restoration of ecological sites damaged during conflicts may be among the means of healing the social wounds they involve.

Claims about justice originate in civil society and through social movements, as well as in judicial proceedings, and several forms and applications warrant mention here. As will be further explored below, the term "environmental justice" emerged from several anti-toxics movement campaigns with a focus upon racial inequality and discrimination. Over time, it has come to include a variety of related objectives, and has spawned related ideals in climate justice, food justice, and justice in energy, water, and transportation. Elements from all of the justice concepts introduced above can be found in these calls for environmental justice (EJ), which develop or employ various conceptions. As David Schlosberg notes of EJ movements, their demands include not only reduced and more socially equitable vulnerability to environmental hazards, and more equitable access to environmental goods and services, but also justice in *recognition* and *participation* (described below), which can be added to the set above.[3]

In examining how justice has been invoked in the context of environmental politics and used to analyze environmental problems, we must be attentive to the plurality of meanings that have been attached to the term. Calling for justice might sometimes involve only identifying an injustice that requires some kind of response, but justice theories also can invoke normative frameworks through which only a particular response is justified. Invoking justice within the context of a social movement or politically contested issue may be a way to mobilize a specific legal power, build a strategic alliance, take advantage of a popular discourse, or associate two or more previously distinct campaigns. In order to keep track of the multiple justice concepts and conceptions at work in this chapter, we shall examine its more conventional meanings and follow how these have been challenged, developed, and transformed, but shall start with the concept's appearance within social movements calling for environmental justice.

## Environmental justice as social movement objective

Before scholars began to theorize environmental inequality through a justice lens, the ideal of justice was mobilized in environmental campaigns to forge a pairing that has been seminal for theorists and practitioners alike. Although the same kinds of problems existed prior to the events that gave rise to the concept of *environmental justice*, thinking about or organizing around them as environmental problems involved a different mindset, constituency, and strategy than would thinking about or organizing around them when they were conceived as justice problems. The emergence of environmental justice as a concept changed that thinking, those constituencies, and that strategy, with activists leading this important evolution of the concept, and justice scholars (whose conventional justice theories were ill equipped for the task) trying to follow. In order to understand how justice has been utilized as a normative concept in environmental politics, and how it has ultimately been developed and adapted for the range of conflicts in which it is now used, we shall trace some of the recent history of the concept.

Race and class have long served as fault lines of environmental inequality in the US and elsewhere. As markers and magnifiers of advantage and disadvantage, they allow the relatively advantaged to count safer environments and more pleasant environmental amenities as among their privileges, with the disadvantaged lacking the power to avoid environmental risks. But the US civil rights movement prioritized campaigns for social and political equality during the 1950s and 1960s, and progressive economic movements to fight poverty and reduce income inequality during that period focused upon employment and income rather than contesting environmental inequalities. While the 1960s were also formative for US environmental policy, with President Johnson's Great Society agenda including traditional social justice imperatives of reducing race and class divisions along with environmental protection initiatives such as the Wilderness Act, their constituencies remained distinct.

The late 1970s and early 1980s brought the two together, however. Organizing by the Love Canal Homeowners Association highlighted the class dimension of vulnerability to toxic waste, as the upstate New York working-class neighborhood exposed to dioxin and other hazardous chemicals was located immediately adjacent to a heavily polluted but inadequately sealed repository for toxic chemicals, but lacked the resources to move. The group's effective advocacy for their relocation and the eventual remediation of the site (of which the Superfund Program is a direct legacy) demonstrated the potential for a form of grassroots activism that the environmental movement had largely eschewed. Led by a working-class mother, Lois Gibbs, rather than professional resource managers, lobbyists, or career politicians, the movement contrasted with the largely affluent white male leadership of the established Washington-based environmental advocacy groups.

As Mark Dowie describes the "fourth wave" of the US environmental movement, Love Canal prefigured a "multiracial, multiethnic, multiclass, and multicultural" movement that manifests in "dogged determination, radical inquiry, a rebellion against economic hegemony, and a quest for civil authority at the grassroots."[4] Apart from these demographic and strategic differences, its focus upon unequal vulnerability to industrial waste helped to bring together conventional environmental concerns with social justice. Not yet wielding the concept of environmental justice or mobilizing legal and political resources, the Love Canal incident and campaign nonetheless brought together a new kind of activism and activist with a new fusion of economic inequality and environmental harm which would, over the next decade, galvanize a new movement, along with a new justice ideal.

## Two environmental justice campaigns

Two watershed events over three years between 1979 and 1982 fused race-based justice advocacy with environment in civil society, spawning movement discourses about environmental racism and linking older civil rights struggles with newer anti-toxics campaigns. The first arose from what would otherwise have been an unremarkable legal contest against the siting of a new toxic waste facility in a middle-class, predominantly African-American, Houston neighborhood. Like other NIMBY protests, the campaign had the singular objective of compelling the selection of some alternative site, which, if successful, would probably have led to the site merely being moved to a poorer neighborhood of color. The campaign was led by attorney and neighborhood resident Linda McKeever Bullard, and assisted by her spouse, a newly appointed sociology professor at Rice, utilizing social science methodologies of his discipline to demonstrate that neighborhoods of color in the city had borne a disproportionate share of the city's toxic facilities (Houston was 25 percent African American, but 82 percent of the metro area's toxic waste facilities were located in predominantly black neighborhoods). The neighborhood's legal challenge (*Bean* v. *Southwestern Waste Management*) sought to utilize anti-discrimination law in opposition to the siting decision, alleging that this record of racially disproportionate siting of waste facilities violated equal protections. They lost, with the judge finding no "purposeful discrimination," despite the statistical evidence presented about patterns of unequal vulnerability in Houston.

That young sociologist was Robert Bullard, who would come to be known as "the father of environmental justice" for his pioneering scholarly work on the subject. Bullard would go on to publish his findings from the *Bean* case in a 1983 article in *Sociological Inquiry* – the first scholarly paper in a new field. His 1990 *Dumping in Dixie: Race, Class, and Environmental Quality* demonstrated empirically that people of color had been disproportionately exposed to toxic hazards across the American South, but argued further that emerging environmental justice movements during the 1980s represented a fusion of civil rights and environmental movements. In it, he served the unusual role of observer and advocate for a social movement that he helped to spawn, nurture, and develop, from both inside and outside the academy, as scholar and citizen.

The second watershed event for the US environmental justice movement came with the 1982 protests against plans to deposit 60,000 tons of PCB-laced soil in Afton, North Carolina. Warren County had been chosen for the toxic waste repository despite its unsuitability on several ecological grounds, including having the highest water table in the state, raising the chances for and impact of a leak of the wastes into groundwater. But Warren County was also the poorest in the state, and the county with the highest percentage of African-American residents. Citing the "environmental racism" on display in that siting decision, civil rights activist Benjamin Chavis of the United Churches of Christ Commission on Racial Justice led civil disobedience actions against the delivery of those wastes to the site in Afton, with protesters stopping trucks that were delivering the toxic soils by physically blocking the roads with their bodies, utilizing tactics similar to those used during civil rights protests in the 1950s and 1960s. Although protesters were again unsuccessful in their primary objective of preventing the waste being delivered to Warren County, they were more successful in discursively associating the view of justice inherent in civil rights struggles with anti-toxics campaigns, galvanizing a new movement with the media attention the event garnered and the organization networks that it mobilized.

Together, the legal strategy of linking anti-toxics campaigns with anti-discrimination law in *Bean*, and the political strategy of utilizing nonviolent direct action steeped in civil rights imagery in Warren County, sparked a broader movement and spawned a concept. It blended grassroots activism led by and focused upon subaltern communities with an environmental politics that impugns a wealthy industrial society for the oft-unseen toxic wastes that are its byproduct, and its tendency to concentrate vulnerabilities from them on poor communities of color. Where the egalitarian justice scholarship of the period focused upon society's least advantaged, it often did so in a deracialized and ungendered context in which disadvantage was understood primarily in individualistic and economic terms, paternalistically treating those falling within the category of claimants to justice as needing to have their claims made by others. The view of justice that emerged was thus transformative for both civil rights and environmental social movements, whose convergence created a new political synthesis. Conceptually, the ideal of justice that scholarly observers drew from this movement was also transformed, adopting a pluralistic rather than singular foundation in justice theory, stressing demands for agency rather than shifting of resources, and identifying structural injustices that defy mere institutional reform efforts.

## Environmental justice movements, discourses, applications

As David Schlosberg observes in his study of EJ movement discourses, the conceptions of justice active in US environmental justice movements were not limited to the redistributive discourse dominant in scholarly theories of justice at the time, but included also demands for participation (or procedural justice) as well as recognition.[5] This pluralistic approach is reflected in the statement of principles adopted through the 1991 First National People of Color Environmental Leadership Summit, which Bullard helped to organize. Participants asserted that EJ principles include "the right to participate as equal partners at every level of decision-making, including needs assessment, planning, implementation, enforcement and evaluation," as well as "the right to ethical, balanced and responsible uses of land and renewable resources in the interest of a sustainable planet for humans and other living things," and that "public policy be based on mutual respect and justice for all peoples, free from any form of discrimination or bias." As a critical and oppositional discourse, this pluralistic focus upon multiple conceptions of justice can be read as a call for change in how justice was theorized as well as practiced, and, in the former regard, we can see its influence on the evolution of justice as a normative concept.

As the concept of environmental justice matured, it evolved to inform challenges to a wider set of environmental inequalities, with movement activists coining related concepts such as food justice and climate justice, and scholars developing frameworks in which such claims could be understood in terms of existing justice concepts (sometimes modifying these concepts to fit this application). How do theories and discourses of climate justice (to be examined in more detail below) build upon and extend the older environmental justice tradition? What features of EJ analysis needed to be transformed in order to accommodate the kinds of justice issues now recognized as inherent to international climate change mitigation efforts? How has the development of environmental justice as a discursive frame for certain kinds of environmental inequality, as well as a scholarly research field, spawned other linkages between justice and environment, as seen in claims about or movements for climate justice, food justice, and other new EJ-inspired hybrids? Since climate justice as a social movement and field of scholarly research is a progeny of the EJ tradition but transforms some of its demands and widens it purview, it is useful to view the concept of environmental justice as having developed over several generations, with successive generations marking significant transformations of the discourse and of the operational justice conceptions in previous ones.

Whereas the early EJ movements noted above were local in their focus, climate justice is international, with advantage and disadvantage conceived along the lines of whole peoples or groups, based on stages of development (global North versus global South, as typically cast). Power imbalances can still be theorized through the lens of race, histories of colonialism, structural economic injustice, and the potentially corrupting role of economic and military power play an explanatory role in marginalization not previously noted. Geography comes to play a larger role in climate justice, as the vulnerabilities of those residing in small island states, sub-Saharan Africa, and other vulnerable regions magnify other inequalities between perpetrators and victims. The absence of common legal and political institutions at the international level complicates the development of remedies, which also become more complex, adding claims for assistance in the building of adaptive capacity and compensation for loss and damage to more familiar demands from earlier EJ movements for injunctive relief and procedural justice. The concepts and conceptions developed and mobilized on behalf of climate victims draw upon a wider pool of normative resources in order to address a wider range of issues. In the remainder of this chapter, we shall examine several such justice concepts as developed in EJ research.

## Environment and intergenerational justice

Given the influence of Rawls in justice theory during the period, and given also limits of his approach in application to environmental problems, environmental political theorists seeking to utilize the justice ideal in normative or critical work on the environment began by engaging the Rawlsian approach (including not only Rawls but also others working on justice theory in the analytic tradition). Sometimes this engagement was more sympathetic, with theorists proposing relatively minor amendments in order to tease out normative implications for environmental politics, but other engagements offered more significant challenges to the existing theoretical tradition, either calling for or developing alternatives to it. As a quite different kind of problem from the economic inequalities that Rawlsian distributive justice theory was developed to treat, environmental inequality prompted several important challenges to any transformations of the justice field within political theory and philosophy, several of which we shall consider below.

One area in which scholars have most successfully challenged and transcended the Rawlsian approach is in intergenerational justice, which occupies a relatively small part of *A Theory of Justice* but gave rise to several important challenges. Justice between generations has been of keen interest to environmental scholars because of the intertemporal nature of many ecological issues, and is widely cited by environmental activists as a key motive or objective for their activism. Pollution stored in a haphazard manner can endanger future persons, as can a pollutant that persists in the air, water, and soil over time. Climate change, in particular, has this intergenerational dimension, since carbon dioxide remains in the atmosphere for over a century after it is first emitted, and the UNFCCC calls for coordinated international mitigation action "for the benefit of present and future generations of humankind." Other environmental problems including overpopulation, the use of nuclear energy and storage of its wastes, and irreversible biodiversity loss or destruction of rare ecological sites involve impacts of an inter- generational nature, prompting the development and application of intergenerational justice principles by scholars.

On justice between generations, Rawls has been relatively less influential than in his intragenerational work, with his "just savings principle" (i.e. that the present generation has a limited obligation to save current resources for the benefit of future others) attracting more critics than sympathetic supporters. Extending the hypothetical contract device of the original position from his derivation of distributive justice principles for contemporaries, Rawls has his readers imagine a parallel thought experiment in which those selecting principles were assumed to be heads of households with natural sentiments toward their progeny, but with the veil of ignorance obscuring generational membership in order to motivate a kind of intergenerational solidarity. This paternalistic standpoint and motivational construct attracted much criticism, as did the relatively modest principle that Rawls defended from this starting point. Since Rawls assumed that continued economic growth would lead future generations to be more generally affluent than the current generation, his concern for the least advantaged that is on display in his difference principle favored using current resources for the existing poor over saving them for a future of relative affluence. He also viewed savings in terms of human rather than nature capital, so the principle did not originally entail environmental conservation imperatives of the kind that his approach might otherwise have warranted. As a result, few environmental theorists have found much use for Rawls, other than as a foil from which to develop more theoretically robust and broadly applicable principles of intergenerational justice.

## Challenges for intergenerational justice: identity and uncertainty

Two research questions stand out among the environment-focused intergenerational justice scholarship for their influence upon environmental theorizing. Population ethics has been a primary concern for those concerned about environmental change since at least 1968, with the work of Paul Ehrlich and Garrett Hardin. Since intergenerational justice asks what the present generation owes future generations (or, to conceive this individualistically, as some do, what persons in the present owe future persons), population interacts with time and environment in these questions. Decisions enabling higher rates of population growth now would be expected to speed resource depletion as human population approached ecological limits, degrading natural resources and leaving the world worse-off for future generations. Both of these population issues challenge conventional accounts of intergenerational justice, which were at the time ill equipped to address them, requiring new theories to treat them.

The first owes to Derek Parfit, whose *non-identity problem* stands as perhaps the most formidable challenge to intergenerational ethics. While, from a zero-sum perspective, we might simply assume that more people and resource use in the present is worse for future persons than lower rates of population growth, Parfit complicates this deceptively simple-seeming question. Consider, he suggests, a policy to stabilize population size out of concern for ecological limits (such as Ehrlich advocated through Zero Population Growth), which would conserve more ecological goods and services for future use. Could we, he asks, justify such a policy with reference to the interests of future persons? Acknowledging that a high population growth rate would degrade the environment in ways averse to human welfare, we could not say that this degradation harmed anyone, since the persons that would come to exist in the future as a result of our current population policies "will owe their existence to this rate of growth."[6]

Since there would be more of them living in an ecologically degraded world, yielding more overall happiness, even if at a somewhat lower average level, Parfit argues that we must concede that such a policy is superior to one that limits population growth rates. Since policies affecting population size would also likely affect the timing of reproductive choices, and thus the identities of those who are born in the future, eventually most of those residing in a future world resulting from high-growth population policies would be entirely different persons than would come to exist in a future world resulting from sustainable growth policies. Eventually all would owe their existence to whatever population policies had been chosen in the past (or our present), so it would be impossible to say of any particular future person that our policies harmed them (since their existence would also be a product of those policies).

Recognizing the unattractive implications of this analysis, which he called the "repugnant conclusion," Parfit called for but did not identify a "Theory X" that could show why it would be ethically preferable to adopt polices limiting human population growth in the interest of ecological sustainability and the improved quality of lives on the consequently less depleted planet.[7] Since Parfit, many writing about intergenerational justice in an environmental context have felt compelled to respond to either the repugnant conclusion or the non-identity problem, yet a compelling candidate for Theory X remains elusive. Scholars of population ethics and intergenerational justice have been faced with a profound challenge in claiming what to most non-specialists is simply obvious: that we ought to protect the environment for the sake of future generations. The problem, most environmental scholars agree, lies not with the notion that we can harm future people with bad environmental policies and practices, but with the limitations of our existing ethical theories, which appear ill equipped to diagnose environmental problems.

## Challenges for intergenerational justice: currency

The second research question at the confluence of environment and intergenerational justice focuses upon the currency of intergenerational justice – that is, the valuable stuff that those of us in the current generation ought to maintain out of concern for its availability to future people. Understanding sustainability to be a profoundly normative concept that informs our obligations to future generations, and apart from questions about whether we can harm or benefit particular future persons, we still need to know what (if anything) ought to be sustained, and why. Can we degrade the environment or deplete its resources but make up for this by producing more wealth that future generations might inherit? If justice requires only sustainable resource use, can we only use renewable resources such as timber or hydroelectric energy, since fossil fuels and other non-renewables cannot be used without depleting them? Like the "currency of justice" debates within distributive justice theory during the 1980s and early 1990s, intergenerational justice theorizing about the environment needs to know what goods are essential for justice.

Recall that the "currency" of distributive justice typically involves a set of goods that are instrumentally valuable for allowing their possessors to form and pursue life plans or visions of the good life, but does not itself presuppose any substantive conception of the good. For Rawls, economic goods like income and wealth are of universal appeal, and so making them central to the social primary goods (his currency) does not presuppose or favor particular conceptions of the good. As he writes, all persons want "meaningful work in free association with others," for which "great wealth is not necessary."[8] Beyond these shared political and economic objectives are subjective preferences that he assumes can be obtained through the social primary goods, but that are not subject to justice principles in distribution and so cannot be unjustly distributed. Rights and liberties, by this account, protect important interests that all share, but are valuable not in themselves but rather because of what they allow us to do with them. They are a means, not an end, and as such, we value them only insofar as they help to generate the ends that we value. If there was some other means that was equally effective at assisting us in realizing a given end, we would be indifferent between those alternative means. For Rawls and other liberal egalitarians, it is this neutrality that makes such goods appropriate for justice in a diverse, pluralistic society.

Some ecological goods and services are instrumental like this. Whatever else we want in life, we need clear air and water. The food that we also need requires arable land and water for irrigation, and we have energy needs related to food, shelter, and mobility that we require some kind of natural resources to supply. None of these presupposes a particular view of the good life or set of values, but none is an obvious candidate for a currency of intergenerational justice. Since all of these instrumental environmental goods depend upon maintaining stocks of *natural capital* from which environmental goods and services can be sustainably generated, scholars have identified sustainable natural resource management as an imperative of intergenerational justice. If the present generation could refrain from impairing the global environment's capacity to yield valuable goods and services into the future, our actions would not imperil future people and so would satisfy the demands of intergenerational justice. From this observation, its currency would seem to be the resource stocks capable of yielding ecological goods and services in perpetuity, if sustainably managed: forests, sinks, fisheries, and other forms of natural capital.

Andrew Dobson, for example, develops a conception whereby justice requires that we protect critical natural capital (defined as "natural capital whose presence and integrity is preconditional for [human] survival"), along with "irreversible nature" and "natural value" (if environmental entities are to be preserved for their own sake, independent of their contributions to human welfare).[9] This position, which refuses to allow key environmental goods to be traded for more human economic goods in what humans maintain for future generations, has come to be known as *strong sustainability*, and rejects this substitution by denying that "all natural goods can in fact be replaced by artificial alternatives."[10] Herman Daly endorses it when he notes that it would be "worthless" to bequeath a fishing fleet but no fish to future generations, but that "the future is always free to make itself miserable with whatever we leave to it." Since we cannot guarantee their welfare, intergenerational justice requires only that we guarantee their future "capacity to produce" in the "form of a minimum level of natural capital, the limiting factor."[11]

Rawlsian justice theory assumes that adequate stocks of natural capital will be maintained over time as a background premise in the moderate scarcity stipulation of the circumstances of justice, but does not treat natural capital as part of the currency of justice in either its distributive or intergenerational conceptions. But since natural capital is causally related to the material prospects of persons and societies, and its degradation or depletion affects the core objective of social justice (to arrange social institutions to promote fair opportunities to live well), its omission from dominant justice theories attracted the interests of environmental theorists, for whom the environment seemed central to justice. Its intergenerational aspects of justice – still conceived in its distributive sense, but now widening its scope to include future persons as claimants upon a common set of social and environmental resources – made the most sense for this extensionist project. Viewing intergenerational justice as complementary to distributive justice within a generation – the former seeks to maintain a social pie over time, while the latter seeks to fairly divide it among claimants within a given time period – theorists applying justice principles to this intergenerational dimension argued that natural capital should be maintained at current levels, or expanded if possible, but not degraded or depleted. It was only later that scholars sought to apply principles of justice to the distribution of environmental goods and services within a given generation. To that important development in justice theorizing, we must now turn.

## Natural resources and the scope and currency of distributive justice

As noted above, distributive justice (that is, principles of justice among contemporaries) takes a set of social goods as its currency: these are to be justly distributed among persons, and injustice arises when they are not. Could these include the kind of environmental goods and services identified within theories of intergenerational justice, allowing some environmental inequalities among contemporaries to be conceived as issues of injustice? Rawls specifically rules out focusing upon what he calls "natural primary goods" (which are qualities or capacities of persons, such as intelligence or dispositions toward health, rather than environmental goods or services). These are inequitably allocated among persons by nature, and so are morally arbitrary products of a "natural lottery" from which entitlements cannot emanate. Since "there is no more reason to permit the distribution of income and wealth to be settled by the distribution of natural assets than by historical and social fortune" (i.e. being born with natural talent is itself a product of good fortune), the "distribution of natural talents" in society should be treated as a "common asset" rather than a source of individual entitlement.[12] Rawls seeks an egalitarian distribution of social goods rather than one that is driven by unequal advantages or disadvantages of birth, and he pays little heed to the unequal access to environmental goods and services noted in chapter 2.

But what about environmental inequality, such as in access to amenities like clean air and water or parks and open space, or in exposure to environmental hazards? Are these not issues of justice at all, even as magnifiers of other sources of injustice (as the increased environmental risk common to poor communities of color magnifies their other disadvantages)? At the collective level, are the wide inequities in natural resource access among peoples and persons a matter of distributive injustice? Do resource-rich persons or peoples have any obligation to share their resource wealth with their resource-poor contemporaries? Are there levels of natural resource deprivation that raise issues of justice apart from any correlative inequalities in social goods? Or does the injustice of the world's poor disproportionately lacking access to clean drinking water get entirely captured by the related fact of their poverty? Nothing in the Rawlsian conception of distributive justice provides any conceptual purchase on such questions, as these kinds of environmental inequalities are beyond its purview. Those looking to this dominant school of justice theorizing within the past half-century of political theory and philosophy will find little support for social movement claims about a wide variety of environmental injustices, at least so long as they remain within the orbit of Rawlsian justice theory.

Of natural resources, Rawls explicitly denies – in an exchange with Charles Beitz on the scope of justice, which we shall consider further below – that inequalities in natural resource access are relevant to justice in a distributive, intergenerational, or international context. Indeed, he denies that resource wealth is necessary for a society to become or remain well-ordered, or that resource poverty can be an obstacle to the development of just institutions – let alone that environmental inequality can become a source of injustice among any society's members. Internationally, resource inequality is not unjust for Rawls because of the limited scope of his principles of international justice, which involve a duty of assistance for rich countries to help developing ones in becoming well ordered. International resource inequality is thus not relevant to this duty, for, as he claims in *The Law of Peoples*, "the crucial element in how a country fares is it political culture – its members' political and civic virtues – and not the level of its resources."[13]

Intergenerational resource inequality that results from one generation depleting natural resources, or degrading the environment to the detriment of future generations, is likewise not a source of injustice for Rawls, since his principle of just savings is again motivated by the duty to bring about or maintain "the full realization of just institutions and the fair value of liberty" and is not subject to egalitarian distribution under the difference principle.[14] According to his just savings principle, each generation "receives from its predecessors and does its fair share for those which come later," with this "fair share" defined in terms of "a fair equivalent in real capital," which excludes the stocks of natural capital discussed above.[15] Rawls acknowledges neither that environmental inequality might exacerbate other inequalities within society, nor that it might be a source of injustice in itself, excluding it altogether from his currency of justice.

Since the question of whether natural resources should be included in the currency of distributive justice overlaps with debates within justice theory about whether its scope should be limited by national borders or must transcend them, we shall consider this question next. Rawls explicitly maintains that his two principles of justice apply within, but not among or between, societies. Its scope is defined by the circumstances of justice, which are "conditions under which human cooperation is both possible and necessary," including moderate scarcity and ongoing schemes of social cooperation.[16] From the assumption that national communities are self-contained cooperative schemes, he sets the boundaries for distributive justice accordingly. Justice requires that social goods (but not environmental ones) be equitably distributed within societies, but not between them. Rawlsian justice theory cannot speak to the injustice of global environmental inequality, including that associated with global problems such as climate change.

## Combining scope and currency in resource access

Conceptual resources do become available by examining some of the scholarly literature in distributive justice theory that has been critical of this omission in Rawls, as well as that which has sought to develop new justice conceptions that are applicable to environmental inequalities. The exchange with Beitz mentioned above originated in his early and largely sympathetic critique of Rawls, challenging the restriction of justice's scope to national boundaries. Notably, Beitz argues from Rawlsian premises in support of a "resource redistribution principle" that would correct for the widely disparate access to natural resources among nation-states, in order to "give each national society a fair chance to develop just political institutions and an economy capable of satisfying its members' basic needs."[17] This imperative to redistribute the world's natural resources, he suggests, is grounded in the "under-lying principle" that "each person has an equal prima facie claim to a share of the total available resources" on the planet. Rawls would later take issue with Beitz' widening of the scope of justice beyond the nation-state because of his disagreement about natural resources belonging among its currency, as potentially relevant to the development prospects of poor countries and thus also the life prospects of their residents.

Ironically, Beitz would go on in the same paper to set the resource redistribution principle (and thus the inclusion of natural resources within the currency of justice) aside, in favor of a global version of the Rawlsian difference principle. Rawls has mistakenly set the limits on the scope of justice at the borders of nation-states on the premise of their economic self-sufficiency, he argues, but increasing global economic integration resulted in the world becoming one "in which national boundaries can no longer be regarded as the outer limits of social cooperation."[18] Beitz is properly credited for his seminal work on global or cosmopolitan distributive justice, maintaining the Rawlsian currency of justice but widening its scope, which usefully allows for the normative analysis of global environmental problems such as climate change. The irony for the development of environmental political theory is that his provoc-ative first challenge to Rawls asserted that natural resources ought to be a part of the currency of justice, but he set this aside in favor of a wider scope but narrower currency of justice. Had he stopped with the first challenge, more attention might have been paid to it than to the full egalitarian cosmopolitanism that he drew from the second challenge, and Beitz might now be better known for his seminal contributions to natural resource justice theory (which remains a relatively smaller research area) than to global justice theory. Both combine in the scholarly treatment of climate justice, which relies upon the global scope of distributive justice but applies its principles to a particular ecological service, thus capturing some of the promise for applied justice theorizing from that early Beitz work.

## On natural resource and climate justice

Whether or not principles of intergenerational justice apply to our management of natural resources, wide disparities in resource access or use among contemporaries suggest another kind of potential injustice. Taking ecological footprints as an indicator of resource use (recall from chapter 2 that they measure aggregate demand for ecological goods and services), we note that the US per capita average of 8.1 global hectares (gha) is nearly seven times larger than India's per capita footprint of 1.2 gha and an order of magnitude greater than Mozambique's 0.8 gha/cap. This per capita average obscures the wide inequality in resource access within countries like the US, where consumption inequality has significantly increased along with income inequality over the past four decades.[19] Given links between resource access and personal wellbeing – perhaps most vividly captured by deprivation of resource-dependent goods such as food, water, and energy – we might look to justice as a theoretical concept to articulate these problems, particularly since the concept has been invoked within social movements (for food, water, and energy justice).

While political theorists have developed accounts of natural resource justice for a variety of resources, including mineral resources, the oceans, and ecological space as a whole, the most developed research on justice issues in natural resource management has concerned the resources associated with climate change (e.g. equity in access to sinks, of pollution impacts, in assignment of remedial costs, related to compensation for loss and damage from degradation, and so on). The emergence of *climate justice* as a scholarly research area and sociopolitical ideal illustrates the wide range of justice concepts and conceptions that are applicable to this natural resource or earth systems governance problem, as well as the value of developing principles in the context of the particular problems to which they can be applied. Responding to the UNFCCC's call for state parties to protect the planet's climate system "on the basis of equity and according to their common but differentiated responsibilities and respective capabilities" (or CBDR+RC), political theorists and philosophers have taken this call as an invitation to theorize how justice principles to which the treaty alludes could be developed and applied to the core normative conflicts in international climate politics.

Framers of the UNFCCC aptly identified several ways in which climate change raises issues of justice in the CBDR+RC principle from Article 3 quoted above. The phenomenon causes inequitable harm within each generation in that the persons and peoples most vulnerable to its impacts are among the least responsible for causing it, and intergenerational harm in that actions or inactions undertaken in the present can significantly and adversely affect future people, since greenhouse gases emitted now remain in the atmosphere for over a century. The call for *equity* invokes the concept of egalitarian distributive justice, with several aspects of the response to climate change involving distributive issues, to be explored further below. The CBDR principle invokes remedial or corrective justice, which initially entailed that "developed country parties should take the lead in combatting climate change and the adverse effects thereof," but which in the further working out of the climate treaty's terms has called for justice principles to guide international burden-sharing in mitigation and adaptation. Finally, the respective capabilities (RC) phrase suggests a role for capacity-based remedial principles.

## Mitigation and burden-sharing equity

*Mitigation* refers to intentional efforts to reduce the human causes of climate change, with reductions in fossil fuel combustion and enhancement of carbon sinks the two primary mechanisms for such efforts. Additional sources of greenhouse gases include methane emissions from agriculture, waste management, and biomass burning, and nitrous oxide emissions from fertilizer use in agriculture. Sinks such as forests absorb carbon dioxide ($CO_2$) and so prevent it from accumulating in the atmosphere and causing its climatic effects, so expansion of natural sink capacity through reforestation projects can remove greenhouse gases after they have been emitted. Artificial sinks like those promised through carbon capture and storage technology would likewise contribute toward mitigation if they become technologically and economically viable. Reducing deforestation or other natural sink degradation mitigates relative to what would occur without the reduction, but any net reduction in sinks contributes to climate change.

Mitigation actions can be technological and infrastructural or behavioral. Transportation accounts for the largest share of US emissions at 29 percent,[20] and these sectoral emissions could be reduced with the adoption of low- or zero-emissions engines on cars, trucks, and buses, trains, ships, and planes without altering any mobility behaviors. Increased use of mass transit, urban development that reduces commuting distances, and changes to modes of transit (including ridesharing and bicycling) can mitigate through behavioral changes. Electricity generation is next at 28 percent, with mitigation actions in this sector including the transition away from fossil fuels such as coal and toward renewable sources like solar, wind or hydroelectric energy, as well as demand-side conservation efforts to improve energy efficiency or otherwise reduce energy use. Other potentially effective mitigation efforts involve increasing energy efficiency in industrial processes as well as commercial and residential buildings, sink enhancement, and changes to agricultural practices to reduce emissions from livestock and fertilizer use.

All of these actions are costly, although not equally so per ton of carbon equivalent in abatement, and with different social impacts, and many of them are considered "no regrets" options in that their ancillary benefits beyond climate change exceed their costs. Those costs can be construed as *burdens* – with climate justice in mitigation concerned with the fair sharing of such burdens – or in terms of resource entitlements. Both involve distributive justice principles, but with different conceptions of what justice requires, based on different conceptualizations of what kind of problem international mitigation presents. Conceptualizing the mitigation problem in terms of either *burden-sharing* or *resource-sharing* allocations influences the selection and use of different justice principles, so we must first consider the main alternatives for doing so.

If all parties were otherwise equal, the fair or equitable way to share mitigation burdens would be to assign costs equally, asking all nation-states to contribute on an equal per capita basis toward total global mitigation costs, whatever those were. The question of which actions to take and where to take them could be detached from who should pay for them, allowing for the most cost-efficient actions to be used to accomplish mitigation objectives, with an international finance mechanism reimbursing countries or private parties for mitigation actions they undertake when equitable cost sharing requires that they be paid for by others. If funds were not globally pooled and disbursed in this manner, equal cost sharing would allow parties to comply merely by meeting a spending rather than an abatement target, inviting abuse by allowing them to spend on actions with high local ancillary benefits rather than actions effective at carbon abatement. Since all parties are not equal – they differ in both their responsibilities and capabilities, as noted in the UNFCCC – this conceptualization of burden sharing gets little traction in climate politics.

Where parties are unequal, equitable burden sharing is often thought to require the use of progressive contributory burdens, whereby those with more of some relevant good contribute more, and those with less contribute less. As in the rationale for progressive income taxes, applying the same tax rate to wealthy and poor households would impose a greater burden upon the poor, given the declining marginal utility of income above a basic needs threshold. One version of the "respective capabilities" principle would assign wealthier countries larger mitigation burdens on grounds that their "capabilities" to mitigate are higher (in that greater wealth allows for revenues to be raised or diverted from other uses and employed to fund mitigation efforts, without having to affect state provision of basic needs), reflecting such a progressive contribution principle.

An alternative conceptualization of mitigation burden sharing that addresses this need to target actual abatement, rather than mere spending, would require parties to reduce their emissions equally. With otherwise equal parties, quantitatively equal abatement (tons per capita reduced) would be the same as proportionally equal reductions to current emissions, but, given the wide differences in current per capita national emissions, only an equal proportional reduction would be tenable. Modest per capita abatement in countries such as the US would exceed the total per capita emissions in some developing countries, which could not possibly abate at the same per capita quantity. A version of the proportionally equal approach, known as *grand-fathering*, was used in the mitigation targets of the 1997 Kyoto Protocol, with developed countries assigned reductions that averaged 5 percent from their 1990 baseline emissions levels. Many found this approach unfair, as it allowed high per capita emitters to maintain their relatively high per capita emissions in perpetuity, while those emitting at relatively low per capita rates were required to continue doing so. Here, burdens would be costs associated with achieving assigned percentage reductions to national emissions, with parties free to decide which actions to undertake, but where the costs incurred by different states might as a result vary widely.

The alternative to burden-sharing equity, which asks what each party needs to change from their status-quo emissions patterns, is equitable resource sharing, or a conceptualization that starts by asking not how much parties are currently emitting, but, instead, what share of the global annual carbon budget each party should receive. Briefly, a global carbon budget would be a cap on overall emissions for a given period (usually a year), which is then allocated among parties like nation-states as national carbon budgets. Since climate change results from accumulated emissions of greenhouse gases, a larger global carbon budget this year would require steeper reductions to future carbon allowances to meet a given mitigation goal, like the 2°C temperature increase limit set under the Paris Agreement. Likewise, allowing one country a larger annual carbon budget would necessitate a lower budget for another country within the constraints of a given global carbon budget. Since these budgets involve the sharing of a resource (sometimes referred to as emissions absorptive capacity, or the quantity of emissions that can be allowed without affecting atmospheric concentrations and causing climate change), resource-sharing approaches seek justice principles to guide their allocation between states and over time.

Conceptualizing the mitigation problem in this way calls attention to the unfairness inherent in current national emissions patterns, which the burden-sharing conceptualization obscures. Why should one developed country (like the US or Canada) be entitled to much more of the planet's sink capacity on a per capita basis (which they implicitly claim through their emissions) than another developed country (like France or Japan)? Why should developed countries in general be entitled to much more of this resource than developing countries? Many climate justice theorists call for equal per capita national emissions allowances for this reason, emphasizing the UNFCCC's invocation of the equity principle while rejecting historical use patterns as a legitimate basis for future allowances. Noting the short-term difficulty in reducing from relatively high per capita levels to a common per capita budget, given time lags between the investment in mitigation actions and their impact on national emissions, some call for what is known as a "contraction and convergence" phase-in of equal per capita allowances over time, requiring developed countries to reduce their emissions (or *contract*) while some developing countries increase theirs with development, until all trajectories *converge* on equitable budgets.

## Adaptation and equity in remedies

The international response to climate change is not limited to mitigation, however, so neither must the development and application of climate justice principles be so limited. Given climate impacts that are already occurring, or now inevitable based on past and current emissions, *adaptation* seeks to insulate humans from their harmful effects. Actions related to this imperative to avoid anthropogenic harming are wide-ranging, from building seawalls or other flood control infrastructure around coastal cities, to conversion to drought-tolerant agricultural systems and relocating displaced migrants. They are also expensive, with a World Bank study estimating their cost at $70 to $100 billion annually.[21] *Compensation* for loss and damage from climate impacts comprises a third category of response. While not all climate-related loss and damage would be compensable under defensible climate justice principles, and the Paris Agreement stipulates that its inclusion in the text of the Agreement "does not involve or provide a basis for any liability or compensation," it is likely to add substantially to adaptation costs, and increasingly so as either mitigation or adaptation imperatives are insufficiently realized. That damage is also likely to be highly inequitable, being most severe in sub-Saharan Africa, India, and Southeast Asia, where per capita emissions are among the world's lowest.

In assigning *remedial liability* (how much various parties should pay) for adaptation and compensation costs, the CBDR (with or without the additional RC for "respective capabilities") and a corrective justice concept are most frequently invoked by climate justice scholars. Drawing upon corrective justice models in law, as well as philosophical theories of moral responsibility, the notion that these remedial costs should be assigned in proportion to national responsibility for climate change has emerged as a point of consensus, if one that obscures its many areas of contestation over the details of its application. While space constrains our full exploration of ongoing debates about how to differentiate the responsibilities of different nation-states for climate change, a brief survey of the main areas of contention should reveal the difficulties in reaching consensus on which climate justice concepts and conceptions to use in this exercise.

A *strict liability* model would assign these remedial costs in proportion to each nation's share of cumulative greenhouse gas emissions over the past 150 years (differences in pre-industrial rates are trivial, and the data are less reliable the further back we go). Claiming unfairness in holding countries responsible for emissions that were not known at the time to involve harmful pollutants (or excusable ignorance), some propose a *fault-based liability* model instead, whereby remedial liability is assigned in proportion only to those national emissions for which countries can be faulted. Here, countries would only be held liable for those historical emissions after the date (often set at 1990, with the first IPCC assessment report) at which ignorance about the harmful effects of emissions was no longer excusing of such fault. Others argue for excusing *survival emissions*, or greenhouse pollution that is necessary for meeting basic human needs, assigning liability in terms of *luxury emissions* (those emissions not associated with basic needs). Under production-based accounting, countries would be assigned liability in terms of emissions from industrial activity that occurs within their borders, while consumption-based accounting would assign these to the country in which the good or service was consumed.

Some call for a hybrid liability model that combines some measure of national emissions with a capacity indicator like per capita income or territorial renewable energy capacity (based on the CBDR+RC principle). Others, recognizing the indirect causality problems discussed in chapter 7 and concerned about assigning liability for harm to agents that cannot be causally linked to it (with fault being related to moral responsibility), advocate using a *beneficiary-pays* liability principle (BPP) instead of the *polluter-pays* conceptions (PPP) above. The rationale for a BPP is that parties now owe to maintain the climate system in proportion to their having used and benefitted from its open access condition, prior to access restrictions being imposed to prevent it becoming a tragedy of the commons. Variations exist with the BPP, from liability for wrongful benefitting to its assigning only for unjust benefits, and different formulae have been proposed to calculate the amount of benefit that various states have received from using an open access sink.

To further complicate matters, some invoke justice principles like these to assign liability for adaptation and compensation costs only, relying upon different burden-sharing or resource-sharing principles for assigning national mitigation duties, while others use a single liability principle or formula for all three kinds of actions. In a critique of all such climate justice approaches that originated with Simon Caney, some maintain that it would be mistaken to develop and apply justice principles to climate change taken in isolation, rather than viewing the bundle of resources and hazards that are associated with climate vulnerabilities or responses together with other goods and bads (or what he terms an "integrationist" approach),[22] viewing them all through the lens of a general account of global justice rather than seeking to respond to only climate change in a just manner. Others conceptualize climate justice at other scales, focusing on agents such as individuals or corporations rather than states. In this relatively young but growing research area, a plurality of justice concepts and conceptions have been mobilized on behalf of several different dimensions of climate change and through multiple ways of conceptualizing its core problems. These are but an illustrative sampling of the ways in which the justice ideal has been invoked and developed within climate justice, which in turn is only a sample of how it has been used in analysis of environmental problems generally.

## Conclusions: environment and the justice ideal

As an ideal that is associated with all seven of the other ideals examined in this book, justice is in many ways the most widely applicable, but also the most challenging to develop for purposes of addressing the environmental crisis or informing the sustainable transition. As this chapter suggests, its multiple concepts and conceptions offer a rich array of normative resources for thinking about environmental inequality, which is fundamental to the human experience of most kinds of environmental change. Movements for environmental justice (including those calling for specific forms of EJ, such as climate justice) articulate concepts and conceptions that have challenged environmental theorists to develop their theoretical models in a way that can help to articulate their negative critiques and positive visions through justice principles, thereby connecting scholarly analyses of environmental justice to previous work on other forms of social injustice.

As we've seen, the concepts and conceptions of justice that have gained the most purchase among scholars or activists in environmental justice have involved the creative use of existing ideas and principles, along with the development of new ones. These new concepts and conceptions have in turn contributed to the social project of trying to realize them in practice, which, in the context of global environmental problems such as climate change, remains a largely unfinished project, but one that has been thoroughly infused with the ideal nonetheless.

# 11 Conclusions: The Just and Sustainable Society

What would it take to ensure that society is both sustainable and just (with justice here standing in for the full set of ideals discussed in earlier chapters, albeit transformed as needed to meet sustainability imperatives)? As noted in the introduction, we can view ecological limits as a disruptive ideal in that prevailing conceptions of these ideals were unable to accommodate this new idea in some of their most popular conceptions, bringing them into conflict with the idea of limits and the sustainability imperatives that it implies. We identified three kinds of responses to the appearance of this disruptive idea: to deny and ignore its factual basis or its normative force (business as usual); to allow it to disrupt and dislodge key social ideals such as equality, justice, and democracy as fundamentally incompatible with limits, instead seeking to mobilize privilege in the service of maintaining environmental inequality under conditions of intensifying scarcity (the eco-fortress); and what I've called the just transition. Here, we shall explore why taking limits, as well as these several ideals, seriously highlights the role that equity and justice must play in that sustainable transition.

Before we consider these normative concepts, we might observe what is required to meet sustainability imperatives, setting aside for the moment how to distinguish just from unjust versions of them. A popular way to conceptualize ecological limits and track progress toward sustainability is through the *ecological footprint*: the ecological goods and services used by a given population (persons, states, humanity as a whole), measured in terms of the amount of land needed to supply its natural resources and absorb its wastes.[1] For humanity as a whole to live sustainably on the planet, its footprint must not exceed the earth's *biocapacity*, or ability to sustainably yield the ecological goods and services that humans use. Indeed, humanity must set aside sufficient biocapacity to support the other 6 million species with whom we share a planet (biodiversity being one of the planetary boundaries), remaining within whatever share of planetary biocapacity gives due regard for the welfare of the more-than-human world.

In 2016, the average human footprint was 2.75 global hectares (the amount of land at average rates of biological productivity that each person would need to support their consumption), compared against a per capita biocapacity of 1.63 hectares, for an ecological deficit of 1.1 global hectares per person (gha/cap). If humanity began borrowing additional ecological capacity once it had depleted what is annually available, this Earth Overshoot Day would have arrived on July 29 in 2019. Defining sustainability in this way, per capita footprints are significantly above what the planet can indefinitely support, and so must be reduced.

How much of that biocapacity may be used by a given people is tendentious, but a robust commitment to the equality ideal at the global level would call for a roughly equal individual entitlement to the planet's biocapacity, disallowing widely disparate per capita footprints to persist among and within countries.[2] But wide environmental inequalities do exist among countries, whether viewed in terms of per capita footprints or of biocapacity. If Australia was entitled to use its sparsely populated continent's biocapacity of 12.3 gha/cap, its per capita footprint of 6.6 would leave an ecological reserve of 5.7 gha/cap. Singapore, by contrast, has less than a tenth of a hectare of per capita biocapacity on its densely populated island, leaving an ecological deficit of 5.8 gha/cap with its otherwise-comparable 5.9 gha/cap footprint. Such wide disparities in per capita resource entitlements would be difficult to justify. Whether reducing to the global per capita biocapacity of 1.1 gha/cap or to its per capita territorial biocapacity of 3.6 gha, the United States needs to significantly reduce its current 8.1 gha/cap footprint, suggesting the scale of reduction in consumption of ecological goods and services needed for a sustainable transition as well as the centrality of equity in this transition.

There are other benchmarks by which the pathway to sustainability may be defined. In the context of climate change, the 2016 Paris Agreement endorsed the target of limiting global temperatures to "well below" 2°C, while pursuing efforts to limit warming to 1.5 degrees. According to the IPCC, the 1.5°C target would require that global emissions be reduced by 45 percent from 2010 levels by 2030, and reach net zero by 2050, while the 2° target would require a 25 percent reduction by 2030, and phase-out by 2080.[3] Put another way, maintaining the 2° cap requires that we limit global cumulative emissions to a trillion tons of carbon over human history, of which 635 billion had been emitted by September of 2019 (most of these since 1950), by which point net zero emissions must be achieved. Based on current trends, the trillionth ton will be emitted in January of 2035, after which further emissions would exceed that temperature target.[4] To meet the more ambitious 1.5° target, renewable sources of electricity would need to reach 97 percent by 2050 (up from 23 percent in 2015), with a corresponding phase-out of fossil fuels, requiring an annual investment of $2.4 trillion (or about a hundred-fold increase over 2018 levels).[5]

Sustainable transition is costly and difficult, but is possible through existing technologies, affordable in comparison to the social and ecological costs associated with business as usual, and necessary for the long-term maintenance of the earth's ecological systems, as well as for the social and political ideals that they make possible. What is needed to balance imperatives of sustainability alongside those associated with social and global justice? In an analysis similar to Raworth's "doughnut" image of the "safe and just operating space" for humanity (as discussed in chapter 4), O'Neill et al. compare 7 indicators of national environmental pressure related to the 9 planetary boundaries (including ecological footprints and $CO_2$ emissions, as well as phosphorous and nitrogen emissions, blue water use, and material footprint [the use of materials – biomass, fossil fuels, metal ores, non-metal ores – in a country's consumption]) against 11 social outcomes, including basic physical needs (nutrition, sanitation, energy access) as well as goals related to development (life satisfaction, education, democratic quality, healthy life expectancy, education, social support, and equality) in 150 countries.[6] The authors find that, while no country presently meets basic needs for its residents within a globally sustainable rate of resource use, such needs could be met for all 7 billion people without transgressing planetary boundaries through transition to sustainable energy, agriculture, and manufacturing systems.

However, egalitarian rather than sufficientarian ambitions for "the universal achievement of more qualitative goals (for example, high life satisfaction)" would require two to six times the planet's sustainably available resources. Such objectives would be achievable through more efficient provisioning systems that "mediate the relationship between resource use and social outcomes," such as efficient technologies or practices. Raworth's doughnut is therefore hypothetically possible: justice of the kind reflected in the Sustainable Development Goals can be achieved within the ecological limits now, albeit not without some global redistribution of resources, and a good life for all may be achieved through more efficient provisioning systems. This finding is remarkable given evidence noted above about how far beyond those boundaries humans have transgressed already. Just transition of the kind promised by sustainable development is possible, but requires major social and technical change. But perhaps this finding's key message for our purposes here lies in its implications for global equity.

The authors call for a shift from a growth paradigm to one of sufficiency (as discussed in chapter 5), since "resource use could be reduced significantly in many wealthy countries without affecting social outcomes," along with the promotion of international and social equity in the form of reduced income inequality and enhanced social support to improve social provisioning. In an ecologically limited world, they note, human development goals have "the potential to undermine the Earth-system processes upon which development ultimately depends," as a decent human life requires more ecological goods and services than does an impoverished one, but such a conflict between the sustainable and the just can be mitigated if "the level of resource use associated with meeting basic needs" is "dramatically reduced" and sustainable development goals can "shift the agenda away from growth towards an economic model where the goal is sustainable and equitable human well-being."[7]

Here, the necessary relationship between a sustainable transition and a just one becomes evident: unless increasingly scarce ecological goods and services are to be monopolized by a few, as in the eco-fortress response, they must be more equitably shared, as well as more efficiently used. A genuinely sustainable transition for all is necessarily a just one, as the desire to preserve ecological goods and services for a few at the expense of the many is a recipe for perpetual conflict, violence, and suffering, which is itself not sustainable. The environmental challenges of the twenty-first century – climate change, biodiversity loss, water scarcity – require the kind of international cooperation that in turn depends upon its terms being made fair to all parties, rather than the more modest unilateral or multilateral efforts that can be imposed by more powerful states onto more reluctant participants.

Conceptions of progress without attention to sustainability alongside some way of defining justice objectives will inevitably undermine themselves, with progress dependent on compelling conceptions of other ideals as well as grounding in ecological limits. Democracy and conceptions of sovereignty that allow for both international cooperation in protection of our shared planet and the self-determination of peoples can likewise be accommodated by this embrace of equity in combination with sustainability, tempered by institutions that ensure responsibility, and motivated by a sense of planetary community. Likewise with conceptions of freedom and equality, which help to constitute the just world that must be made sustainable as a matter of justice, and be just in pursuit of sustainability. Having been disrupted, the question is no longer whether these ideals will change, since, for reasons noted above, they must change if sustainable transition is to occur, and in many cases they are already changing. The question is, rather, how they will change, and whether this change tends toward prolonging or resolving their crisis. Understanding how these ideas and ideals interact and how humans have in the past seen their guiding ideas and ideals be disrupted and transformed should allow those wanting to more actively participate in enabling this transition to more effectively do so, noting its roots in the way that we think about, assess, advocate, and pursue what matters.

# Notes

## 1 Introduction and Approach

1 www.theclimatemobilization.org/climate-emergency-campaign.
2 https://rebellion.earth/the-truth.
3 Damian Carrington, "Why The Guardian Is Changing the Language It Uses about the Environment," *The Guardian* (May 17, 2019), online at www.theguardian.com/environment/2019/may/17/why-the-guardian-is-changing-the-language-it-uses-about-the-environment.
4 William Blake, "London," in *Songs of Innocence and Experience* (London: Basil Montagu Pickering, 1866).
5 Sheldon Wolin, *Politics and Vision: Continuity and Innovation in Western Political Thought* (Princeton University Press, 2016), p. 26.
6 Stephen Skowronek, *Presidential Leadership in Political Time: Reprise and Reappraisal* (University of Kansas Press, 2008).

## 2 Environmental Change and the Sustainability Imperative

1 Mike Hulme, *Why We Disagree About Climate Change* (New York: Cambridge University Press, 2009).
2 John R. McNeill, *The Great Acceleration: An Environmental History of the Anthropocene since 1945* (Cambridge, MA: Harvard University Press, 2014).
3 W. Steffen, A. Sanderson, P. D. Tyson, et al., *Global Change and the Earth System: A Planet Under Pressure* (New York: Springer-Verlag, 2004), p. 131.
4 John Stuart Mill, "On Liberty," in *On Liberty and Other Essays*, ed. John Gray (New York: Oxford University Press, 1991), p. 17.
5 Eleonora Barbieri Masini, *The Legacy of Aurelio Peccei and the Continuing Relevance of his Anticipatory Vision* (Vienna: European Support Centre for the Club of Rome, 2006), p. 8.

6  Donella Meadows, Jorgen Randers, and Dennis Meadows, *The Limits to Growth: The 30-Year Update* (White River Junction, VT: Chelsea Green Publishing Co., 2004), p. xvi.

7  Garrett Hardin, "Lifeboat Ethics: The Case Against Helping the Poor," *Psychology Today* (September, 1974): 38.

8  See Paul Sabin, *The Bet: Paul Ehrlich, Julian Simon, and Our Gamble over Earth's Future* (New Haven, CT: Yale University Press, 2013).

9  Naomi Oreskes and Erik M. Conway, *Merchants of Doubt: How a Handful of Scientists Obscured the Truth on Issues from Tobacco Smoke to Global Warming* (New York: Bloomsbury Press, 2010).

10  Wayland Kennet, "The Stockholm Conference on the Human Environment," *International Affairs* 48(1) (1972): 37.

11  Thomas W. Pogge, *World Poverty and Human Rights*, 2nd edition (Cambridge, and Malden, MA: Polity, 2008).

12  Michael L. Ross, "The Political Economy of the Resource Curse," *World Politics* 51(2) (1999): 297–322.

13  Riley E. Dunlap, Aaron M. McCright, and Jerrod H. Yarosh, "The Political Divide on Climate Change: Partisan Polarization Widens in the U.S.," *Environment: Science and Policy for Sustainable Development* 58(5) (2016): 4–23.

14  Eliza Grizwold, "How Silent Spring Ignited the Environmental Movement," *The New York Times* (September 21, 2012).

15  David Michaels, "Doubt Is Their Product," *Scientific American* (June, 2005).

16  Kim Phillips-Fein, *Invisible Hands: The Making of the Conservative Movement from the New Deal to Reagan* (New York: Norton, 2009), p. 162.

17  David Helvarg, *The War Against the Greens* (San Francisco: Sierra Club Books, 1994).

18  Nan Aron, *Justice for Sale: Shortchanging the Public Interest for Private Gain* (Washington, DC: Alliance for Justice, 1993).

19  National Task Force report on the Rule of Law & Democracy: New York University Brennan Center for Justice, *Proposals for Reform*, vol. II: *National Task Force on Rule of Law & Democracy* (2019): www.brennancenter.org/our-work/policy-solutions/proposals-reform-volume-ii-national-task-force-rule-law-democracy.

20  Garrett Hardin, "Living on a Lifeboat," *BioScience* 24(10) (1974): 566.

21  John S. Dryzek, *The Politics of the Earth: Environmental Discourses*, 3rd edition (New York: Oxford University Press, 2013), p. 40.

22  Peter Christoff, "The Climate State Global Warming and the Future of the (Welfare) State," unpublished paper presented to the Western Political Science Association annual meeting, San Diego, CA, April 18–20, 2019, p. 31.

23  Lisa Sun-Hee Park and David N. Pellow, *The Slums of Aspen: Immigrants vs. the Environment in America's Eden* (New York University Press, 2011).

## 3 Freedom

1 William E. Connolly, *The Terms of Political Discourse*, 2nd edition (Oxford: Martin Robertson, 1983), p. 245.
2 Isaiah Berlin, "Two Concepts of Liberty," in *Four Essays on Liberty*, ed. Isaiah Berlin (London: Oxford University Press, 1969).
3 Ronald Dworkin, "The Jurisprudence of Richard Nixon," *The New York Review of Books* 18(8) (May, 1972): 27–35.
4 Garrett Hardin, "The Tragedy of the Commons," *Science* 162 (1968): 1243–8.
5 Paul R. Ehrlich, *The Population Bomb* (New York: Ballantine Books, 1968), p. 11.
6 Hardin, "Tragedy of the Commons," p. 1246.
7 Hardin, "Tragedy of the Commons," p. 1247.
8 Elinor Ostrom, *Governing the Commons* (New York: Cambridge University Press, 1990).
9 See, for example, Terry L. Anderson and Donald R. Leal, *Free Market Environmentalism*, revised edition (New York: Palgrave, 2001).
10 Richard H. Thaler and Cass R. Sunstein, *Nudge: Improving Decisions about Health, Wealth, and Happiness* (New Haven, CT: Yale University Press, 2008).
11 Ludwig von Mises, *Planning for Freedom* (South Holland, IL: Libertarian Press, 1952), p. 38.
12 The Heritage Foundation / *Wall Street Journal*, *Index of Economic Freedom*, 14th edition (2008), Executive Summary, p. 1: www.heritage. org/research/features/index/chapters/pdf/index2008_execsum.pdf.
13 Alicia Caldwell, "The Tyranny of Low-Flow Showerheads," *The Denver Post* (February 24, 2014).
14 The Foundation specifically targeted proposed rules requiring low-flow toilets and showerheads in its 2008 election guide: www.johnlocke.org/site-docs/agenda2008/agenda2008_web.pdf.
15 www.johnlocke.org/about-john-locke.
16 Ernest Istook, "Thanks to the EPA, Even If You Like Your Shower, You Can't Keep It," op-ed, cnsnews.com, March 24, 2015: www.cnsnews.com/commentary/ernest-istook/thanks-epa-even-if-you-your-shower-you-cant-keep-it.
17 David Boaz, "The Coming Libertarian Age," *CATO Policy Report* 19(1) (1997): 12.
18 John Locke, *Second Treatise of Government*, ed. C. B. Macpherson (Indianapolis, IN: Hackett, 1980), p. 19.
19 Locke, *Second Treatise*, pp. 20–1.
20 Locke, *Second Treatise*, p. 21.
21 Locke, *Second Treatise*, p. 19.
22 This claim is most prominently made in Sir Robert Filmer's *Patriarcha*, which Locke argues against in his *First Treatise of Government*.
23 Robert Nozick, *Anarchy, State, and Utopia* (New York: Basic Books, 1974), p. 169.

24  Nozick, *Anarchy, State, and Utopia*, p. 179.
25  John S. Dryzek, *The Politics of the Earth*, 3rd edition (New York: Oxford University Press, 2013), p. 52.
26  Julian Simon, "Bright Global Future," *Bulletin of the Atomic Scientists* (November, 1984): 15.
27  Julian L. Simon and Herman Kahn, eds., *The Resourceful Earth: A Response to Global 2000* (New York: Basil Blackwell, 1984), p. 1.
28  Definition: condition through which parties to a transaction are made better-off as the result of it.
29  Vandana Shiva, *Water Wars: Privatization, Pollution, and Profit* (Berkeley, CA: North Atlantic Books, 2016).
30  John Stuart Mill, "On Liberty," in *On Liberty and Other Essays*, ed. John Gray (New York: Oxford University Press, 1991), p. 17.
31  Mill, "On Liberty," p. 17.
32  Mill, "On Liberty," p. 75.
33  Mill, "On Liberty," p. 17.
34  Mill, "On Liberty," p. 73.
35  For example, Thomas Princen, Michael Maniates, and Ken Conca, eds., *Confronting Consumption* (Cambridge, MA: MIT Press, 2002).
36  Thorstein Veblen, *The Theory of the Leisure Class* (New York: Macmillan, 1899).
37  Michael F. Maniates, "Individualization: Plant a Tree, Buy a Bike, Save the World?" *Global Environmental Politics* 1(3) (2001): 31–52.
38  Steve Vanderheiden, "Assessing the Case against the SUV," *Environmental Politics* 15(1) (2006): 23–40.
39  Murray Rothbard, *Man, Economy, and the State* (Auburn, AL: Ludwig von Mises Institute, 1993), p. 561.
40  Ludwig von Mises, *Human Action*, 4th edition, trans. Bettina Greaves (Irvington: Foundation for Economic Education, 1996), p. 271.
41  George H. Hildebrand, "Consumer Sovereignty in Modern Times," *American Economic Review* 41(2) (1951): 19.
42  Hildebrand, "Consumer Sovereignty in Modern Times," p. 20.
43  Mill, "On Liberty," p. 14.
44  Mill, "On Liberty," p. 16.
45  Hildebrand, "Consumer Sovereignty in Modern Times," pp. 22–3.
46  Hildebrand, "Consumer Sovereignty in Modern Times," p. 27.
47  Thomas Hobbes, *Leviathan* (London: Penguin Classic, 2017), pp. 186, 188.

## 4 Democracy

1  https://freedomhouse.org.
2  Francis Fukuyama, "The End of History?" *The National Interest* (16) (1989): 3–18.
3  See Andrew Dobson, *Green Political Thought*, 4th edition (New York: Routledge, 2007).

4   Robert E. Goodin, *Green Political Theory* (Cambridge, MA: Polity, 1992), p. 124.
5   Frank Biermann and Ingrid Boas, "Preparing for a Warmer World: Towards a Global Governance System to Protect Climate Refugees," *Global Environmental Politics* 10(1) (2010): 60–88.
6   Rafael Reuveny, "Climate Change-Induced Migration and Violent Conflict," *Political Geography* 26(6) (2007): 656–73.
7   Peter Burnell, "Democracy, Democratization and Climate Change: Complex Relationships," *Democratization* 19(5) (2012): 813–42.
8   William Ophuls and A. Stephen Boyan, *Ecology and the Politics of Scarcity Revisited: The Unraveling of the American Dream* (New York: W. H. Freeman & Co., 1992).
9   Leo Hickman, "James Lovelock: 'Fudging Data Is a Sin Against Science,'" *The Guardian* (March 29, 2010): www.theguardian.com/environment/2010/mar/29/james-lovelock.
10  Brian Barry, *Justice as Impartiality* (New York: Oxford University Press, 1995), p. 150.
11  Goodin, *Green Political Theory*, p. 168.
12  Fritz Sharpf, *Governing in Europe: Effective and Democratic?* (New York: Oxford University Press, 1999). Sharpf was the first to distinguish between input legitimacy, which is a product of the democratic qualities of decision-making procedures, and output legitimacy, which is related to the quality of the decisions themselves.
13  Johan Rockström, W. L. Steffen, Kevin Noone, et al., "Planetary Boundaries: Exploring the Safe Operating Space for Humanity," *Ecology and Society* 14(2) (2009): 32.
14  Kate Raworth, *Doughnut Economics: Seven Ways to Think Like a 21st-Century Economist* (White River Junction, VT: Chelsea Green Publishing, 2017).
15  Michael Saward, "Green Democracy?" in *The Politics of Nature: Explorations in Green Political Theory*, ed. Andrew Dobson and Paul Lucardie (New York: Routledge, 1993), pp. 63–80, p. 77.
16  Henry Shue, "Human Rights, Climate Change, and the Trillionth Ton," in *The Ethics of Global Climate Change*, ed. Douglas Arnold (New York: Cambridge University Press, 2011), pp. 292–314, p. 294.
17  Mark B. Brown, *Science in Democracy: Expertise, Institutions, and Representation* (Cambridge, MA: MIT Press, 2009), p. 93.
18  Robert Pierson, "The Epistemic Authority of Expertise," *PSA: Proceedings of the Biennial Meeting of the Philosophy of Science Association* 1 (1994): 398–405.
19  Roger Pielke, Jr., *The Honest Broker: Making Sense of Science in Policy and Politics* (New York: Cambridge University Press, 2000).
20  Dan Coby Shahar, "Rejecting Eco-Authoritarianism, Again," *Environmental Values* 24(3) (2015): 345–66.
21  Thomas Friedman, "Our One-Party Democracy," *The New York Times* (September 9, 2009), A29.
22  Sarah Manavis, "Eco-Fascism: The Ideology Marrying

Environmentalism and White Supremacy Thriving Online," *The New Statesman* (September 21, 2018).

23  Matthew Phelan, "The Menace of Eco-Fascism," *The New York Review of Books* (October 22, 2018).

24  Ophuls and Boyan, *Ecology and the Politics of Scarcity Revisited*, p. 286.

25  Ophuls and Boyan, *Ecology and the Politics of Scarcity Revisited*, pp. 214–15.

26  American Political Science Association Task Force on Inequality and American Democracy, *American Democracy in an Age of Rising Inequality* (2004), p. 2: www.apsanet.org/portals/54/Files/Task%20Force%20 Reports/taskforcereport.pdf.

27  Terence Ball, "Democracy," in *Political Theory and the Ecological Challenge*, ed. Andrew Dobson and Robyn Eckersley (New York: Cambridge University Press, 2006), pp. 131–47.

28  Walter F. Baber and Robert V. Bartlett, *Global Democracy and Sustainable Jurisprudence* (Cambridge, MA: MIT Press, 2009).

29  Robyn Ecksersley, *The Green State: Rethinking Democracy and Sovereignty* (Cambridge, MA: MIT Press, 2004), p. 140.

30  Eckersley, *The Green State*, pp. 14–15.

31  Robert O. Keohane, "Accountability in World Politics," *Scandinavian Political Studies* 29(2) (2006): 75–87.

32  Karin Bäckstrand, "Accountability of Networked Climate Governance: The Rise of Transnational Climate Partnerships," *Global Environmental Politics* 8(3) (2008): 74–102.

33  David G. Victor, *Global Warming Gridlock: Creating More Effective Strategies for Protecting the Planet* (New York: Cambridge University Press, 2011).

34  Robyn Eckersley, "Moving Forward in the Climate Negotiations: Multilateralism or Minilateralism?" *Global Environmental Politics* 12(2) (2012): 24–42.

35  Daniel Bodansky, "The Copenhagen Climate Change Conference: A Postmortem," *The American Journal of International Law* 104(2) (2010): 230–40.

36  Will L. Steffen, Johan Rockström, and Robert Costanza, "How Defining Planetary Boundaries Can Transform Our Approach to Growth," *Solutions: For a Sustainable and Desirable Future* 2(2) (2001): 59–65.

37  Colin Crouch, *Post-Democracy* (Cambridge: Polity, 2004).

38  John S. Dryzek and Hayley Stevenson (2011), "Global Democracy and Earth System Governance," *Ecological Economics* 70(11): 1865–74.

39  Richard Price, "Transnational Civil Society and Advocacy in World Politics," *World Politics* 55(4) (2003): 579–606.

40  Karin Bäckstrand, "Democratizing Global Environmental Governance? Stakeholder Democracy after the World Summit on Sustainable Development," *European Journal of International Relations* 12(4) (2006): 467–98.

## 5 Progress

1   Yves Charbit, "The Platonic City: History and Utopia," *Population* 57(2) (2002): 207–35.
2   Herman E. Daly and John B. Cobb, Jr., *For the Common Good: Redirecting the Economy Toward Community, the Environment, and a Sustainable Future* (Boston: Beacon Press, 1989).
3   See Jason Kawall, ed., *The Virtues of Sustainability* (New York: Oxford University Press, 2020), and David Macauley, "The Flowering of Environmental Roots and the Four Elements of Presocratic Philosophy: From Empedocles to Deleuze and Guattari," *Worldviews* 9(3) (2005): 281–314.
4   Jacobus A. Du Pisani, "Sustainable Development – Historical Roots of the Concept," *Environmental Sciences* 3(2) (2006): 84.
5   G. H. Von Wright, "Progress: Fact and Fiction," in *The Idea of Progress*, ed. A. Burgen, P. McLaughlin, and J. Mittelstrab (Berlin: Walter de Gruyter, 1997), pp. 1–18, p. 3.
6   C. B. Macpherson, *The Political Theory of Possessive Individualism* (Oxford: Clarendon Press, 1962).
7   John Locke, *Second Treatise of Government*, ed. C. B. Macpherson (Indianapolis, IN: Hackett, 1980), p. 26.
8   Locke, *Second Treatise*, p. 21.
9   Herman E. Daly, "On Wilfred Beckerman's Critique of Sustainable Development," *Environmental Values* 4(1) (1995): 49–55, p. 50.
10   Robert J. Antonio, "Plundering the Commons: The Growth Imperative in Neoliberal Times," *The Sociological Review* 61(2) (2013): 20.
11   John Barry, "A Genealogy of Economic Growth as Ideology and Cold War Core State Imperative," *New Political Economy* 25(1) (2020): 18–29.
12   Charles E. Lindblom, *Politics and Markets: The World's Political-Economic Systems* (New York: Basic Books, 1977).
13   L. Hunter Lovins and Amory B. Lovins, "Natural Capitalism: Path to Sustainability?" *Corporate Environmental Strategy* 8(2) (2001): 100.
14   Charles Wilkinson, "'The Greatest Good of the Greatest Number in the Long Run': TR, Pinchot, and the Origins of Sustainability in America," *Colorado Natural Resources, Energy, and Environmental Law Review* 26(1) (2015): 69–79.
15   Samuel P. Hays, *Conservation and the Gospel of Efficiency* (University of Pittsburgh Press, 1959), p. 267.
16   From *Walden*: "In wildness is the preservation of the world."
17   John Muir, *John of the Mountains* (Madison: University of Wisconsin Press, 1979), p. 317.
18   John Muir, *The Yosemite* (New York: The Century Co., 1912), ch. 16.
19   Aldo Leopold, *A Sand County Almanac* (New York: Oxford University Press, 1949), p. 214.
20   Jedediah Purdy, "The Politics of Nature: Climate Change, Environmental Law, and Democracy," *The Yale Law Journal* 119 (2010): 1131, 1168.

21  William Cronon, "The Trouble with Wilderness," in *Uncommon Ground: Rethinking the Human Place in Nature*, ed. Cronon (New York: W. W. Norton & Co., 1996), p. 85.

22  Rachel Carson, *Silent Spring* (New York: Houghton Mifflin, 1962), pp. 5–6.

23  Bill McKibben, *The End of Nature* (New York: Random House, 1999).

24  David Wells, "Resurrecting the Dismal Parson: Malthus, Ecology, and Political Thought," *Political Studies* 30(1) (1982): 4.

25  William Ophuls and A. Stephen Boyan, *Ecology and the Politics of Scarcity Revisited: The Unraveling of the American Dream* (New York: W. H. Freeman & Co., 1992).

26  Michael H. Huesemann and Joyce A. Huesemann, *Technofix: Why Technology Won't Save Us or the Environment* (Gabriola Island, BC: New Society Publishers, 2011).

27  http://hdr.undp.org/en/content/human-development-index-hdi.

28  Amartya Sen, *The Idea of Justice* (Cambridge, MA: Belknap Press, 2009).

29  http://hdr.undp.org/en/faq-page/human-development-index-hdi#t292n2867.

30  Ronald Inglehart, *The Silent Revolution: Changing Values and Political Styles Among Western Publics* (Princeton University Press, 1977).

31  Martha Nussbaum, *Creating Capabilities: The Human Development Approach* (Cambridge, MA: Harvard University Press, 2011).

32  Breena Holland, "Justice and the Environment in Nussbaum's 'Capabilities Approach': Why Sustainable Ecological Capacity Is a Meta Capability," *Political Research Quarterly* 61(2) (2008): 319–32.

33  Jeffrey D. Sachs, *The Age of Sustainable Development* (New York: Columbia University Press, 2015), p. 12.

34  https://sdg-tracker.org.

35  World Commission on Environment and Development, *Our Common Future* (New York: Oxford University Press, 1987), p. 40.

36  Herman E. Daly, "Sustainable Growth: An Impossibility Theorem," in *Valuing the Earth: Economics, Ecology, Ethics*, ed. Daly and Kenneth N. Townsend (Cambridge, MA: MIT Press, 1993), pp. 267–70.

37  J. D. Ward, P. C. Sutton, A. D. Werner, R. Costanza, S. H. Mohr, and C. T. Simmons, "Is Decoupling GDP Growth from Environmental Impact Possible?" *PLoS ONE* 11(10) (2016): e0164733.

38  Robert Fletcher and Crelis Rammelt, "Decoupling: A Key Fantasy of the Post-2015 Sustainable Development Agenda," *Globalizations* 14(3) (2017): 453.

39  Petter Næss and Karl Georg Høyer, "The Emperor's Green Clothes: Growth, Decoupling, and Capitalism," *Capitalism Nature Socialism* 20(3) (2009): 82.

40  Naomi Klein, *This Changes Everything: Capitalism vs. the Climate* (New York: Simon & Schuster, 2014), p. 25.

41  Andrew Dobson, *Green Political Thought*, 4th edition (New York: Routledge, 2007), pp. 2–3.

42  Giorgos Kallis, "In Defence of Degrowth," *Ecological Economics* 70(5) (2011): 874.

43  Serge Latouche, *Farewell to Growth*, trans. David Macey (Malden, MA: Polity, 2009), p. 31.
44  Kallis, "In Defence of Degrowth," p. 875.

## 6 Equality

1   Peter Singer, "Equality for Animals?" in *Practical Ethics* (New York: Cambridge University Press, 1979).
2   Robert Macfarlane, "The Secrets of the Wood Wide Web," *The New Yorker* (August 7, 2016).
3   Martha Nussbaum, *Frontiers of Justice: Disability, Nationality, Species Membership* (Cambridge, MA: Harvard University Press, 2006), p. 362.
4   Joel Feinberg, "The Nature and Value of Rights," *Journal of Value Inquiry* 4(4) (1970): 257.
5   My focus will be upon the US context, since this is what I know best, but many of my remarks apply also to legal systems in other liberal democratic states.
6   Tim Hayward, "Constitutional Environmental Rights: A Case for Political Analysis," *Political Studies* 48(3) (2000): 569.
7   Hayward, "Constitutional Environmental Rights," p. 559
8   Simon Caney, "Climate Change, Human Rights and Moral Thresholds," in *Human Rights and Climate Change*, ed. Stephen Humphreys (New York: Cambridge University Press, 2009), pp. 69–90.
9   Dinah L. Shelton, *Problems in Climate Change and Human Rights*, GW Law Faculty Publications & Other Works, Paper 1047 (2011): http://scholarship.law.gwu.edu/faculty_publications/1047.
10  Dinah L. Shelton, "Stockholm Declaration" (encyclopedia entry), *Oxford Public International Law* (2008): https://opil.ouplaw.com/view/10.1093/law:epil/9780199231690/law-9780199231690-e1608.
11  Heather C. Lovell, "Governing the Carbon Offset Market," *WIREs Climate Change* 1(3) (2010): 353–62.
12  John Broome, *Climate Matters: Ethics in a Warming World* (New York: W. W. Norton & Co., 2012), p. 52.
13  Jeffrey M. Skopec, "Uncommon Goods: On Environmental Virtues and Voluntary Carbon Offsets," *Harvard Law Review* 123(8) (2010): 2065–87, 2086.
14  Jonathan Aldred, "The Ethics of Emissions Trading," *New Political Economy* 17(3) (2012): 343.
15  Aldred, "The Ethics of Emissions Trading," p. 345.
16  Simon Caney, "Just Emissions," *Philosophy and Public Affairs* 40(4) (2012): 255–300.
17  Michael Walzer, *Spheres of Justice: A Defense of Pluralism and Equality* (New York: Basic Books, 1983), p. 19.
18  Thomas Princen, *The Logic of Sufficiency* (Cambridge, MA: MIT Press, 2005), p. 7.

19   Adam Smith, *An Enquiry into the Nature and Causes of the Wealth of Nations* (1776), part 2 art. 4.
20   J. R. McNeil, *The Great Acceleration: An Environmental History of the Anthropocene since 1945* (Cambridge, MA: Harvard University Press, 2014).
21   Oxfam, *Extreme Carbon Inequality* (2015): www.oxfam.org/en/research/extreme-carbon-inequality.
22   A. Y. Hoekstra and A. K. Chapagain, "Water Footprints of Nations: Water Use by People as a Function of Their Consumption Pattern," *Water Resources Management* 21 (2007): 35–48.
23   Kenneth Pomeranz, *The Great Divergence: China, Europe, and the Making of the Modern World Economy* (Princeton University Press, 2000).
24   Timothy Noah, *The Great Divergence: America's Growing Inequality Crisis and What We Can Do about It* (New York: Bloomsbury, 2013).
25   Tom Athanasiou, *Divided Planet: The Ecology of Rich and Poor* (Athens: University of Georgia Press, 1996), p. 299.
26   Tom Athanasiou and Paul Baer, *Dead Heat: Global Justice and Global Warming* (New York: Seven Stories Press, 2002), ch. 5.
27   Clark Wolf, "Contemporary Property Rights, Lockean Provisos, and the Interests of Future Generations," *Ethics* 105(4) (1995): 791–818, p. 812.
28   Wolf, "Lockean Provisos," p. 812.
29   Hillel Steiner, *An Essay on Rights* (Cambridge, MA: Blackwell, 1994), pp. 271–2.

## 7 Agency and Responsibility

1   John S. Dryzek, "Democratic Agents of Justice," *The Journal of Political Philosophy* 23(4) (2015): 363.
2   Mary Ann Warren, *Moral Status: Obligations to Persons and Other Living Things* (New York: Oxford University Press, 1997), p. 3.
3   Christopher D. Stone, "Should Trees Have Standing? – Toward Legal Rights for Natural Objects," *Southern California Law Review* 45 (1972): 450–501.
4   Claudia Card, "Genocide and Social Death," in *Genocide and Human Rights*, ed. J. K. Roth (London: Palgrave Macmillan, 2005), pp. 238–54.
5   As an ideology, fascism rejects the priority of individual rights over the collective that is common to liberalism, sometimes calling for the sacrifice of individuals for the sake of the state. In Mussolini's *Doctrine of Fascism* (1932), for example, he casts the "Man of fascism" as someone willing to engage in "the sacrifice of his own private interests, through death itself" for the sake of the state.
6   James E. Lovelock, "Gaia as Seen Through the Atmosphere," *Atmospheric Environment* 6(8) (1972): 579–80.
7   Lynn Margulis, *Symbiotic Planet: A New Look at Evolution* (London: Weidenfeld & Nicolson, 1998).

8   Stephen Gardiner, *A Perfect Moral Storm: The Ethical Tragedy of Climate Change* (New York: Oxford University Press, 2011).

9   Derek Parfit, *Reasons and Persons* (New York: Oxford University Press, 1984), ch. 3.

10  Carbon Disclosure Project, *The Carbon Majors Database* (CDP Worldwide, 2017): https://climateaccountability.org/carbonmajors.html.

11  Michael P. Vandenbergh, "Private Environmental Governance," *Cornell Law Review* 99(129) (2016): 129–99.

12  Susan Clayton, Susan Christie, Kirra Krygsman, and Meighan Speiser, *Mental Health and Our Changing Climate: Impacts, Implications, and Guidance*, American Psychological Association, March, 2017: www.apa.org/news/press/releases/2017/03/mental-health-climate.pdf.

13  Steve Vanderheiden, "Climate Change and Free Riding," *Journal of Moral Philosophy* 13(1) (2016): 1–27.

14  Michael F. Maniates, "Individualization: Plant a Tree, Buy a Bike, Save the World?" *Global Environmental Politics* 1(3) (2001): 33.

15  Michael Walzer, *Just and Unjust Wars* (New York: Basic Books, 1977), p. 300.

16  David Miller, "Holding Nations Responsible," *Ethics* 114 (2004): 240–68, p. 243.

17  Miller, "Holding Nations Responsible," p. 260.

## 8 Community

1   For example, Robert E. Goodin "What Is So Special about Our Fellow Countrymen?" *Ethics* 98(4) (1988): 663–86.

2   Michael J. Sandel, *Liberalism and the Limits of Justice* (New York: Cambridge University Press, 1982).

3   Benedict Anderson, *Imagined Communities: Reflections on the Origin and Spread of Nationalism* (New York: Verso, 1983).

4   Anderson, *Imagined Communities*, pp. 6–7.

5   Robyn Eckersley, *Environmentalism and Political Theory: Toward an Ecocentric Approach* (Albany, NY: SUNY Press, 1992).

6   George S. Sessions, "Anthropocentrism and the Environmental Crisis," *Humboldt Journal of Social Relations* 2(1) (1974): 71–81.

7   Rachel Carson, *Silent Spring* (New York: Houghton Mifflin, 1962), p. 85.

8   James Lovelock, *The Revenge of Gaia: Earth's Climate in Crisis and the Fate of Humanity* (New York: Perseus Books, 2006), p. 153.

9   Bryan G. Norton, "Environmental Ethics and Weak Anthropocentrism," *Environmental Ethics* 6(2) (1984): 131–48.

10  Aldo Leopold, *A Sand County Almanac* (New York: Oxford University Press, 1948), ch. 22.

11  Leopold, *A Sand County Almanac*, pp. 223–4.

12  Peter Singer, *Animal Liberation* (New York: HarperCollins, 1975).

13  Val Plumwood, *Feminism and the Mastery of Nature* (New York: Routledge, 1993).

14   Lynn White, "The Historical Roots of Our Ecological Crisis," *Science*, new series, 155(3767) (1967): 1203–7.
15   Lucas F. Johnston, *Religion and Sustainability: Social Movements and the Politics of the Environment* (New York: Routledge, 2013).
16   Ronald Sandler, *Character and Environment: A Virtue-Oriented Approach to Environmental Ethics* (New York: Columbia University Press, 2007).
17   Kyle P. White, "Indigenous Climate Change Studies: Indigenizing Futures, Decolonizing the Anthropocene," *English Language Notes* 55(1–2) (2017): 153–62.
18   Karsten A. Schulz, "Decolonizing Political Ecology: Ontology, Technology and 'Critical' Enchantment," *Journal of Political Ecology* 24(1) (2017): 125–43.
19   Plumwood, *Feminism and the Mastery of Nature*.
20   Bonnie Roos and Alex Hunt, *Postcolonial Green: Environmental Politics and World Narratives* (Charlottesville: University of Virginia Press, 2010).
21   See Kenneth E. Boulding (1966), "The Economics of the Coming Spaceship Earth," in *Environmental Quality in a Growing Economy*, ed. Henry Jarrett (Baltimore, MD: Resources for the Future / Johns Hopkins University Press, 1966), pp. 3–14; and R. Buckminster Fuller, *Operating Manual for Spaceship Earth* (Southern Illinois University Press, 1969).
22   Wendell Berry, *What Are People For?* (San Francisco: North Point Press, 1990).
23   http://extremeicesurvey.org.
24   Ed Abbey, *One Life at a Time, Please* (New York: Henry Holt, 1988), p. 43.
25   Murray Bookchin, *Social Ecology vs. Deep Ecology* (Burlington: Green Program Project, 1988), p. 4.
26   Sierra Club Population Report, Spring 1989 (www.susps.org/history/popreport1989.html).
27   Sierra Club Population Policies (www.sierraclub.org/policy/conservation/population.asp).
28   Sierra Club Population Policies.
29   Glen Martin and Ramon McLeod, "Ecology Groups Wrestle with Population Pressure," *The San Francisco Chronicle*, February 23, 1998, p. A1
30   Avery Kolers, *Land, Conflict, and Justice* (New York: Cambridge University Press, 2009), p. 132.
31   Robyn Eckersley, "Environmentalism and Patriotism: An Unholy Alliance?" in *Patriotism: Philosophical and Political Perspectives*, ed. Igor Primoratz and Aleksander Pavković (Burlington, VT: Ashgate, 2007), pp. 183–200, p. 196.
32   Bill McKibben, "How Extreme Weather Is Shrinking the Planet," *The New Yorker* (November 26, 2018).
33   Avner de-Shalit (2011), "Climate Change Refugees, Compensation and Rectification," *The Monist* 94(3) (2011): 310–28.

34  Peter Singer (1972), "Famine, Affluence, and Morality," *Philosophy and Public Affairs* 1(3) (1972): 229–43.
35  Peter Singer, *One World: The Ethics of Globalization* (New Haven, CT: Yale University Press, 2002).
36  Singer, as a *consequentialist*, defines right and wrong in terms of outcomes only, and so would reject any such distinction between doing and allowing, but other moral philosophers disagree. For a critique, see Bernard Williams, "Negative Responsibility: and Two Examples," from *Utilitarianism: For and Against*, ed. Williams and J. J. C. Smart (New York: Cambridge University Press, 1973).
37  Andrew Dobson, "Thick Cosmopolitanism," *Political Studies* 54 (2006): 165–84.
38  Terence Ball, "Democracy," in *Political Theory and the Ecological Challenge*, ed. Andrew Dobson and Robyn Eckersley (New York: Cambridge University Press, 2006), pp. 131–47, pp. 143–4.
39  In his "Letter from Birmingham Jail," *The Atlantic* (August, 1963), King wrote: "Injustice anywhere is a threat to justice everywhere. We are caught in an inescapable network of mutuality, tied in a single garment of destiny. Whatever affects one directly, affects all indirectly."

## 9 Sovereignty

1  Alex J. Bellamy, *Responsibility to Protect: The Global Effort to End Mass Atrocities* (Cambridge: Polity, 2009).
2  Joseph Nye, *Soft Power: The Means to Success in World Politics* (New York: Public Affairs, 2004).
3  Allen Buchanan, *Secession: The Legitimacy of Political Divorce from Fort Sumter to Lithuania and Quebec* (Boulder, CO: Westview Press, 1991).
4  Sarah Song, *Immigration and Democracy* (New York: Oxford University Press, 2018).
5  Thomas Pogge, "'Assisting' the Global Poor," in *The Ethics of Assistance: Morality and the Distant Needy*, ed. Deen Chatterjee (New York: Cambridge University Press, 2004).
6  Kristian Skagen Ekeli (2004), "Environmental Risks, Uncertainty and Intergenerational Ethics," *Environmental Values* 13(4) (2004): 421–48.
7  Elizabeth Kolbert, *The Sixth Extinction: An Unnatural History* (New York: Henry Holt and Co., 2014).
8  Aline C. Soterroni, Aline Mosnier, Alexandre X. Y. Carvalho, *et al.*, "Future Environmental and Agricultural Impacts of Brazil's Forest Code," *Environmental Research Letters* 13(7) (2018): 074021.
9  "Bolsonaro fears that combating global warming takes Brazilian sovereignty out of the Amazon," says expert: *UOL News*, October 31, 2018: https://noticias.uol.com.br/ultimas-noticias/rfi/2018/10/31/bolsonaro-teme-que-combate-ao-aquecimento-global-tire-soberania-brasileira-da-amazonia-diz-especialista.htm?cmpid=copiaecola.
10  William J. Snape III, "Joining the Convention on Biological Diversity:

A Legal and Scientific Overview of Why the United States Must Wake Up," *Sustainable Development Law & Policy* (Spring 2010): 6–16, 44–7.

11    Robert F. Blomquist, "Ratification Resisted: Understanding America's Response to the Convention on Biological Diversity, 1989–2002," *Golden Gate University Law Review* 32 (2002): 493–586, p. 533.

12    "Statement by President Trump on the Paris Climate Accord" (June 1, 2017): www.whitehouse.gov/briefings-statements/statement-president-trump-paris-climate-accord.

13    Eric A. Posner and David Weisbach, *Climate Change Justice* (Princeton University Press, 2015).

14    Full text: "Trump's 2018 UN Speech Transcript," *Politico* (September 25, 2018): www.politico.com/story/2018/09/25/trump-un-speech-2018-full-text-transcript-840043.

15    Jean Bodin, *On Sovereignty: Four Chapters from The Six Books of the Commonwealth*, ed. and trans. Julian H. Franklin (New York: Cambridge University Press, 1992), p. 6.

16    Joan Cocks, *On Sovereignty and Other Political Delusions* (New York: Bloomsbury, 2014), p. 31.

17    Nico Schrijver, *Sovereignty over Natural Resources: Balancing Rights and Duties* (New York: Cambridge University Press, 1997).

18    Thomas Pogge, *World Poverty and Human Rights*, 2nd edition (Cambridge, and Malden, MA: Polity, 2008), p. 336.

19    www.cbd.int/doc/c/d9d0/7a53/95df6ca3ac3515b5ad812b04/sbstta-21-inf-09-en.pdf.

20    Bill McKibben, "How Extreme Weather Is Shrinking the Planet," *The New Yorker* (November 26, 2018).

21    Karen T. Litfin, "The Greening of Sovereignty: An Introduction," in *The Greening of Sovereignty in World Politics*, ed. Karen Litfin (Cambridge, MA: MIT Press, 1998), pp. 1–27, p. 8.

22    Allen Buchanan, "Theories of Secession," *Philosophy and Public Affairs* 26(1) (Winter, 1997): 31–61, p. 47.

23    http://responsibilitytoprotect.org/ICISS%20Report.pdf.

24    Cocks, *On Sovereignty*, p. 36.

25    Frank Biermann and Ingrid Boas, "Preparing for a Warmer World: Towards a Global Governance System to Protect Climate Refugees," *Global Environmental Politics* 10(1) (2010): 60–88.

26    Catriona McKinnon, "Endangering Humanity: An International Crime?" *Canadian Journal of Philosophy*, 47(2–3) (2017): 395–415, p. 405.

27    McKinnon, "Endangering Humanity," p. 403.

28    Robyn Eckersley, *The Green State: Rethinking Democracy and Sovereignty* (Cambridge, MA: MIT Press, 2004), pp. 231–2.

## 10 Justice

1    John Rawls, *A Theory of Justice* (Cambridge, MA: Harvard University Press, 1971), p. 302.

2  https://climatejusticealliance.org/just-transition.

3  David Schlosberg, *Defining Environmental Justice* (New York: Oxford University Press, 2007).

4  Mark Dowie, *Losing Ground: American Environmentalism at the Close of the Twentieth Century* (Cambridge, MA: MIT Press, 1995), p. 207.

5  Schlosberg, *Defining Environmental Justice*.

6  Derek Parfit, *Reasons and Persons* (New York: Oxford University Press, 1984), p. 384.

7  Parfit, *Reasons and Persons*, p. 390.

8  Rawls, *A Theory of Justice*, p. 290.

9  Andrew Dobson, *Justice and the Environment* (New York: Oxford University Press, 1998), pp. 41–54.

10  Marcel Wissenburg, *Green Liberalism: The Free and Green Society* (London: UCL Press, 1998), pp. 103–4.

11  Herman E. Daly, "On Wilfred Beckerman's Critique of Sustainable Development," *Environmental Values* 4(1) (1995): 49–55, p. 50.

12  Rawls, *A Theory of Justice*, pp. 74, 101.

13  Rawls, *A Theory of Justice*, p. 117. He elsewhere (p. 108) suggests that, with the exception of Arctic Eskimos, there are no societies in the world in which resource scarcity poses an insurmountable obstacle to becoming well ordered.

14  Rawls, *A Theory of Justice*, p. 290.

15  Rawls, *A Theory of Justice*, pp. 288, 290.

16  Rawls, *A Theory of Justice*, p. 126.

17  Charles R. Beitz, "Justice and International Relations," *Philosophy and Public Affairs* 4(4) (1975): 370.

18  Beitz,"Justice and International Relations," p. 374.

19  Orazio P. Attanasio and Luigi Pistaferri, "Consumption Inequality," *Journal of Economic Perspectives* 30(2) (2016): 3–28.

20  https://www.epa.gov/ghgemissions/sources-greenhouse-gas-emissions

21  The World Bank, *Economics of Adaptation to Climate Change: Synthesis Report* (2010): http://documents.worldbank.org/curated/en/646291468171244256/pdf/702670ESW0P10800EACCSynthesis Report.pdf.

22  Simon Caney, "Just Emissions," *Philosophy & Public Affairs* 40(4) (2012): 255–300.

## Conclusions: The Just and Sustainable Society

1  Mathis Wackernagel and William E. Rees, *Our Ecological Footprint* (Gabriola Island, BC: New Society Publishers, 1996).

2  For a fuller discussion of this claim, see Steve Vanderheiden, "Allocating Ecological Space," *Journal of Social Philosophy* 40(2) (2009): 257–75.

3  IPCC, "Summary for Policymakers," in *Global Warming of 1.5°C. An IPCC Special Report on the Impacts of Global Warming of 1.5°C*

*Above Pre-industrial Levels and Related Global Greenhouse Gas Emission Pathways, in the Context of Strengthening the Global Response to the Threat of Climate Change, Sustainable Development, and Efforts to Eradicate Poverty* [ed. V. Masson-Delmotte, P. Zhai, H.-O. Pörtner et al.] (in press, 2018): www.ipcc.ch/sr15.

4   http://trillionthtonne.org.
5   IPCC, "Summary for Policymakers."
6   Daniel W. O'Neill, Andrew L. Fanning, William F. Lamb, and Julia K. Steinberger, "A Good Life for All Within Planetary Boundaries," *Nature Sustainability* 1 (2018): 88–95.
7   O'Neill et al., "A Good Life for All," p. 93.

# Index